Thinking with
James Carey

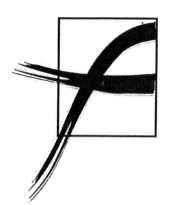

Intersections
in Communications
and Culture

Global Approaches and Transdisciplinary Perspective:

Cameron McCarthy and Angharad N. Valdivia
General Editors

Vol. 15

PETER LANG
New York • Washington, D.C./Baltimore • Bern
Frankfurt am Main • Berlin • Brussels • Vienna • Oxford

Thinking with
James Carey

ESSAYS ON
COMMUNICATIONS,
TRANSPORTATION,
HISTORY

Edited by
Jeremy Packer and Craig Robertson

PETER LANG
New York • Washington, D.C./Baltimore • Bern
Frankfurt am Main • Berlin • Brussels • Vienna • Oxford

Library of Congress Cataloging-in-Publication Data

Thinking with James Carey: essays on communications, transportation, history /
edited by Jeremy Packer and Craig Robertson.
p. cm. — (Intersections in communications and culture; v. 15)
Includes bibliographical references and index.
1. Communication. 2. Culture. 3. Carey, James W. I. Packer, Jeremy.
II. Robertson, Craig. III. Series.
P90.T438   302.2—dc22   2005018066
ISBN 0-8204-7405-3
ISSN 1528-610X

Bibliographic information published by **Die Deutsche Bibliothek**.
Die Deutsche Bibliothek lists this publication in the "Deutsche
Nationalbibliografie"; detailed bibliographic data is available
on the Internet at http://dnb.ddb.de/.

Cover design by Joni Holst

The paper in this book meets the guidelines for permanence and durability
of the Committee on Production Guidelines for Book Longevity
of the Council of Library Resources.

© 2006 Peter Lang Publishing, Inc., New York
275 Seventh Avenue, 28th Floor, New York, NY 10001
www.peterlangusa.com

Printed in the United States of America

Table of Contents

Acknowledgments   vii

Introduction   1
    JEREMY PACKER AND CRAIG ROBERTSON

1. From New England to Illinois: The Invention of (American)
Cultural Studies   11
    JAMES CAREY IN CONVERSATION WITH LAWRENCE GROSSBERG, PART 1

2. Between Cultural Materialism and Spatial Materialism: James Carey's
Writing about Communication   29
    JAMES HAY

3. For a Pragmatist Perspective on Publics: Advancing Carey's Cultural Studies
through John Dewey . . . and Michel Foucault?!   57
    CHRIS RUSSILL

4. Rethinking Dependency: New Relations of Transportation
and Communication,   79
    JEREMY PACKER

5. Communication Scholarship as Ritual: An Examination of James Carey's
Cultural Model of Communication   101
    GRETCHEN SODERLUND

6. Transportation and Communication: Together as You've
Always Wanted Them   117
    JONATHAN STERNE

7. Technology and Ideology: The Case of the Telegraph Revisited   137
    JOHN DURHAM PETERS

8. *The Public and the Party Period*   157
   JOHN NERONE

9. *A Ritual of Verification? The Nation, the State, and the U.S. Passport*   177
   CRAIG ROBERTSON

10. *Configurations of Culture, History, and Politics*   199
   JAMES CAREY IN CONVERSATION WITH LAWRENCE GROSSBERG, PART 2

List of Contributors   227

Index   229

Acknowledgments

This book originated as a mid-afternoon panel at the 2001 annual meeting of the National Communication Association. We would like to thank the Critical Cultural Studies Division not only for sponsoring that panel but more generally for giving a space within NCA for the approach to communication that this volume spotlights. In the journey from panel to book, we have been assisted by numerous people. First and foremost, our contributors, who responded promptly to the numerous final deadlines that a project like this creates—and responded with thoughtful and insightful essays. We benefited enormously from the enthusiastic support we have received from Cameron McCarthy and Damon Zucca, our editor at Peter Lang. Miranda Brady, our research assistant, provided critical editorial assistance over the final 12 months of this project. We are also very grateful for the generous funding provided by the Babson College Board of Research and Penn State College of Communications. Finally we are indebted to James Carey, whose gracious support has been integral to this project from its beginnings as a conference panel four years ago; support we hope will continue in the form of the ongoing conversations of which this volume is only a part.

Introduction

JEREMY PACKER AND CRAIG ROBERTSON

"Opening his books is like reengaging an extended conversation: they are not merely things to read but things to think with."

—James Carey[1]

After crowning Harold Adam Innis the twentieth-century's preeminent theorist of communications, describing his work as "maddeningly obscure, opaque, and elliptical," and, via an Oscar Wilde allusion, restoring Marshall McLuhan to a subordinate position in the hierarchy of the Toronto School, James Carey concludes the first paragraph of his homage to Innis with the above epigraph. This single sentence sums up this book's relation to Carey.

The essays that follow "think with" the writings of James Carey in the form of an "extended conversation." This is not due to any stylistic insufficiency in Carey's work that necessitates clarification but because the force of his ideas, the breadth of his work, and the far-ranging effect he has had on the field has drawn each of us in our own ways to his ideas. The authors collectively engage in what we see as Carey's most inspiring accomplishment, his unrelenting, and often combative dialogue with a widely cast and historically deeply flung net of social theorists, communications scholars, and historians. Our contributors continue this tradition by "thinking with" James Carey and dialoguing with his writing. While this volume is intended as an acknowledgment of the impact James Carey has had on the field of communication, it is not a festschrift in name or tone. As John Peters comments in his essay, "though I hesitate to criticize a friend and mentor who has done so much in so many ways to advance my own thinking and career, the only proper tribute for a street-fighter and democrat, both of which Carey fiercely is, is a direct confrontation."[2] Thinking *with* James Carey does not mean thinking *as* James Carey. Yet, how Carey thinks *about* communications, transportation, and history has clearly inspired the conversations that follow.

These conversations can be fit into Carey's set of concerns regarding communication, culture, technology, and transportation. However, we argue, that it is only through history that Carey gains the perspective and footing for his larger project—a critique of the trajectories of communications practice and the academic field of communications and, most important, a critique of the political ramifications of both. Yet, the object and forms of the histories Carey writes and so often references are widely varied. Significantly he makes it quite apparent that he has little time for much of what has passed for historical work in the field, particularly journalism history, which he read in the 1970s as endlessly retelling a narrative of the progress toward, or regression from, "freedom and knowledge."[3] Carey's foci and statements regarding the importance of historical research are bountiful yet purposeful. They reveal an understanding of the stakes of doing "history" and of what such histories might look like. In his version of the culturalism versus structuralism debate he has invoked "history" as specificity to challenge universal theories of communication. He advocates "history," care of Harold Innis and John Dewey, as a strategy to critique the present.[4] Carey also isolates "lived experience" as a critical historical problematic to endorse the North American bias of his chosen mentors.[5]

His varied deployment of "history" comfortably fits within his belief that "Eclecticism can be a virtue and it never is the worst of intellectual sins."[6] We humbly suggest the essays in this book, clearly eclectic and whose sins the reader will have to discover, attack a number of problems that concerned Carey in new ways. Loosely grouped, these problems are: How do we construct an intellectual history for the field of communications? How have relationships, historical and theoretical, between communications and transportation configured thought and practice for communications? How has communications figured into the uniquely American experience of nation building and the production of a continental community? Though clearly not an exhaustive list of Carey's concerns, we feel these intellectual threads not only knit together the tapestry of texts the authors have chosen to think with but engage with what remain the most vexing and stimulating of Carey's essays on communications.

On the Intellectual History of the Field

Engaging in the creation of an intellectual history of a discipline is fraught with so many dangers as to seemingly doom any such attempt to wide-scale derision if not wholesale dismissal. Yet such attempts are necessary. Carey makes clear that the formation of a canon and official history of a field is the creation of intellectual and political weaponry; an arsenal used to justify the contemporary tactics of those who dominate the field's terrain. One form of counter-attack against such domination according to Carey is historically grounded intellectual history. He states, "We need a model [of communications] that is thoroughly historical and reflexive: a model in which the history and intentions of the observer are part of the history and meanings of the observed."[7] Carey is here arguing that we can't treat the history of our field as if its changes exist according to an internal set of debates. Rather, interested researchers produce communications scholarship. As Carey succinctly puts it, "All scholarship must be and inevitably is adapted to the time and place of its creation. That relation is either unconscious, disguised, and indirect or reflexive, explicit, and avowed."[8] His engagement, then, with the history of thought regarding communications must be grounded in terms of the very historical context from which such ideas themselves arose. Communications theory is never to be ahistorical and communications history is never to be atheoretical. It is this healthily complex relationship among the historical, the theoretical, the history of theory, and the politics of the creation of such histories that we believe has led to Carey's profound effect upon the field. The first three chapters in this book are the most explicit in reworking this terrain. How they do so and in what ways this relates to Carey's more general project of communications' intellectual history will benefit from some contextualization of its own.

Carey asks that we begin by always recognizing the situatedness of our theorists and their theory. To this end we begin the book with something of an intellectual biography in the form of an extended conversation between Carey and Lawrence Grossberg, one of Carey's most well-known and influential students. But this is not done in the spirit of what Michel Foucault derides as a history of philosophy but rather as a means to actively engage with the living biography that is Carey's ongoing thought. As Carey makes very clear regarding his relation to leftist politics, the important role of the Catholic Church in his own biography tells only part of the story. For him the church provided much more than just a set of guiding principles or explanations; more significantly it was a means for negotiating and overcoming the daily struggles of working-class life. This is to say that we can 1) not simply import "Catholic thought" into Carey's writings on the history of ideas about communications any more than we can 2) read his work itself as a mere part of the very teleological procession that he has so resolutely dismissed as both a form of practice and a standard history of said thought. Thus, situating thought is not only to trace ideas but to establish the historically grounded political investments of such thought. Carey's discussion of his own biography helps us recognize that his concerns about communications were grounded in a series of ongoing political struggles—over the direction of the discipline, over how class struggle was bound into practical cultural practices of daily existence, and how such concerns regarding class have fallen out of the national debate and conceptions of leftist politics. But this turn to the biographical only tells a small part of the story of the situatedness of Carey's thought and the ongoing theoretical debates taking place over such forms of thinking.

More broadly, the type of intellectual histories that Carey himself wrote was aimed to bring into bold relief not only why the contemporaneous state of so much communications scholarship was theoretically and politically bankrupt but also how the importation or reengagement with other strains of intellectual work could invigorate the field. He provided just such a scathing examination of the official history of the field of mass communications. Carey argued it worked in the "disguised" mode to "focus, justify, and legitimize a twentieth-century invention, the mass media, and to give direction and intellectual status to professional teaching and research concerning these same institutions . . . it was invented with a political purpose: an attempt to cast loyalties, resolve disputes, guide public policy, confuse opposition, and legitimize institutions."[9] As he says, it was "hardly an innocent history."[10] But then neither is Carey's counterhistory in which the Chicago School figures prominently, not to say that we do not promote this history. Therefore, we should also always question how we approach any counterhistories.

In chapter 3, Chris Russill offers an intellectual history that examines the relationship between John Dewey and Michel Foucault and, by extension, James Carey; a history at which, as he notes, Carey would seem initially to bristle. Russill argues that in order to reinvigorate the public, something demanded by Carey via Dewey, it is necessary to rethink the public through a Foucauldian conception of problematization. Furthermore, contra-Carey, Russill maintains that Foucault is not anathema to a Deweyan project but is in fact necessary given our current understanding of the public. If Russill is correct that Foucault not only read Dewey but that his work on power and politics is dependent upon Dewey, do we need to re-approach Carey's conception of American cultural studies?

Carey has worked over the past forty years to keep alive the vision and concerns of a number of scholars who he continues to believe have great relevance to contemporary political and cultural concerns. The most prominent figures of Carey's intellectual history come from North America; the Canadians Harold Innis and, in a somewhat conflicted manner, Marshall McLuhan; select members of the Chicago School most clearly exemplified by John Dewey; and American historians of technology such as Lewis Mumford. Yet, as James Hay makes evident in his essay, situating the thought of Carey demands a host of excursions through European sociology and British cultural studies, a point Carey by no means shies away from as he makes clear in the interviews. Hay untangles the strands of thought Carey tied together in his 1975 formulation of the transmission and ritual models of communications. Furthermore, Hay, with greater detail than Carey provided in the original, articulates the political and theoretical context in which Carey formulated his canonical essay. Hay ultimately makes an argument for adding, among others, the work of Henri Lefebvre to the mix of social theorists who can help communications scholars avoid what he sees as the pitfalls of thinking too stridently within the dichotomies of ritual/transmission and time-bias/ space-bias. The rigid distinction between these two spheres of activity, associated technologies, and the political commitments each is seen as engendering comprise in many ways the focus of this volume's second grouping of essays. It should be noted, however, that Carey himself revisits this distinction in some detail in the conclusion of his dialogue with Grossberg found in chapter 10. We would argue that this ongoing demand, by both Russill and Hay, to integrate and juxtapose European theory with communications theory is one means to carry forward one of Carey's most important contributions to the field.

Approaching the Divide: Communications and Transportation

The second grouping of essays addresses in some detail, and in a different fashion from Hay, the conceptual and historical split between transportation and communication. For Carey, the advent of the telegraph negated (or at least began the process of negation) communication's dependence upon transportation technologies: "The simplest and most important point about the telegraph is that it marked the decisive separation of 'transportation' and 'communication.'"[11] Jeremy Packer's and Jonathan Sterne's essays engage more directly with the materiality of the split to assess how such conceptions have affected the topics of communications scholarship and the theoretical concerns organizing such scholarship. Both authors caution against an overemphasis upon this "separation," but more important ask how, following from Carey's work, this physical separation has proliferated as a conceptual separation. Gretchen Soderlund, through a historical account of white slavery as a form of cultural transport/transmission, draws upon a different strain of French anthropological thought (i.e., Levi-Strauss as opposed to Carey's use of Emile Durkheim) to elucidate how the binarism of transmission/ritual deflects attention away from differential understandings of how communications operates to strengthen community ties even as it promotes unequal power relations. This allows Soderlund to foreground gender, as she argues "women have been the invisible media through which social linkages are formed."[12] Underlying these essays is a feeling that something has been lost in the choosing of sides that seems implicit to the dichotomy of transmission/ritual. (To be fair to Carey, he makes evident in the final chapter of this book that he is in agreement with such a concern.)

If we recognize this statement that his contextually strategic distinction has been treated as an overly deterministic feature of communications practice, the perceived limits of Carey's initial distinction, which these authors investigate, fills in some conceptual and historical schisms; schisms that, despite Carey's best intentions, have formed to split these two not-so-disparate elements of communications practice. From such a perspective, these essays are not working in opposition to Carey but rather continuing work started by Carey more than thirty years ago. This is a problem that nearly all the authors, and Carey, feel has been insufficiently addressed.

Another similarity shared by these essays, and Robertson's, is that they all partake in Carey's eclectic style of tackling a problem faced by communications theorists through an overlooked historical aspect of communications practice. Soderlund treats the white-slavery scare of 1907–1911 as a way of investigating how women are a medium of exchange. Sterne examines the infrastructural templates used to trace preceding communication technologies infrastructure. But, the historical specificity of Sterne's analysis is a means for addressing how the field of communications has tended to overemphasize the symbolic dimension over what he terms "organized movement and action." Sterne maintains that it is a conceptual split between the individual and the social in the scale of analysis that allows for the very story of transportation and communications "splitting" to be told. In a related fashion, Packer provides a brief history of mobile communications as the linkage of communications and transportation technologies that runs backward from the mobile phone, to CB, to police radio, and ultimately to the train/telegraph couplet with which Carey began. He emphasizes that such historical couplings reveal a double dependency. First, transportation has become increasingly dependent upon communications at the behest of safety and security. Second, this linkage depends upon a conceptualization of how to use transportation and communication technologies to "govern at a distance"—that is ensure the smooth flow of power relations across increasingly vast distances through the exertion of as little direct action as possible.

Nineteenth-Century U.S. History as Communications History

Carey's argument for the separation of communications and transportation is made in his most famous essay on communications history, his story of the telegraph, first published in 1983.[13] It is a very specific kind of history, in which Carey uses the telegraph as an "analytic prism"[14] into the nineteenth century. This approach to writing the history of communications can be read through one of Carey's important arguments: that the history of the United States is the history of communication. Our final set of essays provides three very different responses to the problem of writing communications history within this framework. These essays utilize the telegraph (John Durham Peters), the emergence of professional journalism (John Nerone), and the development of the passport (Craig Robertson) to foreground three concepts critical to Carey's history: technology, the public, and culture.

Carey positions the nineteenth century as critical because it is the period in which the transmission capacity of technologies eclipsed a local community's ability to define itself. The importance of this history to his formulation of the transmission and ritual models is made explicit in essays written subsequent to his 1975 canonical essay (and his 1983 rescue of the telegraph from obscurity).[15] Instead of ritual and transmission, Carey has come to write of self-representation (the problem of identity) and social representation (the problem of scale). He outlines a post-Revolution United States where the definition of the country—its geography, culture, and political institutions—was up for debate. This is specifically a story of a "crisis of representation"[16]; it is through this argument that the history of the United States becomes the history of communication. In response to this specific "historical" problem of representation, technology was seen to provide both the material and metaphorical solution to the production of a national community. Therefore, what Carey viewed as the fundamental process of communication—the basis of the construction of social reality through self-representation (ritual)—got marginalized within the idea of communication as social representation (transmission).

Robertson takes on this articulation of representation and culture in terms of tension between the local and the national. He foregrounds the problem the federal government encountered as it sought to govern over ever-increasing distances in the nineteenth century. He analyzes this, using the increased use of standardized identification documents as an example of a federal challenge to local practices of individual identification. While this fits into Carey's narrative of the decline of the local, Robertson argues that Carey's symbolic definition of culture limits our ability to understand this both as a cultural practice and a problem of the transmission of information. Therefore, through a Foucauldian-influenced conception of cultural practices as a distinctive set of knowledge, expertise, and techniques, he offers "verification" as a framework to critically analyze transmission.

This contrasts with Carey, whose privileging of the symbolic as ritual, is rooted in his commitment to an American tradition of democratic thought. Carey, therefore, articulates his historical argument for the decline in the local to a project to cultivate democratic life through the restoration of the "public" (the label for the form of interaction necessary for community and democracy to exist). Carey, a Deweyan, writing against the dominance of a transmission model, refuses to detach community from face-to-face interaction; whatever the scale, democracy depends on the foundations of group life.[17] Nerone engages this normative use of communications history in an attempt to offer an alternative history of the decline of the public that speaks directly to Carey's project of making the present more thinkable and, therefore, a site of action. He does this by moving the debate and analysis of the public and the public sphere away from access to representation. For Nerone, the impact of pessimistic histories of the public can be lessened with the recognition that the "public" has always mediated the people; the public is always represented. Thus, he argues that "sad histories" about the decline of participation and the rise of spectacle need to be rethought "merely" as changes in an ongoing system of representation.

Peters also calls for a history of continuities not ruptures through his close reading of Carey's telegraph essay. While he recognizes why and how Carey used the telegraph for a particular project, Peters seeks to clarify the telegraph as a technology outside of Carey's complex articulation of technology and culture. He outlines a history of the telegraph as media history, not U.S. history. Locating the telegraph in a media history that had occurred, and was occurring, outside the United States, Peters proposes telegraphy (a cluster of practices involving distance writing) as a more useful organizing point than the telegraph.

It may now be even more apparent that this book is festschrift in neither form nor tone. Yet it is with great respect that all the authors have attempted to think with Carey. The book maintains that spirit by allowing Carey the last word in a second interview in which he addresses a number of the issues the authors have raised. Specifically, he revisits the ritual and transmission models—explaining why they have mattered and what their effect has been on the field—and contemporary politics. The interview also provided Carey with an opportunity to address criticism regarding his stated American cultural studies "provincialism." Most important for us, this interview allowed Carey to dialogue with the authors and the field more generally regarding what new directions it has taken and will continue to take. This concern over the seriousness of our charge as scholars has been at the heart of all of Carey's writing, and it has inspired all of us to take that charge seriously. To that end, we are grateful that Carey has allowed us to think along with him as each of us contemplates the future of communications through communications' past.

Notes

1. James Carey, "Space, Time, and Communications: A Tribute to Harold Innis," *Communication as Culture: Essays on Media and Society* (Boston: Unwin Hyman, 1989), p. 142.
2. John Durham Peters' essay in this volume.

3. James Carey, "The Problem with Journalism History" in Eve Stryker Munson and Catherine A. Warren, eds., *James Carey: A Critical Reader* (Minneapolis: University of Minnesota Press, 1997), p. 88.
4. From Innis, the use of the "oral tradition" as a counterpoint to modern communication technologies. From Dewey, more generally, "history from the standpoint of the present." For a discussion of Dewey see Chris Russill's essay in this volume.
5. James Carey, "The Language of Technology: Talk, Text, and Template as Metaphors for Communication," in *Communication and the Culture of Technology*, ed. Martin Medhurst, Alberto Gonzalez, and Tarla Rai Peterson (Pullman, WA: Washington State University Press, 1990); James Carey, "Commentary: Communications and the Progressives," *Critical Studies in Mass Communication* 6 (1989): 264–82.
6. James Carey, "The Ambiguity of Policy Research," *Journal of Communication* 28 (Spring 1978): 119. See also Munson and Warren, *James Carey: A Critical Reader*, p. 111.
7. Carey, "The Ambiguity of Policy Research," p.119.
8. Carey, "Space, Time, and Communications: A Tribute to Harold Innis," p. 148.
9. James Carey, "The Chicago School and the History of Mass Communication Research," in Eve Stryker Munson and Catherine A. Warren, eds., *James Carey: A Critical Reader* (Minneapolis: University of Minnesota Press, 1997), p. 14.
10. Ibid., p. 14.
11. Carey, "Technology and Ideology: The Case of the Telegraph," *Communication as Culture: Essays on Media and Society* (Boston: Unwin Hyman, 1989), p. 213.
12. Soderlund, chapter 5 in this volume.
13. Carey, "Technology and Ideology: The Case of the Telegraph," *Prospects* 8 (1983): 303–325.
14. Peters' essay in this volume.
15. Carey, "Communication and the Progressives"; Carey, "Introduction," *Communication as Culture: Essays on Media and Society* (Boston: Unwin Hyman, 1989), pp. 1–9; Carey "Afterword: The Culture in Question," in Eve Stryker Munson and Catherine A. Warren, eds., *James Carey: A Critical Reader* (Minneapolis: University of Minnesota Press, 1997), pp. 308–340; Carey, "The Sense of an Ending: On Nations, Communications and Culture," in Catherine A. Warren and Mary Douglas Vavrus, eds. *American Cultural Studies* (Urbana, IL: University of Illinois, 2002), pp. 196–238.
16. Carey, "The Sense of an Ending," p. 210.
17. Carey, "Communications and the Progressives," p. 273.

1. From New England to Illinois: The Invention of (American) Cultural Studies

JAMES CAREY IN CONVERSATION WITH LAWRENCE GROSSBERG, PART 1

Grossberg

We're all very grateful and honored that you agreed to do this. You haven't agreed to do many interviews in your career. Let me tell you what I plan to do. In the first part of the interview I want to talk about your biography, which remains a kind of black hole for many, even for many of your students. In the second part of the interview, there are three major areas in which I want to raise questions: first, the question of cultural studies and the ritual approach to communication; second, issues of technology; and third, issues of contemporary politics. I didn't want to tie the interview too tightly to the chapters because I think there are lots of questions people would like to hear you talk about. So, having said that, let me start with the most obvious question. Could you tell us a little about your background, growing up in Rhode Island, your family background, and so on?

Carey

I grew up in a rather traditional Irish Catholic family in the north end of Providence, along the Woonasquatucket River where the textile mills lined its banks. My family arrived just before and after the Civil War. They became railroad workers on the lines constructed throughout New England. When railroad construction played out, they, like most other workers, went to work in the mills that lined the banks of the river and railroad largely between Worcester, Massachusetts, and Providence. Providence was the end of the line, in a way; that's where they settled in my generation. My grandparents are all from Massachusetts. We grew up in what was an urban village, where generations of people in the same family lived in the same or adjacent houses. It was ethnically homogeneous. The only contact with outsiders was meeting Jewish merchants and peddlers who came through or the occasional Protestant who ventured into the neighborhood to visit an old church of his youth. It was there that my mother and father and my five sisters grew up. I was the second of six children, born in 1934. It would be improper to describe my family as poor in the modern sense, but we were damaged very badly by the Depression and only started to recover during the war. I remember that my father was making eighty dollars a week working in the local shipyard during the war. The day after the war ended, he was laid off and was out of work for two years and finally got a job at twenty-five dollars a week, so it was that kind of up-and-down existence. You just never knew when the work was going to play out.

The rule of the family was that when you were twelve and had your confirmation, you were expected to earn enough money to support yourself in all but room and board. However you did it, you had to carry your own weight. All the women worked in the mills. My mother and aunts were trade union organizers when they weren't in the mill. They had educations through the eighth or ninth grade. My grandparents didn't go to school, except my grandmother went to the first grade before she went into the mills. But the family was very active politically in all the social movements of the times, particularly the trade unions, organizing textile workers and rubber workers and even the mineworkers at one point.

It was by all the measures that I have a fine, interesting childhood. I have no great scars that come from all of this. But it was a premodern childhood. The first refrigerator that we had in the house was about 1946 or 1947. Before that there was Larry the iceman who provided the ice for the icebox. The refrigerator arrived one day from Sears with a coin box on it. You had to put a quarter a day in the refrigerator to keep the damn thing running. That was the installment plan! It was like having a pay telephone in the house. So we were late to the consumer goods culture, which had developed far beyond that. My family never owned an automobile nor held a driver's license. It wasn't until my generation that we started to live a more characteristic middle-class life in terms of what one owned and what one did.

Grossberg

Were you the first child in your family to go to college?

Carey

I was the first child, maybe not the first in the neighborhood, to go to college. There were a couple of World War II veterans that went off to a college that was organized up at Lake Champlain on the New York–Vermont border, one of these emergency universities put up to accommodate veterans seeking an education under the GI Bill. But I was certainly the first in my own family and one of the very first in the neighborhood.

Grossberg

And what was it that motivated you to go to college?

Carey

I wish I could say it was something within me, but it was something within my life situation. When I started school in the first grade, a doctor came into the school and gave a physical examination to all new students to make sure you didn't have TB or another contagious disease. He diagnosed me as having congenital heart disease at a time when the heart was a real dark continent of medicine. The only treatment they knew at the time was to isolate you from other children by keeping you out of crowded places like schools. So I was kept at home and did not go back to school until I was fourteen, in the equivalent of the ninth grade. I started going two hours a day at that point, and then when I was fifteen, I started regular schooling in the tenth grade. Before I was fourteen, I had some homeschooling from a teacher who would come from the Providence Board of Education for an hour a week. It was all very modest, but it was enough that I knew something. But I was simply not allowed to be in school, and I was in and out of hospitals because the treatment at that time was rest. I guess the longest tour of duty was eleven months in a rest hospital for children with cardiac problems of various kinds. So when I started high school, what was then known as the Department of Vocational Rehabilitation said, "What are we gonna do with this person? He can't go in the army; he can't work in the textile mills or the factory system. What the hell is he going to do with his life?" "Well, he should learn how to be a secretary." So I took bookkeeping and shorthand and typing. The only boy in the class with thirty girls, and, therefore, I was thought of as quite a priss. However, at the same time, I showed very untrained but instinctive talent in English, History, and the required courses in the curriculum that I was allowed to take. And so in my junior year, Vocational Rehabilitation started talking about going to college as an alternative to secretarial work. By my senior year, I started to take more "college courses." I was just woefully behind. I could write, but I couldn't parse a sentence. I was terrible at foreign languages. I was good at geometry but bad at arithmetic. There are a lot of skills you build up in school over the course of time. I didn't know any of those things, and as I said in one of my essays, looking back at it, I think of myself as an affirmative action admit before there was an affirmative action system. They said, "What else are you gonna do with this person?" and so the Department of Vocational Rehabilitation sent me off to the state college with a "full disability scholarship"—they paid my room and board on campus, as well as the modest tuition.

So in the fall of 1952, I arrived on the campus of the University of Rhode Island scared to death and completely unprepared for college. I enrolled in the College of Business because it was the only place that would admit someone who didn't have languages or many of the other requirements. I tried at the end of my first semester to switch to the College of Liberal Arts. I'd fallen under the spell of a philosophy professor named Oliver Smith that I'd taken a course with as an elective my first semester. He was a productive scholar, but he was also an extraordinary teacher. It was a course in social/political philosophy and each day he would come into the class and say, "Today I'm Plato," "Today I'm Hegel," and then he would simply enact these philosophers. He wouldn't talk about them, he would enact them, and we would say finally at the end, "But, what do you believe, Professor Smith?" and he would say, "Why do you care what I believe when you now know what Hegel believed, what Plato believed?" He was a very inspirational teacher and was capable of opening a world that was completely foreign and unknown to me. So because of him I tried to transfer to Liberal Arts, but they said, "You have to go back to high school and take all these courses." But, I was too anxious to get on with life. So I stayed in Business largely taking economics and business administration courses.

I found six or so faculty members whom I thought were just tremendous, and I took course after course from them in philosophy, English, economics, statistics, and speech. In statistics I had a great teacher who was an Eisenhower statistician during World War II. He would set us to work on the problems of the invasion of Normandy. He'd say, "Alright, where are we going to put the battleships? Where we gonna station them? What kind of distribution pattern do you get when shells fire? Where do you want them to land? How many of our own people are we gonna kill with friendly fire?" I learned one lesson. Friendly fire is calculated into the whole business of war. It's not some damn accident. It's a matter of statistical probability. But these courses were completely outside of the world I was presumably being trained for—to go off and work for, as an example, a department store.

Anyway, I graduated and ended up doing quite well to my astonishment, and probably the astonishment of my family even more. The motivation was provided by fear of failure, the fear of going back to the neighborhood and saying, "I flunked out." I thought that would be the greatest embarrassment. This was negative reinforcement, not some high idealism. But I fell in love with the academy and liked many things about it.

When I decided to go to graduate school, I took the safe route. I had written for the student newspaper and the yearbook and had written a few successful things on a minor scale. And so I decided to go someplace where I could write journalistically or even do advertising. That led me to apply to Michigan State and Illinois, and I was accepted at both places, but I went to Illinois for whatever reason.

Grossberg

And you met your wife Bette at this time?

Carey

Yes, she was a bit ahead of me at the University of Rhode Island. We met there on a blind date, the way you do at universities. She was the class of '54; I was the class of '56. But I had to drop out for a year and work to support my family, so I didn't get my degree until '57. In the summer of 1957, I graduated and fortuitously at the same time I went to a hospital in Providence to be examined again. A young intern by the name of Max Bloom listened to my heart and said, "I know exactly what's wrong with you." The first time anyone did. So I was then operated on twice in July of 1957. The problem was never completely cured, but it was ameliorated. I did not have a good prognosis at the time. And once that was out of the way, we immediately decided to get married and then in the fall of '57 went to Illinois.

Grossberg

And when was the first child born?

Carey

Nine months and seven days after that.

Grossberg

Good Catholic.

Carey

We struck out at Vatican roulette!

Grossberg

So you and Bette arrived in Champaign, Illinois, and you studied journalism in the College of Communications?

Carey

Well, I studied a number of things . . .

Grossberg

. . . in the Institute of Communication Research?

Carey

No, the Institute at that time was part of the Graduate College. There was a separate committee on Communications that ran a communications Ph.D. program also out of the Graduate College. But, they were separate entities altogether. I enrolled in the master's program in the College in journalism and advertising. I actually took as many courses in economics as anything else. And indeed when I got to the Ph.D. I sat for preliminary examinations in economics separate from communications. In the course of my electives, I took courses from George Gerbner, Dallas Smythe, and Jay Jensen. They encouraged me to think seriously about the academic life, to think seriously about doing something other than journalism. I gradually drifted that way, in part, because the teachers were more interesting, even when I disagreed with them, which I often did.

Grossberg

Who was the "wise man" who told you to read Dewey?[1]

Carey

Jay Jensen. It was as much his philosophical interests and his constant forcing them upon others that cultivated in me an interest in all sorts of scholars. He gave me a very broad philosophical reading list. But he said he thought that

I should start with Dewey, for I would find in Dewey a congenial mind.

Grossberg

Was this during your Ph.D. work?

Carey

During my Ph.D. work . . .

Grossberg

But you didn't use it at that point . . .

Carey

No, I didn't use it at that point. I mean, I started reading at home and it took awhile.

Grossberg

Was Jay your Ph.D. advisor?

Carey

I'm trying to remember now. Yes, he was. It's a little confusing because I actually wrote two dissertations. I wrote one that later became the Innis and McLuhan article.[2] In 1960 Marshall McLuhan came to campus for the summer. He was then unknown, but he had written this manuscript *Understanding Media,* which in its original form was a report to the United States Department of Education that argued that media, particularly television, should be studied seriously in schools. It was a very strange document. But, it was commissioned by the National Association of Educational Broadcasters, which eventually became PBS in another evolutionary cycle. The head of the Educational Broadcasters, Harry Skornia, was on the faculty at Illinois. So, Marshall came and spent the summer with Harry, revising this manuscript, trying to get it in shape. I'd already shown an interest in Innis, whose work Dallas Smythe had introduced me to. Harry started to invite me over to his house in the evening for drinks and conversation on the porch. That started to shape and configure my thinking, and so I wrote a dissertation on Innis and McLuhan, which was not very good, so I didn't turn it in. Then I went off and did something on the economics of communications. It was much safer because no one could understand it, including me. At least the committee couldn't understand it, and they figured I could, or at least they deferred to me. I mean there are good things in it, but nonetheless, it was not a great piece of work.

Grossberg

Can you be more specific? What was it about?

Carey

It was a very formal piece of work. What I did was to ask this question: If we stated what you might call fundamental postulates and theorems of economics and then tried to match them with certain postulates and theorems of communications (largely derived from information theory and the behavioral stuff that was being done at the time), what kind of overlap would there be and what kind of integration was possible? There were some parts that were interesting and some parts that didn't make any sense at all, that still don't make any sense. But it was a useful exercise for me. That's the one I submitted. George Gerbner said to me at the end of my final exam, "I disagreed with everything you say, but I'm not going to fail you." And, I wanted to say, "Well, I disagree with everything you say, and I'm not going to fail you either," but I didn't have the balls to say that at that point in my life.

Grossberg

Did you ever tell him that?

Carey

Yes, our conversations became sharper over the course of time but also mutually supportive. As we became better friends, the more sharply we focused the disagreements.

Grossberg

Was there an economist you were talking to when you wrote this?

Carey

There were two. One is recently deceased: Paul Wells, whose first year at Illinois was my first year. He was a new Ph.D. from Stanford and I took two or three courses from Paul, the standard master's/Ph.D.-level economic theory. There was also a very, very great teacher, though not a great economist in an original sense, by the name of Dwight Flanders. He had taught for years at the military academy at West Point and offered an absolutely smashing course on macro and micro economics. He became a big supporter and friend of mine. There were also a variety of people in the history of economic thought and in Marxist economics. There was still some residue of Marxism in the College of Business at the time, though much of it had been driven out during the McCarthy era. It disappeared subsequently. I also took some work in the philosophy of science and the history of science and the "soft" social sciences. It was a relatively open curriculum, beyond that first year, so I did a variety of things. I took a few courses from Fred Will in philosophy, which absolutely mystified me. Fred, like his son [George], was a baseball fan. We'd be reading Wittgenstein, and he would say, "Let's think about the infield fly rule in baseball. What would Wittgenstein say about that?" And then Fred would lapse into silence, and I didn't have a thought in my head [laughter]. But I learned a lot from him anyway, even though I was unprepared for work at that level of analytic philosophy at the time.

Grossberg

And then, when you finished your Ph.D., you got a job at Illinois?

Carey

I turned in the second dissertation in '62 and got the degree in January of '63. I had offers from the journalism schools at Northwestern and Berkeley and from Illinois and a few others. The Northwestern job paid about five thousand dollars a year. We would have died in Evanston with four children on that kind of salary, so I turned it down. I was very interested in Berkeley because the center of hostility to the Journalism program at Berkeley was in the Sociology department, which perhaps was at its apogee with Goffman and Neil Smelser, Seymour Martin Lipset, and a comparable group of stars. They wanted someone who could be in journalism but could talk to the sociologists. I was twenty-eight years old. It would have been very challenging. But I stayed in Illinois, where I was in the Department of Journalism, but I was to teach the communications courses that were offered out of Journalism as electives.

Grossberg

In one of your essays, you write that "In the fall of 1963, I suggested the label cultural studies, for. . . ."[3] What happened? Between '62 having submitted a dissertation on economics and information studies in communication and a previous dissertation on McLuhan and Innis, what happened to get you to cultural studies?

Carey

It was a matter of ecology; the claim originally was nothing more than that. The Illinois program at the time was divided between macro and micro studies. There was the macro proseminar, and there was the micro proseminar. On the micro side there was Charlie Osgood and many psychologists, information theorists, etc. In the macro half of the class there was Gerbner, Smythe, Jensen, Bill Albig (who was a sociologist), and a changing cast of characters, largely sociologists who came and went after a few years: Bennett Berger, Joe Gusfield, Murray Edelman. Some of these people were doing literary type of work; some were reading Kenneth Burke (who, when Marie Nichols retired, was not being read over in the Speech department); some were trying to do politics, but not on the behavioral model dominant in political science as it was understood at that time. They all lectured in the macro proseminar about large-scale problems. It might be worth saying that many of the people we are talking about, who were very important, particularly in sociology at Illinois, came from the University of Chicago. They were classmates of Goffman; they were part of this post–World War II group. They were largely urban and Jewish at a time when the university was very Scandinavian.

Dallas intensely disliked anyone who was not a Marxist, either a Stalinist or a Maoist, or whatever he was at that particular time. And, therefore, he defined Marxism as the science of society and the other stuff that everyone else did as history in order to make it inconsequential. In other words, you could either do serious intellectual work, science on a behavioral formal or Marxist model, or you could do history. History was to many like poetry: a lot of fun, fairly engaging, but you can't make any serious claims for it or from it. While the micro people could live with Dallas, strangely enough— and that may have been because they shared certain political beliefs that had nothing to do with their intellectual work—they were less happy with these irregular people, who came and went. And, so I said to myself, "I have to find a name for these irregular historians, sociologists and then to try to convince the Marxists to join with us. I had read, over the course of that summer (probably as part of dissertation work), *The Logic of the Cultural Sciences* by

Max Weber. This was my first introduction to that hermeneutical, *verstehen* tradition, if you will, in its European form. I liked "cultural science" as a name, but I didn't want to use the word "science." Osgood and the other hard-nosed scientists would castrate me. So, I started to think of this assorted group of scholars under the umbrella name of cultural studies.

Cultural studies was then little more than a term to describe the perceived commonalities in the work of Joe Gusfield, Jay Jensen, Erving Goffman, Thomas Kuhn, symbolic interactionism and the Chicago School of Sociology, Kenneth Burke, Leslie Fiedler and a small group of literary critics, and, of course, Marshall McLuhan and Harold Innis, along with those Marxists willing to associate with a group largely affiliated in opposition to positivism and positive science. This was a strange group to patch together, against their will, if they knew about it, but nonetheless I carved out a section of the proseminar under the label "cultural studies." I didn't realize at the time that others were using the same title elsewhere to describe their work. Though a few years earlier, following some disagreements with George Gerbner on the nature of popular culture, he came to me one day with a copy of Raymond Williams's *Culture and Society* and said, "You ought to read this, you'll find this much more to your liking." I think he recognized the affinity from the outside.

Grossberg

So Gerbner introduced you to the British tradition?

Carey

Yes, maybe out of exasperation.

Grossberg

When did you become aware of the American studies people in the '60s like Leo Marx and Alan Trachtenberg and people who were on a path similar to yours?

Carey

It was, believe it or not, through John Quirk. John is the illusive figure in this story. He was a political radical during the '60s and probably today. He was an undergraduate who took a couple of courses from me in the mid-1960s at the time of the first of the Vietnam teach-ins.

John was a very strange fellow, deeply, profoundly intelligent who at nineteen seemed to have read everything. He never graduated from the university. He was a kind of autodidact, who disappeared into Chicago after dropping out and I could not find him today. When he dropped out of school prematurely, we began a genuine and richly rewarding collaboration. He taught me much and introduced me to a wide variety of literature, particularly in American studies. He was also very active politically but sometimes in odd and strange ways. He used to go around picking up, not only the official documents of the university but also deeply revealing private documents that were just thrown out in an age before the shredder. He used these documents to challenge, and sometimes to humiliate, the university administration, finding lies and contradictions in official pronouncements and rank hypocrisy in their dealings with students. Anyway, he first pointed out Leo Marx to me in some work he did in a course of mine, and that is when we started to do some work together. There were aspects of the literature that he commanded better than I did. So it was a genuine collaboration, albeit an unfulfilled one. As I said, I couldn't find John now. He just disappeared into the underlife of Chicago. He was very smart but also very difficult to work with because of periodic bouts of mental instability. That made it a tough and exhausting collaboration. He could only work under the worst deadlines. So, two days before we had to get our piece into *The American Scholar,* he arrived in town and we worked forty-eight hours without sleeping.[4] I concluded that he could only work at break-neck speed and with the closest of deadlines.

Grossberg

Between the time Gerbner gave you *Culture and Society* and the time I got there in '70, did you have any contact with Stuart Hall?

Carey

I read *Culture and Society* and admired it very much, and then I read *The Long Revolution* and whatever other things I could get my hands on at the time. Williams was, of course, not very well known in 1960. When you found his stuff reviewed, it tended to be in political science journals, not in literary journals. When I published the piece on Innis and McLuhan, later in the '60s, Richard Hoggart wrote me a note in which he said how much he liked the piece, and we started to correspond a bit. I sent him the course outline I was using to teach something called cultural studies. It was largely reading Durkheim, and Weber, and Goffman and the Chicago School, a variety of people I was interested in. He sent me back a reading list from Birmingham, which had many similarities. They were trying to break out of literature and into social theory and social thought, so there was a kind of enormous unplanned convergence. That gave me more confidence in using the label cultural studies, because they had already named their program the Center for Contemporary Cultural Studies. And, Stuart saw this stuff as it went back and forth, too. I'd read the early book he had done with Paddy Whannell on the popular arts. So, I came to know, distantly and largely by correspondence, this cast of people, and I admired many things they were doing.

Grossberg

You talked a little about Gerbner and Smythe. What about Herb Schiller when he arrived at the Institute? What was your relation with Gerbner, Smythe, and Schiller?

Carey

These were all quite different personalities, but all were in their way splendid teachers, particularly George and Dallas. Troubles came at dissertation time, however. There were many reasons for not wanting to work with Smythe, but the major thing was that he was an authoritarian personality—you did things his way, or you didn't do them at all. Dallas was the most difficult. There were a number of unwritten dissertations at Illinois, dissertations that foundered on the rock of Dallas Smythe saying, in effect, it is not ideologically correct.

George Gerbner was more generous and tolerant, but he wanted his students to work on his project, for example, what was later called the Cultural Indicators Project. I always got nervous around George because he, too, had an Eastern European authoritarian streak to his personality. But he did recognize that I did not want to think the way he thought about these matters, cut me some slack and, in later years, was supportive of many of the things I wanted to do, particularly administrative projects.

I had a worse relationship with Herb Schiller, though perfectly congenial on the surface. Dallas Smythe was a charming man. Unfortunately, he could charm you out of your socks, before you knew what happened. I never found Herb charming. I suppose I found Herb less straightforward in what he did. He was a very hard-line Marxist of a certain kind, who was always looking for a fight. He stated his views in ways designed to antagonize and alienate everyone but true believers. But he was supremely bourgeois. When the troubles began at the campus in the 1960s, Herb couldn't be bothered. He was home reading the *New York Times* and clipping articles for his next book. And, if he rose to speak in a public forum, it was only to attack and alienate everyone there, not to deal with any of the problems we were struggling with: some very important problems on questions of student rights and access to the campus by political figures who were being kept off because of the nature of their beliefs. In other words, Herb was not interested in political work which he left to others, nor was he a good academic citizen. I encountered Herb as a bourgeois Marxist; a particularly unattractive example of the breed who speaks of fiery rebellion and lets other people go out and take risks and clean up in the aftermath but doesn't take any risks himself.

I found Tom Guback to be the same. Tom was a good teacher of small numbers of students, but he was a completely irresponsible faculty member. His classes characteristically met for the first session with twenty students enrolled. By the second meeting only three enrollees remained (or thereabouts, I exaggerate) with the others driven into the classes of colleagues. Guback had a kind of ideological orthodoxy to him, and, yet, he had a cultivated private life. That's fine but he never thought about the contradiction between that life and his claims to be conducting some kind of revolutionary struggle.

Grossberg

How much of your relationship to Marxism over the years was shaped by these relationships with people like Dallas and Herb?

Carey

Well, it certainly was partly shaped by them, but it was formed during a particular time, and other people influenced me as well, particularly Sidney Hook, whom I admired, especially his early works. Hook was unusual because he was so close to Dewey. I didn't agree with him as he got older. But there was another aspect to my relation to Marxism—very much from my experience of life itself. When I reflect back on it, there is a kind of continuous tension between myself, Marxism, and the theory of culture that centers on issues of religion

For my family, trying to decide where to cast its political allegiances during the 1930s, there was of course FDR and the Democratic Party, and there was the Communist Party, which was active in Providence in trade union circles as it was everyplace else, and there were the Catholic Workers and the pacifists. I'm really attributing a mature thought to an immature mind; I understand that. But, I know that the old IWW I came to admire later on, and my family admired, had the slogan that said, "If you don't come in on Sunday, don't come in on Monday," meaning Sunday does not belong to the church but to the party. That was the attitude of the Communist Party as well. And, like Stuart Hall much later, I think that was a gross misunderstanding of the practical role religion at large played in people's lives.

Where to hold political meetings? We held them in the basement of the church. I mean, it was the only space available to us. I mean, they gave space to the Communist Party to come harangue us when they wished to do that. But, religion answered, in addition to metaphysical questions like what happens to me after I'm gone; it answered questions like: How do you bury the dead? How do you consecrate the ground? How do you retain memory of people? These are practical problems when your grandparents are dying, and you have to ask, how are we going to do this? The CP had no answer for that. They kind of recommended leaving the dead on the porch until they disintegrated. To do more was rank superstition. This produced a tension in the family. We were not theological Catholics; we were ritual Catholics and organizational ones. That is to say, we found satisfactions in the rituals of the church. We found meaning in it at many bad times. The church would also help us take care of all sorts of problems that the political system couldn't help us with: problems with children, problems with the great difficult moments of life—birth, death, and this sort of thing. And so, on these questions, on the practical side of life, I was always tempted to say things like until Marxism gets an adequate theory of culture, read as a theory of religion, an understanding of religion beyond the opiate of the people, it is not going to get very far in attracting to it the numbers it needs to be effective politically.

So, I may have felt much different about Marxism, but I encountered it in its Stalinist phase. When Dallas said, "I want all the graduate students to lie down on Friday afternoon on the Illinois Central tracks near the power plant to protest American policy toward Cuba," we all thought: That goddamn engineer may not see us! I mean this was the director of the program. That's what I mean by a certain authoritarian spirit which I don't think works very well with most Americans at that stage in their life and which deformed Marxism.

And deformed it unnecessarily, you know. So Tom Guback would tell his students that they did not have to see anything in or about a movie except that it is an MGM picture, and that's a Warner Brothers picture, and they are both from Hollywood studio systems. But, if you said to him, "Isn't it interesting that different capitalist cultures produce different kinds of representations of the real?" (Now, maybe this is not a big problem in relation to where the world is going, but it's interesting.) But he would simply tell the students that it was absurd to even be interested in that sort of thing except as a pleasant diversion. Marxism could have held onto the core of the economic analysis but still given the "theory" enough freedom that you could bring into it other kinds of questions, which, if nothing else, are interesting and which are satisfying to a variety of different types of personalities, whose attention is arrested by different kinds of phenomena.

Grossberg

Your description here brings to mind something you wrote about Innis—when you talk about Innis as an essayist and you say the essay for Innis was an essay because it was both tentative and urgent.

Carey

That's right.

Grossberg

But, I wanted to turn that back on you. Is that why you're an essayist? Because you certainly are an essayist as opposed to . . .

Carey

Well, I mean, one reason is that the essay is what I think I do best, and maybe if I did other things better, I'd do something else. I admire people who can write big books, who can control them. I've tried it; I've written some of them, but they're unpublished. But a book also makes a claim for a certain kind of arrest and finality. An essay is something you can keep revisiting, "Did I get it right? Let me try it again from a different point of view." For me, it's a more fluid form of thought; things are kept in a contingent frame of thought..

Grossberg

I have one small biographical question. In your move from Illinois to New York were you conscious that you were following Dewey's path, when he moved from the University of Chicago to Columbia University in the early twentieth century?

Carey

Yes, I was in one sense. I mean, there were two reasons behind the move. One is the obvious one that I gave at the time. After thirty years at Illinois, twenty of them as dean and department head, I could have settled into a very comfortable life at Illinois with minimal demands and had a good time and made a lot of money and all, but, partly, I wanted to be challenged by a new environment by coming to New York where I was less in my element. Some-where I'd have to start all over again. I didn't want to retire in that sense, as attractive as it was. And secondly, if I had been looking for all those years at the metropolis from the hinterland and indeed if many of the criticisms in the manuscripts about me reflected where I was and where I was looking, it was time to look the other way, to try to see the hinterland from the metropolis, to try to see life more from within it. So it just seemed to me it would open up other avenues of exploration that would lead in the long run, one hopes, to more balanced and nuanced understandings.

Grossberg

Following that, I think people thought—just as Dewey when he moved to New York, in a way, entered into a more public life—part of the expectation, which you might have had (and I think others had), was that when you came to New York you might have taken up the journalistic kind of writing you had practiced earlier. That you would take on a much more public voice, which you would have access to, especially through Columbia. But you haven't.

Carey

No, I haven't really. I've done some of it, and I've certainly done a lot on the speaking and lecturing side of it. I've written for *The Columbia Journalism Review* . . .

Grossberg

But, you haven't written for the *New York Times* a lot, which one would have thought . . .

Carey

No, I've had some tensions with the *Times*. I was offered the possibility of writing the media column for *The Nation* at a time when Victor Navasky was trying out some people. I've now been offered a permanent column in *The Columbia Journalism Review* if I want it. The column scares me. It's like being married to a nymphomaniac. You finish one, and it's ready to start up again. There's no rest. I do get a little afraid of taking it on in the midst of other things. And, some of the stuff that I have done publicly in New York, I've not found satisfying in some ways. I don't want to go on Sean Hannity. Why should I go take his goddamn abuse? I've been on CNN a number of times. But you're often sitting in an airless room by yourself, formerly down at One Penn Plaza, and you're connected to Los Angeles and Atlanta, where there are four or five other people, and you've got this simulated conversation where you're just staring at a red light. This doesn't engage me, and I'm not very happy doing it. And I realize, I guess I always have known it, that New York life is very wired. Nothing happens spontaneously here. And so when you get asked to do things, they have preselected you to play a role, and it's usually a role in which you're going to look bad to make the other people they've preselected look good. So there are real defects in this system of public discourse. I've enjoyed writing some stuff for *The Nation* and doing some interviews for *The Nation* and in a variety of other places. But, I haven't done as much. Now it's in part because, as you know, I'm a teacher in the sense that the first thing I think about when I get up in the morning is "What's my class today?" "What do I have to say?" I mean its just part of me, that's all. I hope I do more, but we'll see.

Notes

1. "When I decided some years ago to read seriously the literature of communications, a wise man suggested I begin with John Dewey." James Carey, *Communication as Culture: Essays on Media and Society* (New York: Routledge, 1989), p.13.
2. James Carey, "Harold Adams Innis and Marshall McLuhan," *Antioch Review* 27 (Spring 1967): 5–39.
3. James Carey, "Reflections on the Project of (American) Cultural Studies," in Marjorie Ferguson and Peter Golding, eds., *Cultural Studies in Question* (London: Sage, 1997).
4. James Carey and John Quirk, "The Mythos of the Electronic Revolution, Parts 1, 2," *American Scholar*, 39 (Spring, Summer, 1970): 219–41, 395, 424.

2. Between Cultural Materialism and Spatial Materialism: James Carey's Writing about Communication

JAMES HAY

Transporting Cultural Materialism and Historicizing the "Spatial Bias" and the Geography of Communication Studies: Two Models of Communication, Then and Now

During the 1970s and 1980s, James Carey's distinction between a cultural model and a transportation model of communication became a prominent framework in the United States for cultural studies of media and communication and, more generally, for explaining the objectives of communication studies. Although Carey had argued since the early 1960s that *culture* had become too often overlooked and simplified in North American communication studies, his 1975 essay, "A Cultural Approach to Communication," and his 1977 essay, "Mass Communication and Cultural Studies," developed an argument about the need to rethink *communication* (as ritual rather than as transmission/transportation) and to install a "cultural model of communication" in a disciplinary discourse that had come, in his opinion, to overemphasize communication as transmission and transportation.[1] Although Carey acknowledged that these two views can be seen as transpositions of one another, his attempt to define a cultural model of communication as an alternative to a transmission/transportation model often led him in these essays to underscore their difference.[2] In that Carey considered communication as ritual to have become a *minor* definition in U.S. communication research, Carey's essays mined a disciplinary knowledge in order to underscore not only that communication studies rested upon this minor definition but that recognizing this minor definition's relation to the primary objectives of communication research would lead communication studies to pose an alternative set of questions.

In this chapter (and particularly in this section), I am interested in discussing some of the tensions and contradictions of Carey's distinction between the ritual and transmission models of communication and in focusing upon those instances where his binarism breaks down—especially as these tensions and contradictions represent points of intersection, and as these intersections represent a framework for an analytic of communication concerned with the relation between temporality and spatiality, history and geography, and (to use Carey's terms) ritual and transmission. Describing this analytic (one of the primary objectives of this essay) requires acknowledging at the outset several points about Carey's formulation of these two models. First, while contrasting a transmission and a ritual model of communication may have been a useful and even necessary rhetorical strategy and intervention in the 1970s, the distinction has been read more as a binarism than as a framework for thinking about the multiple (situated and changing) ways that communication is modeled through the lives of various populations and classes. Along these lines, the distinction also has been cited in efforts to justify fundamental incongruities (particularly in the United States) between communication science, political economy of media, and cultural studies. During the 1990s, Carey sought to clarify and amend the early versions of his argument about communication as transmission and ritual, in part to qualify and/or dispel particularly this latter assumption. (As Luigi Pirandello dramatized, such are the perils of designing models that assume a life of their own, tormenting their "inventor.") Casting Carey as inventor or author of a "ritual model of communication" (whether one sees communication research as a science or interpretation) is also a bit misleading. His modeling of communication involved *translating* (introducing or reintroducing from other continents, earlier periods, and various disciplinary knowledges)—literatures that were marginal and ostensibly anathema to communication research, even as his proposal was having a significant impact on how those doing communication studies in the United States thought about what they were doing and even as his proposal was mobilizing and legitimating something called cultural studies in U.S. communication departments. (And, in 1985, as a new assistant professor at the University of Illinois, where Carey was dean of the College of Communication, I counted myself among the individuals caught up in his way of posing questions about the legacy of U.S. communication research and about how cultural studies mattered differently in the United States than elsewhere.)

In later responses to his 1970s essays, Carey has been adamant that he considered a ritual model of communication to be primarily a response—an intervention and an alternative—to the dominance and authority of positivism in U.S. communication research and policy and to a growing interest in cultural studies in U.S. communication research. But, he has been less inclined (until this book) to use and reflect upon transmission and transportation as the key terms/issues that they were in the 1970s essays.[3] In "Reflections on the Project of (American) Cultural Studies" (1997), he outlines five primary objectives for having described a ritual model of communication, as he has since the 1970s, in relation to the positivist strain of U.S. communication research (behavioralism and social psychologism), political economy of media, and cultural studies. One objective, he states, was to emphasize that "the constitution of ritual form through communication is pulled off, first of all, by embedding *conceptions* of time and space, duration and extent, history and geography, into the model and artifacts of the process [of communication as practice] and then *living,* in a consummatory fashion, the very conceptions therein embedded" (italics mine).[4] Although this stated objective and its relation to the other objectives are not elaborated further in the 1997 essay, they are (as I intend to explain in this chapter) crucial to his early essays' contribution not only to communication research and policy and to cultural studies in the United States but also in fashioning what I have described as a *spatial materialism* and a spatial materialist view of communication and media.[5] This spatial materialism is more or less congruent with Carey's claim (in the 1997 essay) that "the emphasis [in a ritual model of communication] on language, culture, and meaning does not exclude issues of power and conflict; instead it attempts to *locate* them . . . to locate the mechanisms by which differentials of power and intractable conflict are buried, deflected, resolved, exercised, and aggregated into interests."[6]

In order to elaborate what I mean by a spatial materialism of communication and culture and why Carey's writing is relevant to this perspective, I begin by considering a particular facet of Carey's writing. As an intervention—a critique of the dominant paradigm of U.S. communication studies and a proposal for an alternative analytic of communication—Carey's account of the ritual view of communication was about correcting the "spatial bias" of U.S. communication research and policy through an awareness and analysis of (cultural) *history.* In the 1970s and 1980s, Carey's essays affirmed that critiquing the dominant paradigm—emphasizing how its (re)production occurred within a cultural history—involved recognizing and rethinking the geography of communication studies.

For Carey, cultural/historical analysis served to denaturalize the subjects, objects, and objectivity that communication research as positivist science assumed about its project, and thus served to denaturalize the dominant position that this research paradigm had achieved in the United States following the Second World War. In his explanation (and embedded historicization) of both models, Carey pointed to twentieth-century communication studies' perpetuation of nineteenth-century thinking about the spatiality of communication. In his opinion, the dominant view of communication as "persuasion, attitudinal change, behavior modification, and socialization through the transmission of information" was inseparable from the nineteenth-century desire to "use communication and transportation to extend influence, control, and power over wider distances and over greater populations."[7] For Carey, the dominant view of communication in U.S. research and policy thus understood space in the terms of nineteenth- and twentieth-century frontier projects (terrestrial space, air space, outer space)—that is, as a container to be filled and an empirically verified and calculated distance to be overcome and managed. And, in these terms, communication had been understood and developed as a basis simultaneously for *settlement* (reconciling the distance between two points/individuals, making way for a population) and for population *management*. The spatial bias of communication research and policy (a conception of space supporting a particular model of communication research and particular objectives of communication policy) thus relentlessly wed communication technologies to the ideal of progress—a progress that could be measured and, through measurement, settled/managed peacefully. (Unless, of course, one views the technologies of measurement as instrumental for an ongoing war of expansion waged under the banner of progress and settlement.)

For Carey, calling attention to the spatial bias of communication research and policy—the disposition toward a *present-mindedness* and an idea of *progress* measured in terms of managing distance and geographic frontiers—involved not only recalling the *historical* conjunctures and imperatives of this bias but also calling attention to the displacement of communication as *ritual*. Carey also emphasized the *temporality* (communication's repetition/reproduction in daily life, the conventionalization of language and meaning, and communication as "a process through which a shared culture is created, modified, and transformed"[8]) of ritual. This emphasis was central to Carey's *constructionist* view of communication as a form of representation, and as such promised to correct the *intentionalist* and *reflectionist* conceptions of representation perpetuated by a transmission model of communication. However, Carey's account was decidedly more historicist than were many structuralist and semiotic analyses in cultural criticism—an inclination that he shared with the voices of early British cultural studies (such as Raymond Williams and Richard Hoggart) whom he admired. As such, a ritual model of communication was a means of introducing historical flux, process, and conjuncture to an understanding/analysis of communication as transmission, and a means of recognizing that communication practice pertained to cultural histories that were no longer recognized by much of communication/media research.

This historicist (or cultural historicist) view of the spatial bias in communication research was evident, for instance, in Carey's argument that both transmission and ritual models developed over centuries through Western religion—through a knowledge and cultural practice that was not reducible to political or economic institutions. Citing Emile Durkheim's *Elementary Forms of Religious Life,* Carey's description of communication as a ritual most clearly acknowledges the historical connection between communication and Western religion (and thus the intersection of communication research and anthropology). Yet, in "A Cultural Approach to Communication" he also discusses "the moral meaning of transportation," which he emphasizes in order to acknowledge the religious dimension of the spatial conception of communication in the United States (for example, telegraphy as instrumental to manifest destiny), and thus to acknowledge both the cultural and territorial/territorializing (Western) dimension of communication as transportation. Pointing out the relation between religion and communication as transmission underscores the historical interrelation (not just the distinction) between two understandings of communication—one about transportation and the other about ritual.

Carey's historicization of the ritual and transmission models of communication also placed communication research within the *modern* problematic that Weber famously described in his account of the prestige of science and rationality through Western religion, and that Ferdinand Tonnies notably explored in his distinction between gemeinschaft and gesellschaft, that is, the displacement of the premodern conception of *oeconomia* (household management) by modern *political economy,* and the formation of modern *society* around the displacement of *community* (a collectivization, propinquity, and sharing that Tonnies described as the "extended family table"). Carey's rationale for supporting a ritual/cultural model of communication (as I explain below) was prone to valorize communitarianism and forms of "fellowship"—forms of spiritual expressivity/practice that, as he pointed out, were anathema to scientific positivism and that contributed to the "derangement" in models of communication and community in contemporary life.[9] He also claimed that the dominant paradigm of communication research was grounded more in science than religion,[10] a view that perpetuated not only the nineteenth-century arguments of Tonnies and Durkheim but the 1950s debates in the United States about science and culture famously elaborated by C. P. Snow. However, Carey also extracted from Durkheim a more subtle point (to which I return below) that "society," regulated by utility and contract, "could not work *without* the integrative mechanisms of Gemeinschaft" (italics mine).[11]

In elaborating what he meant by a ritual model of communication, Carey therefore called attention to twin structured absences in communication policy/research. First, he noted the failure to understand media/communication as a cultural form (communication as expressive and formally complicated) or as a cultural practice (communication as integral to and pro-

ductive of certain "ways of life"). And, second, Carey recognized the failure
to understand its objects and objectives as having developed out of long and
short histories. Such histories include twentieth-century communication
research's perpetuation of nineteenth-century dispositions, communication
research and technological development as "modern" and as supporting programs of modernization, the development of communication science out of
long-standing Western religions, and similarly the "moral meaning of transportation" (and transmission) in the relocation and expansion of Western
religions/cultures. In both senses, culturalism mattered to Carey because it
historicized U.S. communication research's spatial bias. By emphasizing ritualization, long historical processes, the productive/transformative capacity of
culture (culture's role in "making history"), and understanding the imperatives of communication, research, and policy through historical ways of life,
culturalism countered communication research's inability to see communication as anything but expansion, territory, and control.[12] It challenged the
social authority and legitimacy of U.S. communication research by turning
attention to the *history* of the present and of the present-mindedness of the
dominant paradigm. It shared with structural anthropology an interest in
denaturalizing modern rationality as well as science's presumption of a direct
access to nature and truth—the "spatial bias" of U.S. communication
research referring both to the research's conception of communication as
transmission (involving sender-message-receiver) and to the research's social
authority and legitimacy that accrued through the symbolic form of its
method (science's implication in a system of representation).

However, casting culture as a dimension of communication that had
been *forgotten* by communication research, Carey's emphasis on time and history—and on culture as community and fellowship—also carried a nostalgic
charge. The return of culture to communication analysis offered a path to
recognizing and restoring community and fellowship through a research program that valued expansion and modernization, leaving scant room for recognizing "common cultures"—either as a research object, as a condition for
its own knowledge, or as an objective in the present. Like many modern
social theories, Carey's ritual mode (particularly in its early versions)
lamented the loss of community to the self-interest, privatization, and utility
of "society" (and to the insularity of communication science's increasing disciplinarity).

> The object, then, of recasting our studies of communication in terms of a ritual
> model is not only to more firmly grasp the essence of this "wonderful" process
> but to give us a way in which we rebuild a model of and for communication of
> some restorative value in reshaping our common culture.[13]

Invoking Tonnies's contrast between premodern *oeconomia* and modern
"economy" in order to challenge the spatial bias of communication research,

Carey thus viewed culturalism's historicizing project as a potential framework for preventing self-interest from "overtaking the entire household of the social."

The historicist perspective about the longevity and dominance of a spatial bias in U.S. communication research and policy, and about the need for a (forgotten) ritual model of communication, involved for Carey a reassessment of the legacy of the Chicago School, which he considered to be as much a "resource" for a latter-day culturalism in U.S. communication research as it was a turning point when a culturalist view of communication was sidetracked, overwhelmed by the spatial bias of the dominant paradigm. While his distinction between a ritual and a transmission model of communication relies upon numerous theoretical references and resources, his most cogent early elaboration of this distinction, in "A Cultural Approach to Communication," opens by considering the significance to communication research of John Dewey's statement, "society exists not only by transmission, by communication, but it may fairly be said to exist in transmission, in communication."[14] The ambiguity of this statement bespeaks Carey's ambivalent account of the Chicago School's legacy, and the statement serves as an anchor for the essay's rationale about fashioning a ritual model of communication by re-articulating (or refashioning) particular impulses from social research that he associates with the Chicago School. The impulses that he found most worth recovering were the Chicago School's sociology of community life—a research program that was concerned with, among other things, the emerging and residual forms of communication that accompanied the migration of ethnic populations (that is, communication as one of many practices informed by and shaping community and "common culture"). He also supported their research's preoccupation with the ordinariness (the *commonness*—the everydayness and sharedness) of culture and communication and gleaned from this impulse the basis for an early kind of social science in the United States about the cultural production of the real and the ordinary.[15]

The importance that Carey attributed to the Chicago School in charting a relation between a ritual and a transmission model of communication had less to do with valorizing an indigenous lineage of communication research in the United States, a move that would have affirmed his research's universalizing tendency (its spatial bias), than with considering the Chicago School as a laboratory shaped by a changing geography/map of social analysis, as well as by competing models of "mapping" communication. It is worth following the implications of how his preoccupation with history involved a changing geography of social analysis because, although his distinction between two models of communication valorized historicism, this valorization involved locating U.S. social and communication research in relation to European and Canadian historiography.

In one sense, Carey considered European and U.S. conceptions of communication as having developed out of "quite different kinds of intellectual puzzles" and as having produced "two different metaphors for communication,"[16] which Carey, through his formulation of the two models of communication, sought to bridge and/or to play against one another. In another sense, Carey found the intersection of these two puzzles and metaphors in the early Chicago School research. The changing geography of social research, and the tension that he attributed to the emergence of communication research through the Chicago School between a deepening spatial bias and an impulse toward cultural sociology and toward a culturalist communication research, involved the application of European (particularly German) social theory by researchers at the Chicago School. Carey viewed this approach as, like his own work, framed in terms of a dualism between community and society, and in terms of cultural formation in urban, industrialized, and "mass-mediated" agglomerations. He saw it as less about social critique or cultural criticism, less engaged with the theories of power running through the work of Marx, Tonnies, Weber, Simmel (with whom Robert Park studied), Kracauer, or the culturology of the early Frankfurt School, and decidedly more committed to affirming the progressive possibilities of community and communication in the multiethnic U.S. city and liberal democratic government. Carey (not alone) rightly notes the incongruity between European social theory's critical accounts of modern industrial, scientific, and political *rationality* and the Chicago School's commitment to developing a social *science* (sociological mappings) of community, culture, and communication—a science that (as Carey notes) was readily adapted to the aims of liberal democratic politics in the United States.

In mapping the research of the Chicago School in terms of its appropriation of European social theory, Carey may have ignored the universalist assumptions of both European and U.S. (that is, Western) accounts of modern society, even as he implied that the spatial bias of U.S. communication research contributed to its provincialism—if not an exceptionalism—with respect to European social theory and with respect to that research's attention to highly localized communities in U.S. cities (such as the agglomeration of ethnically and racially defined "communities"/settlements in early-twentieth-century Chicago). The matter of provincialism and cosmopolitanism is further complicated given that race and ethnicity were more a focus of Chicago School social research than of European social theory and cultural criticism. The Chicago School's attention to racialized communities made the U.S. research about both localization and migration/displacement (of population and culture) and about the adaptation of "old cultures" to modern, urban environments. (Carey's advocacy for a ritual model of communication thus recognized U.S. communication research's difference/dis-

tance from European social critique and cultural criticism [European cultur-
ologies of modern life], while emphasizing, as was more typical of European
social critique and cultural criticism, that a ritual model heightened recognition of the historical contingency of knowledge and beliefs.) Carey also
defended the Chicago School's not having emphasized (as had European
Marxism and some of the prominent European social theories) class, economy, capitalism, and industrial rationality as the fundamental determiners of
modern life and culture, and as having emphasized instead a more diverse
array of conditions shaping modern life.

During the 1970s, Carey's historical account of the spatial bias of U.S.
communication research (and of the latency within this research paradigm of
a ritual model of communication that he associates with the Chicago School)
described a changing geography/map of social analysis that had as much to
do with the trans-Atlantic, cross-cultural currency of European social thought
in the early twentieth century as with British cultural studies and Canadian
media/communication studies. Carey's account was less a defense or lioniza-
tion of the Chicago School (since he undoubtedly viewed it as caught up in
and propelling some of the dominant impulses of U.S. communication
research and policy that he rejected) than an effort to think historically about
the territorialization and deterritorialization of theory and analysis that made
possible, or impeded, the introduction of a ritual model's emphasis on temporality and history (on cultural analysis) in U.S. communication research
and policy. During the 1970s, his reading of the Chicago School to elaborate
what he meant by a ritual model of communication occurred through reviews
and citations of writing by Williams, Hoggart, Stuart Hall, Clifford Geertz,
and Harold Innis.[17] As such, Carey's prescriptions about a ritual model were
as much about rethinking/recalling tendencies of the Chicago School in
order to justify the relevance in the United States of a non-U.S. analytic of
communication as they were about envisaging a kind of cultural study of
communication in light of the deeply rooted disposition of U.S. communication research/policy that developed out of the Chicago School.

Explaining the significance of the Chicago School through writing from
outside the United States figured into Carey's explanation of a ritual model
in various ways. For instance, Carey's review-essay about Geertz's newly published *The Interpretation of Culture* dwelt upon Geertz's Chicago School
pedigree as well as Geertz's openness to structuralism and social semiotics
that had been informing studies of culture and communication in Europe
since the 1950s. Carey's assessment of Canadian Harold Innis's legacy for
U.S. communication studies also stressed both his affiliation with and inclination away from the trends of the Chicago School since the 1930s.[18] In
"Culture, Geography, and Communication: The Work of Harold Innis in an
American Context," after pointing out that Innis studied somewhat later at

the University of Chicago than the period that Carey finds exemplary and thus refuting Marshall McLuhan's opinion that Innis "should be considered as the most eminent member of the Chicago group headed by Robert Park" (p. 75), Carey describes Innis's importance as an alternative perspective with respect to the social psychology and behavioralism that became the dominant paradigm in U.S. communication research: "Innis provided in communication studies, at a moment when no one else in the United States was doing so, a model of scholarly investigation that was historical, empirical, interpretive, and critical" (p. 79). Although Carey adopted Innis as a frequent and relatively crucial reference point in his conception of two models of communication,[19] Carey's greatest affinity in explaining/justifying a ritual model (aside from Innis) was undoubtedly with Raymond Williams's culturalism and, by the 1970s (when Carey cited him frequently), Williams's representation/advocacy of a *cultural materialism*. Since the 1950s (particularly in *Culture and Society* and *The Long Revolution*), Williams had argued for understanding art and literature (the nineteenth-century models of culture) as communication and had described communication as the basis for modern formations of community (a term that Carey adopted to explain what the transmission model had overlooked), while rejecting (as Carey notes in his review of Geertz's book) "mass communication" as the subject of communication studies because the term/subject "creates unacceptable limitations on [communication] study and a certain blindness as well."[20] Both Dewey and Williams provided Carey with useful reference points for a culturalist view of communication because both understood communication as a basis for community and because both viewed communication as "modeled" as much by science as by "common cultures" and the daily practices of community life.

On the Train Tracks of Historical Materialism: The Passage from Cultural Materialism to Spatial Materialism

Carey's two models of communication (as part of his critique of the positivism and "spatial bias" of U.S. communication research and policy) reproduced Innis's historical schema of "time-biased" and "space-biased technologies" (and their societies), though the expression "spatial bias" figured much more prominently in Carey's argument than did the expression "time bias."[21] Carey described communication research's spatial bias unfavorably (as a "bias"), while attributing various benefits to a culturalism that understood communication historically as ritual. Correcting the spatial bias was tantamount, according to Carey, to achieving "cultural stability"—the "balance" that Innis associated with healthy civilizations, and for Carey (as for Innis) this correction involved recognizing and engaging with something lost in modern Western societies' spatial bias. For Carey, Innis's "achievement"—his most important contribution to thinking in the United States about communication—was that he historicized the "present-mindedness," utilitarianism, organicism, and positivism of a research that had become integral (in its method and regime of truth) to the United States' expansionism and empire. Even though Innis's history of communication technology relied upon a grand, overarching explanation (space-biased technologies/societies replacing time-biased ones), Carey also considered Innis's historicism to be a foil to systems-theory and to philosophical universalisms that Carey associated with the legacy of Hegelianism (or Hegel's version of a historical dialectic). Carey thus pointed out that Innis "attempted to *restore* to economics and communications an *historical* model of analysis. . . . The historical imagination checked off the bias of the theoretical one."[22]

While Carey's culturalist view of communication was beholden to the connection that Innis made between communication and culture (as in Innis's *Strategy of Culture,* 1952), Carey undoubtedly found Raymond Williams's cultural historicism (and his historicization of the meanings of "culture," "communication," "community," and other key words for a sociology of culture) to be a useful framework for explaining/adapting Innis's historicization of "space-biased" societies and for rationalizing the objectives of a ritual model of communication as an alternative to the positivism and spatial bias of U.S. communication research.[23] Williams's writing about culture (like Hoggart's and E. P. Thompson's) had developed out of a British tradition of Marxist historicism and historiographic debate.[24] By the 1970s, Williams's formulation of a sociology of culture reassessed the aims of Marxist historical materialism in terms of a cultural materialism. Relying on the then recent translations of Volosinov and Gramsci, Williams's cultural materialism conceived of language, communication, and culture as material social *praxis* and thus as an important terrain of political struggle, and in those terms cultural materialism emphasized that formations of rule (hegemony) needed to be understood as process (historically contingent on the mobilization of social classes through culture). Culture, as such, was defined and practiced in historical contexts, and cultural production was socially and politically transformative, a means of "making history." A cultural materialism allowed Williams, following Gramsci in particular, to avoid the economic determinism of "mechanistic" versions of Marxist historical materialism by emphasizing that culture is a robust, variegated field of "production"—of making and doing in different spheres of activity and experience. During the 1970s, Williams's (and British cultural studies') Gramscian rationale about a *cultural politics* thus supported and extended his markedly historicist explanation that structures of dominance occurred through "emerging" and "residual" cultural practice.[25]

By charting Carey's formulation of the two models of communication as I have in the preceding section (that is, by charting how they were designed within and about a historical geography of thought), I want to underscore not only that Carey's argument was about the *geography* of thought about communication during the 1970s (particularly in his effort to locate the "spatial bias" of U.S. communication research) but that—in his rejection of this spatial bias, in his frequent citation of Williams and Innis, and in his effort to reintroduce certain tendencies of the early Chicago School in order to rationalize a culturalist perspective of communication—his rationale involved a binarism with a *historical* bias for thinking about communication, culture, and the objectives of cultural studies. This historical bias has emphasized not only the temporality of culture and communication but also the importance of cultural historicism as a corrective to a predominant spatial bias.

As I have suggested above, Carey was just as complicit during the 1970s in this historicist view of culture and communication as was Williams (and, for that matter, British cultural studies).[26] This disposition, however, seemed most pronounced (most ostensibly a "bias") when Carey counterposed ritual and culture to a "spatial bias" and when his account of a ritual model was cast in terms of what was lacking (and what was at stake as a result of this absence) in the dominant paradigm of U.S. communication research and policy. Without using Williams's terms, Carey's proposal for a cultural study of communication emphasized how a "dominant" research paradigm was predicated upon "residual" and "emerging" ways of structuring reality and life.[27]

In some respects, I find a culturalism that cast its proposal so bluntly in terms of relations of time-space and as a corrective to the *"spatial* bias" of communication research and policy (identified as the *dominant* paradigm in U.S. research and policy) to be both a strength and a shortcoming of Carey's argument, especially compared with British cultural studies from the 1970s and 1980s, which Carey frequently invoked. As a way of considering the implications of this historical bias in Carey et al.'s cultural materialism, of explaining why I see Carey's conception of a spatial bias to be important but inadequate, and of working toward an alternative model/analytic, let me briefly summarize a few of the implications of Carey's having contrasted/counterposed two models of communication. Doing so underscores my debt to and restlessness with Carey's intervention.

Counterposing two models as Carey did led him to beg three interrelated sets of questions that were (and still are) worth considering, and that I pose in order to explain (through Carey, as he was prone to do with others' voices) a spatial materialism of communication. The first set of questions concerns the "cultural politics" of a ritual model of communication and its relation to a cultural materialism (or a "materialist" conception of cultural historicism in communication research). If the transmission/transportation model of communication is prone to reduce communication to control and if a cultural model emphasizes the generative potential of communication and culture on one another, is control anathema to a cultural model? Does the distinction between these two analytics make it impossible to conceive of control except in terms of the transmission of information from one point to another? What kinds of questions has or should a cultural model of communication ask about power? If "society," regulated by utility and contract, "*could not work*" without the integrative mechanisms of Gemeinschaft" (Carey's statement, op cit., italics mine), how are culture and community instrumentalized, governmentalized, and made useful—made to work and made to make the technologies of power/control workable? A second set of questions (related to this first set of questions) is whether transmission (the spatial bias of communication research) is the best or only way of thinking about power and control. Or does ritual offer a more useful way of thinking about power and control as they pertain to communication and/or culture? What are the implications of posing communication (and/or media) as the central (mediating?) term between models of power conceived as transmission and ritual? Third (and the reason that I ask the questions above), is the binarism itself an impediment to thinking about power as a historico-geographic—a temporal and spatial—problematic, which after all was one of Carey's objectives?

As suggested by the title of this section, these questions mostly pertain to Carey's response (after Innis, and alongside Williams) to historical materialism and his engagement with a cultural materialism (or, as phrased above, a materialist conception of cultural historicism in communication research). Although Carey's critique of positivism was not grounded in or primarily responsive to Marxist theory, it was certainly cited approvingly, and was congruent with, early German social theorists such as Tonnies and Weber as well as historians of the political economy of communication and culture such as Innis and British cultural studies. Through references to all this writing, Carey rejected equating culture and ideology and rejected reducing communication and culture to matters of the state and markets. His historicism arguably was about the inadequacy of the base-superstructure metaphor as a framework for universalizing explanations of power and/or communication. As noted above, he emphasized that the two models were mostly about formulating a critique of and an alternative to the *positivism* of communication research rather than this research's implication in economies and in the reproduction of relations of production. Yet, in so doing, they also were his way of formulating a critique of and an alternative to the scientism of earlier Marxist critiques, and a ritual model introduced a culturalist terminology for describing "the reproduction of the relations of production." How, in other words, was the spatial bias of modern societies "ritually" reproduced through communication (and presumably other practices)?

My title for this section invokes Perry Anderson's *In the Tracks of Historical Materialism* (1983), wherein he argued that Marxist theory offered a historiographic perspective about theory and philosophy and a perspective that should be (in part) about the tendency to construct "internal" histories of Marxism and about the changing and multiple contexts of Marxist thought. This historicism, by focusing upon the ongoing production of thought/ knowledge, thus called into question the universalist applications and scientific aspirations of Marxist theory and asked to what extent Marx's history of the emergence of capitalism adequately explained power in the second half of the twentieth century. Anderson pointed out that historical materialism "involved no element of complacent positivity—as if truth were henceforward guaranteed by time, Being by Becoming, their [Marx and Engels'] doctrine immune from error by mere immersion in change."[28] Others writing in Britain during the 1970s (such as Ernesto Laclau and those associated with British cultural studies) sought, mostly through Gramsci's writing, a more radical historicization and a more robust version of overdetermination than had been suggested by Althusser's structural Marxism.[29] In so doing this latter group, particularly British cultural studies, wondered whether historical materialism left the door open wide enough for anything but a single (economic) motor of history—whether historical materialism impeded an analytic that began by considering the *material*/practices for formations (assemblages) of power, that understood this material to be heterogeneous and irreducible to a single material/determination, and that therefore never assumed in advance that the analytic could predict exactly how power was assembled.[30]

Carey's early versions of the two models of communication were more or less engaged with these debates about the historical materialism of Marxist thought and analysis—were more or less "in the tracks" of historical materialism (and on the same track as—tracking—a cultural materialism). I say "more or less" because, while his description of the two models (and his historical accounts of communication research, journalism, and telegraphy that followed) was consonant generally with British cultural materialism's historicism and with the other concerns that I have cited above, his early explanations of the two models is less clear about how ritual or culture is productive of the spatial models and techniques of control upon which empire and the territorializing programs of modern Western societies have been carried out.

In one sense, Carey's distinction is fundamentally about power—about the "dominance" of a particular paradigm in communication research and policy in the United States, about the spatial "bias" of this paradigm's conception of communication in terms of U.S. territorialization and of the myth of progress upon which the science of communication had been deployed, and thus about the instrumentality of communication research and policy in the United States' conception and ongoing enactment of its own modernity.[31] Beyond his polemic about two models of communication, his analysis of telegraphy in nineteenth-century U.S. expansion also demonstrated that the capacity to expand through transportation and communication was imbricated with the capacity to govern—an argument that supported his view of the spatial bias of communication research. His essays on telegraphy and on Innis deal with the relation between centers and margins, though not until the 1990s (as best I can tell) does Carey begin to reassess the two models in these terms.[32]

In another sense, however, Carey's historical bias about communication and culture (that is, his formulation of a distinction, particularly in the early essays, that casts communication as cultural ritual in order to emphasize the role of communication/technology in establishing continuity between present and past, in negotiating with or reproducing the past in the present, and in the productive, transformative capacity of cultural forms and practices for shaping the future, for making history) tends to place questions of power more in terms of the strategic interests of communication research and policy than in terms of ritual, daily life, and culture (aside from occasional instances when, in arguing against economic determinism and the term "mass communication," he suggests that cultural struggle and resistance occur from localized community-based means). As such, the ritual model is (to use Michel de Certeau's expression) a *tactical* response and obliquely (less conspicuously than in British cultural studies) an argument about culture as a set of tactical responses to the utility and calculation—to a scientific and political economic rationality and rule—of modern societies. Culture could not simply be added to communication research; the cultural historicism that understood communication as ritual made the positivism and spatial bias of communication untenable.

My interest in Carey's conception of power in his account of the two models is selective. That is, I am interested primarily in how power gets ascribed to transmission and to a spatializing perspective but not as directly to ritual and culture—in how power is explained as expansion and territorialization rather than as occurring through sharing, participation, association, fellowship, and community (the qualities that he attributes to communication as a condition for a "common culture")—even as ritual and culture are implied to be productive of communication as transmission, of the spatial bias of communication research and policy, and of communication networks' imbrication in transportation networks.

One implication (with which I will have to deal rather schematically but which is addressed more thoroughly by other chapters in this volume) is that if culture is primarily about sharing, participation, association, fellowship, and community, and if communication is about the process (rituals) through which culture is created, modified, and transformed, then communication (the regularity/ritual of communicative performance) becomes the primary way that culture is regulated. Culture is regulated by a history that it has produced through (communicative) rituals/performance. Carey thus devoted considerable energy during the 1980s and particularly the 1990s to arguing that he never intended to counterpose culture and economy, or political economy and cultural studies of media—that he had intended, rather, to point out culture's irreducibility to markets and state control while pointing out that its impact in modern life was its productive relation to them. One might also legitimately ask whether understanding culture's regulation as historical (as bound by and transformed primarily through communicative ritual) adequately acknowledges the technical, institutional, and governmental dimension/modalities of ritual, representational/symbolic practice, and culture. While Carey emphasized that culture is the cumulative effect of multiple practices/rituals in the daily lives of particular populations and classes (thus arguing that making history is overdetermined), the binarism has little to say about how power is *exercised* as/through ritual in daily life, and how these rituals are not only governmentalized through institutions but instrumental to the way that individuals and populations control themselves. Furthermore, culture, the meaning and ritualization of which is primarily communicative and linguistic, has mostly a representational content and thus, as Tony Bennett has argued about a similar trend in cultural studies, suggests that the social is "the product of a mobile set of relations of signification [or in Carey's formulation, "communication"] whose 'fixings' of the social through the relations between the different discursive positionalities that they effect is always provisional, incomplete, and on the way to being unfixed again."[33]

Another implication, with which I want to conclude because it is most pertinent to my thoughts about a spatial materialism, has to do with the binarism's counterposition of space and time, geography and history—and (following from my questions in the preceding paragraph) with whether/how we should understand Carey's cultural historicism as a historical (or cultural) materialism. As I have explained in other writing, a spatial materialism was most vividly at issue and elaborated in the writing of Henri Lefebvre during the 1960s and 1970s, though Lefebvre (to my knowledge) never used the expression spatial materialism to define his perspective. I ascribe that term to Lefebvre's perspective for numerous reasons: because of his interest in correcting the abstractness of space (particularly pronounced in modern science) by emphasizing that space is a social practice (produced somewhere); because of his interest in correcting (and overcoming the opposition between) Marxism's economism and semiotics'/structuralism's textualism (that is, in overriding the base/superstructure binary) by emphasizing the overdetermination of spaces (as variously lived and practiced) and, in turn, the productivity of space (as a third term irreducible to neither economic or symbolico-cultural determination/production); and because of his interest in rethinking Marx's historical dialectic in these terms (that is, as a history of spatial practice and production, as a historical account of how space is a condition for "making History"). In all these respects, Lefebvre's historical perspective about space, and his spatial perspective about history, gestured toward an analytic that was neither a historical materialism or a cultural materialism.

Lefebvre's contribution to the debates that comprised the "post-Marxist" moment and geographic contexts included *The Survival of Capitalism* (published in French in 1973, and translated into English in 1976). In this book (never a touchstone for British post-Marxists, British cultural studies, or Carey), Lefebvre lamented the abstractness (including among Marxists) of scientific accounts of capitalism, arguing instead that the capitalist reproduction of relations of production should never be *assumed* to take particular paths or to have particular effects but needed to be endlessly "discovered." This sense of discovery makes necessary, he argued, an analytic that begins with everyday life—a terrain both in flux and in order. Using a figure of speech remarkable for its multiple connotations, he suggested that capitalism only could be understood by an "explorer" who studied the "reproduction of relations of production" as if it were a *continent*—"a totality which has never been systematized or achieved, is never 'over and done with,' and is still being realised" (*Survival of Capitalism*, p. 7). In this kind of analysis, returning the dialectic to history and avoiding the abstractness of space were one in the same objective, achieved through recognizing that space—the various sites and scales of sociality, making, and doing—is "reproduced" and "reproductive."[34]

Although Lefebvre was not prone to discuss the production of space through electronic media or communication technology, his writing about space (particularly in *The Production of Space*) revised, and in part rejected, the semiotic and structuralist literature about making meaning, representation, art, and culture. The spatial materialism that he outlined considered the relation between spatial representation (as one form of production/work, one kind of social practice) and the spaces/sites of representation, and between "works of art," the production of meaning, and spatial production. Through this vein of his writing about space, he likened contemporary architecture and city planning to "mass media" (*The Production of Space*, p. 131). All these insights are useful for communication/media studies because the insights are not preoccupied with the media usually considered by this discipline and because they situate the more commonly considered "media" in environments of multiple socio-spatial practices and challenge the abstractness of space in scientific research (such as the dominant paradigm of communication research that Carey described) by calling attention to the social space of representation and reproduction.

Although Carey counterposes two models of communication (thus countering the "spatial bias" of communication research with a cultural historicist perspective that casts the *"reproduction* of relations of production" as "ritual") and although by counterposing two models Carey's argument tends to generalize/homogenize the modeling or representation of space (as a dominant tendency in U.S. communication research), rather than dwelling upon the multiplicity of spatial representation of cultural/representational space, his most often cited explanation of these two models offers a way of thinking about communication as ritual that complicates the binarism (in a way consonant with Lefebvre) and that (to my knowledge) has been overlooked in the numerous references to Carey's work. Significantly, the single example of communication as cultural ritual that Carey offered in "A Cultural Approach to Communication" was the map (and secondarily, the architectural blueprint): "The map stands as a representation of an environment capable of clarifying a problematic situation . . . guiding behavior and simultaneously transforming undifferentiated space into configured—that is, known, apprehended, understood—space."[35] According to Carey, maps can be drawn, sung, or danced, and they are not only produced in various ways and forms but are productive of worlds/geographies by providing templates for navigation—for a way of being mobile, of moving through a world that is mapped and traversed, for coming and going as "daily and hourly" ritualized activity.

In one respect, Carey's point about ritual/communication as mapmaking is about the ontology of the maps produced by a transmission model of communication. Like structuralism and semiotics in the 1970s, Carey's ritual model of communication emphasizes that communication and the models produced by communication research are representations—partial and strategic formulations of an environment that become templates for living within the environment. The scientism of communication research and policy assumes their direct access to Nature—the physical bodies of land ("continents") and communicators—and thus makes the space of communication abstract, not just beyond representation but a representation that (in Baudrillard's terms) is inseparable from the nature/environment being mapped.

There is however another implication of Carey's description of ritual/ communication as map that bears more directly on my references to Lefebvre. While maps and mapmaking are clearly what are at stake in understanding the "spatial bias" of communication research, Carey's emphasis on the map as ritualized communication (which is also imbricated in routines of movement/transport) gestures not only toward the representational practices of communication science (that is, communication research's explanation of social relations as *map*) but also toward the microscales (the everydayness) of mapmaking and thus toward the common, formulaic, little, everyday ways that space is produced and becomes productive as/through communication.

Through the example of the map, Carey thus underscores that communication as transmission (that is, communication as the *calculable* distance between points or communicators) rests upon the diverse, everyday production of space—as ritualized representation *and* movement. Understood this way, a cultural approach to communication entails not simply countering a spatial bias in communication research with a cultural historicism but introducing a dialectical understanding of the production of space as central to communication research—an analytic wherein spatial representation and the spaces of representation are mutually constitutive, wherein space (and the spatial bias in communication research) is historically lived, practiced, and produced through bodies in motion.

There are several consequences of reading Carey's account of communication as transportation and ritual in relation to a spatial materialism. One concerns the question of power and control. If ritual refers to the little, common, everyday practices through which communication and representation are lived and thus regularized (in the sense of regulated and regulating), then a cultural approach that understands communication as mapmaking needs to consider how the ritualized sites and paths, and the most common, everyday technologies of mapping and moving through daily life, are regulated, are productive of regulations, and (in both senses) negotiate regulations. This perspective avoids the binary logic arising from Carey's early formulation of the two models, which he considered to be (in part) an intervention into the dominance and spatial bias of U.S. communication research and its conception of media power as transmission.

Second, though Carey's formulation may have called attention to cultural and historical foundations of communication science and its spatial bias, his effort to introduce (or reintroduce) ritual as an *alternative* way of thinking about communication suggested that a "cultural approach" was anathema to empirical research, and that communication as ritual was incommensurate with the technical knowledge and rationality of the dominant form of communication research. If a transmission model of communication makes measurable the space of communication, does a ritual model of communication (communication/ritual modeled as/through everyday mapmaking) necessarily fail to account for how the everyday making of maps—the everyday production of space—occurs through or reproduces specific (historically and geographically situated) rationalities and technologies of space? Do not regularized/ritualized practices in daily life reproduce not only the relations of production but the technical knowledge (that is, the *technology*) and rules of mapmaking and movement? Lacking in Carey's account, therefore, is a sense of the interdependency of the science and rituals of (communication as) mapmaking and of traveling/transport—of science (in Foucauldian sense) as a rationality and technical knowledge that is lived in ritualized/regularized forms of communicative behavior and mobility.

Third, a spatial materialist reading of Carey's two models, instead of counterposing culture as ritually produced, and economy as the ever-expanding networks of transport, would recognize the materiality (the "making") of ritual and science, without assuming that mapmaking or the networks of transport are fundamentally economic (or "economic" as the political economy of media and communication has been prone to explain the world). Not only are there many forms of making and doing that need to be understood historically—through a cultural historicism/materialism that understands the multiplicities of "production" up through daily life—but the big spatial projects, the "continental" projects (the projects forging networks, roads, bridges, houses, cities, nations, and empires) have been made and lived through specific, but multifarious and differentially distributed, resources and technologies. Ritual as mapmaking, as Carey later pointed out, is not reducible to making meaning, and his passing reference to communication/ritual as dance (embodied and even technologized forms of movement) suggests one way of beginning to recognize the enactment, performance, and living of space through various media/technologies of communication, which are also forms of transport and mobility.

Fourth, a spatial materialism of communication would not counterpose geographic and historical understandings of transport and ritual, nor would it counterpose empire building or continent mapping and the everyday, varied making of maps and paths, or the various mobilities in daily life. To see space as produced through the rituals of daily life (including the ritualization of communication) is to acknowledge not only Doreen Massey's point (that places are never fixed because they are processes and because they are linked—"extroverted"—through daily movements into and out of those places)[36] but also that the production of space involves the production of temporalities. A spatial materialism of communication therefore seeks to understand communication/media, and their power, in terms of how and where these technologies matter within and are made productive of orderings of time and space. Whereas Carey's explanation of two models of communication seems mostly content to contrast (scientifically abstracted) space/empire and history (the past, the everyday, and cultural reproduction), and thus to contrast networks of power and control (which he sees as too often explained in terms of trade and economy) with the "wonderful" processes that have a "restorative value in reshaping our common culture" (*Culture as Communication*, p. 35), his historical geography of telegraphy in the United States gestures toward an analysis interested in locating the technology of communication within the changing production of time and space.[37]

Finally, while Carey may be most recognized in North America for having introduced a "cultural approach" to communication, this chapter has sought to underscore how his explanation of a cultural model offered a way of thinking about the interdependency between the territorialization and ritualization of communication, and between communication and transport/mobility. Although Carey's formulation cast geography and history, transport and ritual, domination and community in an overly binary rationale, which tended to perpetuate the very modern logic that he criticized, his formulation also underscored the spatial and temporal (geographic and historical) production of culture, economy, and communication in a way that certainly was not typical of communication research or cultural studies in the United States during the 1970s and 1980s. To the extent that (as Carey pointed out about telegraphy) modernity has been predicated upon the separation of communication and transportation (or, for that matter, of communication as transmission from communication as ritual), what is needed is an analytic of communication informed by the *countermodern* objectives of a spatial materialism.

Accomplishing this not only would involve avoiding the binary distinctions between political economy and cultural studies, between communication science and cultural studies of communication, between empirical and critical studies of communication but (perhaps most important) would recognize that communication as transportation *and* ritual poses a variety of questions that a study merely of "communication" or of its "media" has not addressed and has difficulty addressing. That Carey formulated an argument about two models of communication within an emerging regime of portable and mobile forms of communication makes it necessary not only to rethink his formulation in terms of these developments but also to rethink how communicative practice shifts constantly (and unevenly around the world) within the paths of daily life, and through the various *attachments* of communication technologies to bodies and various *materials* and material production across different spheres of activity. The mobility and portability of communication technology require, perhaps more than ever, an analytic that recognizes the rituals of communication as maps that move and are danced.

Notes

1. "American studies are grounded in a transmission or transportation view of communication. We see communication basically as a process of transmitting messages at a distance for the purpose of control. The archetypal case of communication, then, is persuasion; attitude change; behavior modification; socialization through the transmission of information, influence, or conditioning or, alternatively, as a case of individual choice over what to read or view. . . . By contrast, a ritual view conceives communication as a process through which a shared culture is created, modified, and

transformed. . . . A ritual view of communication is directed not toward the extension of messages in space but the maintenance of society in time . . . ; not the act of imparting information or influence but the creation, representation, and celebration of shared even if illusory beliefs. If a transmission view of communication centers on the extension of messages across geography for purposes of control, a ritual view centers on the sacred ceremony that draws persons together in fellowship and commonality." "Mass Communication and Cultural Studies," in *Communication as Culture,* (Boston: Unwin Hyman New York, 1989), pp. 42–43.

2. "They obviously derive from differing problematics; that is, the basic questions of one tradition do not connect with the basic questions of the other." *Communication as Culture,* p. 43.

3. See, for instance, "Reflections on the Project of (American) Cultural Studies," *Cultural Studies in Question,* ed. Marjorie Ferguson and Peter Goulding (Thousand Oaks, CA: Sage, 1997).

4. James Carey, "Reflections on the Project of (American) Cultural Studies," p. 11.

5. I long have been indebted to writing by and conversation with Lawrence Grossberg about the idea of a spatial materialism. For Grossberg's use of the term, see "The Space of Culture, the Power of Space," *The Post-Colonial Question: Common Skies, Divided Horizons,* eds. Ian Chambers & Lidia Curti, London: Routledge, 1996, pp. 169–188. For my use of the term, see Hay, "Afterword: The Place of Audience Studies," *The Audience and Its Landscape,* eds. James Hay, Lawrence Grossberg, Ellen Wartella, Boulder: Westview Press, 1996; Hay, "Piecing Together What Remains of the Cinematic City," *The Cinematic City,* ed. Dave Clarke, New York: Routledge, 1997; Hay, "Locating the Televisual," *TV and New Media,* vol. 1:1 2001; Hay, "Toward a Spatial Materialism of 'the Moving Image': Locating Screen Media within Changing Regimes of Transport," *Cinema & Cie.*

6. James Carey, "Reflections on the Project of (American) Cultural Studies," p. 10.

7. "Mass Communication and Cultural Studies," reprinted in *Communication as Culture,* pp. 42–43.

8. Ibid., p. 43.

9. "Cultural Approach to Communication," reprinted in *Communication as Culture,* p. 34.

10. Ibid., p. 32.

11. James Carey, "Communication and Economics," *James Carey: A Critical Reader,* eds Eve Stryker Munson & Catherine A. Warren, Minneapolis: Univ. of Minnesota Press, 1997, p. 70. (This essay was reprinted from *Information and Communication in Economics,* ed. Robert Babe, Boston: Kluwer, 1994, pp. 321–336.)

    This was arguably a vein of critical theory being formulated in the United States by members of the former Frankfurt School (e.g., Kracauer, Arendt, and Marcuse) who, after Weber, viewed scientific, industrial, technological, and political rationality as nothing short of the modern guise of religion, though Carey energetically refuted that his conception of communication as cultural practice and ritual had anything to do with ideology.

12. "The United States . . . at all levels of social structure pursued what I call high communications policy, one aimed solely at spreading messages futher in space and reducing the cost of transmission. That is what Innis meant by exploiting the spatial bias of modern communication. Communication was seen, in other words, solely in the envelope of space and power. That communication might be seen as something else,

as container of human interaction that allows for persistence and growth of culture, is a view that never entered United States policy," James Carey, "Culture, Geography, and Communications: The Work of Harold Innis in an American Context," *Culture, Communication, and Dependency: The Tradition of H. A. Innis,* eds. William H. Melody, et al., Norwood, NJ: Ablex, 1981.

13. Carey, *Communication as Culture,* pp. 34–35. I add the thought about disciplinarity because "common culture" in Carey's statement refers as much to the interdisciplinarity required by a ritual model for the culture of communication research as it does to the need to overcome the self-interest that he associates with modern societies.

14. Carey, "Cultural Approach to Communication," pp. 13–14.

15. While Dewey's penchant for emphasizing that modern society was a "great community" undoubtedly provided a key reference point for the communitarianism of Carey's advocacy of a ritual/cultural model, Carey rejected the Chicago School's description of society through organic analogies (i.e., of parts synergized into/by a whole body), which he viewed as their inheritance of nineteenth-century science that continued (through them) as a characteristic of twentieth-century social psychologism. In a move that captured the ambiguity of Dewey's statement above (and of the modern contradiction that society is "made to work" through community), Carey emphasized instead that the community life researched by the Chicago School was multiple and varied, "tied together across space, attenuated in time, and existing relative to one another *not* as variants on an explicitly shared culture but . . . as 'veto groups' . . . with little relation . . . except the exercise of power and manipulation" (*Communication as Culture,* p. 162).

16. James Carey, "Communication and Culture: Review Essay of Clifford Geertz, *The Interpretation of Culture,*" *Communication Research,* April 1975, p. 177.

17. See, in particular, Carey's review-essay of Clifford Geertz's then newly released *The Intrpretation of Cultures* (Ibid.,: 173–191), which he begins with a summary of his recent participation in a 1973 conference in London, "The Future of Communication Studies," and of the conference's interventions by Raymond Williams and Stuart Hall. Although Geertz is a U.S. anthropologist, Carey considered his "views toward communication . . . [to be] more European than American and . . . connect with what is called in Germany the 'cultural sciences' and, less pretentiously perhaps, in England 'cultural studies.'" Also see his review of Richard Hoggart's *On Culture and Communication* in *Commonweal* (16 March 1973), p. 42, and "Canadian Communication Theory: Extensions and Interpretations of Harold Innis," *Studies of Canadian Communications,* ed. Gertrude Robinson and Donald Theall (Montreal: McGill University Programme in Communications, 1975), pp. 27–59.

18. In "Culture, Geography, and Communication: The Work of Harold Innis in an American Context," Carey refutes Marshall McLuhan's opinion that Innis "should be considered as the most eminent member of the Chicago group headed by Robert Park" (p. 75).

19. I want to make two points about how Carey's work was engaged with Innis's. One is that Carey's conception of *two* models of communication, and Carey's references to the transmission model as having a "spatial bias," riffs upon Innis's argument (for example, in *Empire and Communications,* 1950) that modern Western societies conceive of communication in terms of space and power rather than in terms of time and forms of human interaction that Innis associated with premodern oral cultures. Second, references to Innis are so integral to Carey's essays that in a recently published

retrospective about Innis (*Harold Innis in the New Century: Reflections and Refractions,* ed. Charles Acland and William Buxton [Montreal: McGill University Press, 1999]), the number of references to Carey that appear in the book's index are exceeded only by those for Innis and McLuhan.

20. Carey, "Communication and Culture," p. 176.

21. Innis considered "time-biased" and "space-biased" societies to be imbalanced—organized around certain instabilities. The former suffered from its inability to solve problems of space, and the latter, problems of time. He characterized the former as prone to institutional decentralization, and the latter, to institutional centralization.

22. Carey, "Culture, Geography, and Communications," pp. 79–80.

23. Like Carey, Williams emphasized the ambiguity (the tension between two meanings) of the term "communication" in modern discourses about communication systems and communication theory. In summarizing the emergence of a modern conception of communication as an "abstract, general term" for the development of roads, canals, and railways, Williams noted in *Keywords* (1976) that:

> The *communication industry,* as it is now called, is thus usually distinguished from the *transport industry: communications* for information and ideas, in print and broadcasting; *transport* for the physical carriage of people and goods.

> In controversy about communications systems and communication theory it is often useful to recall the unresolved range of the original noun of action, represented at its extremes by *transmit,* a one-way process, and *share* (cf. *communion* and especially *communicant*), a common and mutual process. (pp. 72–73)

24. For an account of this tradition, see Dennis Dworkin, *Cultural Marxism in Postwar Britain: History, the New Left, and the Origins of Cultural Studies* (Durham, NC: Duke University Press, 1997).

25. To sum up and elaborate a bit further, Williams's cultural materialism had several intersecting objectives. For Williams, a cultural materialism was a historical analytic concerned with the materiality of culture, which he conceived as culture's practice/production within social relations and conditions (culture as particular formal practices—*ways* of making and doing—within the "whole social material processes"). He developed the term during the 1970s as part of the debates about (post-)Marxism; in *Marxism and Literature,* cultural materialism is a "sociology of culture"—an analytic that reassessed Marxism by rethinking the material(ity) of art as medium and mediation. Cultural materialism also figured into his outline of an historical approach/analytic to television [*Television: Technology and Cultural Form,* wherein he pointed out that TV developed within various material practices (new regimes of privacy and mobility) and argued against understanding TV either as mass communication or as medium]. In these projects, Williams's cultural materialism refuted not only the primacy of economic determinism (arguing instead that the modalities of "production" *in* social experience have been more complex and heterogeneous than suggested by the mechanistic variants of historical materialism) but also technological determinist histories of communication, which he (like Carey) associated with the work of McLuhan. Having stressed in *Culture and Society* (1959) the importance of

rethinking older aesthetic definitions of culture by recognizing a relation between culture and communication, Williams argued in both of the 1970s books against understanding a medium and mediation as intermediate communicative substances (what Carey would call mediation as "transmission"). "Medium," he notes, is often and wrongly abstracted, understood as the formal traits that define a practice; a cultural materialism emphasizes and begins with the practices of working with and on certain materials (e.g., literature not as formal conventions but as the practices of writing, publishing, reading, etc., that are part of an array of material processes). A cultural materialist view of "medium" also became the basis for an alternative conception of mediation, or an avoidance of the term, particularly as it has pertained in Marxist thought to the relation between materiality and immateriality/ideology, base and superstructure, society and art (as separate or opposed spheres of activity within a totality). A cultural materialism rejected the idea that mediation was only or primarily about distortion (as in ideological criticism of "the media"); it emphasized instead that mediation is constitutive/constituting of objects "in the object itself, not something between the object and that to which it is brought" (Adorno quoted in Raymond Williams, "From Reflection to Mediation," *Marxism and Literature,* New York: Oxford Univ. Press, 1977, p. 98) and a *substantial* and *"positive* process in social reality" (Williams, "From Reflection to Mediation," p. 100).

26. This "historical bias" had to do in part with British cultural studies (BCS)'s development through the work of historians such as Williams, Thompson, and Hoggart during the 1950s and 1960s but also with BCS's investment during the 1970s in Gramsci's conception of Marxism as a "philosophy of praxis" that relentlessly emphasized the temporality (contingency and process) of power/rule as hegemonic formation. As I explain below, the two models of communication also are quite similar to Innis's historiographic framework for explaining the political economy of communication.

27. For Williams's most cogent explanation of why "emergent" and "residual" are crucial terms for thinking about the contingency, unevenness, and historical process of cultural and hegemonic dominance, see Williams, "Dominant, Residual, and Emergent," *Marxism and Literature* (Oxford, England: Oxford University Press, 1977).

28. Perry Anderson, *In the Tracks of Historical Materialism,* London: Verso, 1983, p. 11.

29. See, for instance, Raymond Williams, *Marxism and Literature* (already cited); Ernesto Laclau and Chantal Mouffe, *Hegemony and Socialist Strategy,* London: Verso, 1985; Stuart Hall, "The Problem of Ideology: Marxism Without Guarantees," *Marx: 100 Years On,* ed. B. Matthews, London: Lawrence & Wishart, 1983. (Reprinted in *Journal of Communication Inquiry,* 10: 2, 1986, pp. 28–44, and in *Stuart Hall: Critical Dialogues in Cultural Studies,* eds. David Morley & Kuan-Hsing Chen, London: Routledge, 1996.)

30. For Williams and Carey, cultural historicism (and the historical practice *of* a cultural materialism) emphasized the materiality and productivity of *culture* (as both "communication" and "a whole way of life"; as a *relation* between communication and common, everyday practice; and as a way of recognizing a more robust, poly-form sense of productivity as "common" *making* and *doing,* through communication and everyday life). For Williams, a cultural materialism thus rethought (a historical materialist account of) power/hegemony as communicative and ordinary practice (as historical process understood in this way). For Carey, a cultural historicism of communication provided an alternative to the "spatial bias" (the preoccupation with

expansion and territorial control) in U.S. communication research and policy—a bias which Carey ascribed as much to political economic critiques of communication industries and policy as to the more dominant forms of empirical research upon which communication industries and policy relied.

31. As a response to the positivism of U.S. communication research after World War II, his description of a ritual model provided a useful way to point out the cultural-historical contingency and overdetermination of scientific truth claims and of communication research's assumption that communication could be understood as relatively organic, circumscribed systems of behavior whose effects could be readily calculated. His cultural historicism pressed questions about the relation between science and culture (a discussion not confined to communication studies) from his disciplinary field (U.S. communication studies). His cultural historicism was also about transforming the disciplinarity of communication studies through alternative/marginalized histories—no small matter for a discipline/science that was just beginning to establish an awareness of its own disciplinarity through the construction of competing pedigrees and historical trajectories of research that could be used to teach communication studies. In the 1970s, Carey's account of the Chicago School emphasized and valorized a period before social research became the model in the United States for the social scientific and behavioral tendency of communication research. Carey's account of the Chicago School thus countered the version of history that had become canonical for the predominantly social scientific and behavioral paradigm; for an example of the latter, see Jesse Delia, "Communication Research: A History," *Handbook of Communication Science*, eds. C. Berger & S. Chafee, Thousand Oaks, CA: Sage, 1987, pp. 20–98.

32. For a useful assessment of how Innis's writing might be brought to bear on current discussions about centers and margins, see Jody Berland, "Space at the Margins: Critical Theory and Colonial Space after Innis," *Harold Innis in the New Century*, eds. Acland and Buxton.

33. Tony Bennett, "Culture and Governmentality," *Foucault, Cultural Studies, and Governmentality*, eds. Jack Bratich, Jeremy Packer, and Cameron McCarthy (Albany, NY: SUNY Press, 2003), pp. 52–53.

34. In *The Production of Space*, Lefebvre sums up his interest in rethinking spatially the reproduction of relations of production and historical or dialectical materialism (what I am calling his spatial materialism), when he states that "historical materialism . . . will be deepened [by broadening] the concept of production so as to include the production of space as a process whose product—space—itself embraces both things (goods, objects) and works [including art, architecture, representations of space]. . . . The study of space offers an answer according to which the social relations of production have a social existence to the extent that they have a spatial existence; they project themselves into a space, becoming inscribed there, and in the process producing space itself. . . . Space itself, at once a product of the capitalist mode of production and an economic-political instrument of the bourgeoisie, will now be seen to embody its own contradictions . . . [and thus] to designate . . . another mode of production" (pp. 128–129).

35. Carey, *Communication as Culture*, p. 27.

36. See, in particular, Doreen Massey's discussion of "power geometry" in terms of the street where she lives in *Space, Place, and Gender* (Minneapolis: University of Minnesota Press, 1994), p. 149 ff.

37. His essay about how telegraphy developed through a changing production of time and space and through the decoupling of communication and transportation could be read as a version of Armand Mattelart's later account of "communication" as "invented" through a swarming of scientific discourses and experiments seeking to rationalize circulatory systems and of projects/experiments that understood transport as an issue of communication (and vice-versa). See Mattelart, *The Invention of Communication* (Minneapolis: University of Minnesota Press, 1996). See also *Harold Innis in the New Century*, eds. Acland and Buxton.

3. For a Pragmatist Perspective on Publics: Advancing Carey's Cultural Studies through John Dewey . . . and Michel Foucault?!

CHRIS RUSSILL

William James used to say the great fact about a person is their vision. This is certainly true of James Carey. Although it grates harshly against the temper of times in the academy to say so, Carey has mapped a metaphysics of democracy, one linked integrally to many of the best aspects of American pragmatism. Yet this vision has fallen on hard times in terms of both everyday democratic practice and its special Deweyan sense of metaphysics as criticism. In fact, Carey himself has sounded a death knell for cultural studies as an intellectual and political project. Cultural studies will, no doubt, survive in some form, perhaps not unlike those feudal-times theme restaurants complete with witty menu items, costumes, and rude serving wenches. But is Carey's vision lost or fatally flawed?

Carey's Project

For Carey, the general task of cultural studies has remained relatively constant: "to contest a body of theoretical and empirical work carried forward in the name of positive science *and* to contest the project of social reconstruction carried forward, implicitly or otherwise, in the name of positive knowledge."[1] One finds the general contours of this program as early as his 1974 call for a cultural approach to journalism history, in which the twofold task is formulated as "a thoroughgoing critique of the behavioral sciences and the permeation of our studies and our students' thought with historical consciousness."[2] In 1975, Carey broadens this call in his famous article, "A Cultural Approach to Communication," only this time with Dewey's views of communication at the forefront. However, Carey's use of Dewey here is more inspirational than elaborated, as Carey draws important distinctions in terms of communicative traditions (oral/written) and models (ritual/transmission), while claiming "the most viable though still inadequate tradition of social thought on communication comes from those colleagues and descendants of Dewey in the Chicago School: from Mead and Cooley through Robert Park and on to Erving Goffman."[3] Carey does, of course, return to Dewey repeatedly in order "to extend, however gently, his pragmatic conception of mass communication."[4]

What is worth elaborating and advancing in Carey's project, however, is its broader social theoretical vision and not particular moments of exegesis (McLuhan and Innis, Dewey), distinction drawing (oral/literate cultures, transmission/ritual models), or arguments (telegraph separates transportation and communication, economic and communicative paradigms contradict each other in their conception of resources). As useful as these intellectual tools often are in Carey's hands, they have sometimes been put to spurious use by advocates and critics alike and sometimes draw attention away from the context and purposes for which Carey put them to work. At other times they serve as a veiled intellectual vocabulary for fighting out moral and political differences. Carey, on the other hand, has repeatedly insisted on the importance of making explicit the social theoretical assumptions informing any such formulation or use of these intellectual tools. This has been crystal clear, stated in no uncertain terms by Carey, yet oddly ignored. Nor has Carey's point been made obscure by general theoretical pronouncements about power/knowledge. His criticism of McLuhan's communication theory, of policy applications, of graduate education, and of communication research have all taken place on the terrain of social theories and in contestation of a quite specific one: utilitarianism.

We find this as early as 1969, when Carey calls for a "general theory of communication," one capable of handling the twin social tendencies toward massification and differentiation and able to overcome utilitarianism via "new norms and procedures for the process of public communication."[5] Initial formulations of the task were "primarily intellectual at the outset," requiring "a body of work that had sufficient weight and reach to clear a space, a legitimate and central space, in the academy for work that was, broadly, historical, critical, interpretive and empirical."[6] But this necessary first step is by no means a sufficient condition for cultural studies. In Carey's view, the intellectual project was guided by an alternative social theory able to forward a political program capable of engaging "conventional liberal/capitalist thought."[7] But what is this social theory and how can it be advanced? Can Carey's vision for cultural studies guide an effective project of social reconstruction able to combat scientism, recover history, and advance Dewey's theory of public communication?

Carey's Outline of the Problem at Present

Today, finding conservatives "in the political saddle virtually everywhere, forcing all political positions to contest on the terrain they have defined," Carey believes the days of cultural studies "are numbered except as an irrelevant outpost in the academy."[8] Sensing that a "deep political cynicism" lurks behind these conservative triumphs, Carey suggests, interestingly enough, that Americans "have decided to go it on their own, to seek market-driven, private solutions to every collective problem and thereby to eliminate the need of the state or public life in every possible way."[9] The situation is not new or at least not unanticipated. Dewey himself once put the matter as a choice between a public or market socialism, one perhaps stated more simply today as a choice between the Chicago School of old (Dewey) and the Chicago School of present (Becker).

But this really does state things too simply. All this is interesting, and not merely sad, for conservative political triumph and market-driven solutions are not of a piece, unless we wish to speak loosely of the neoliberal hegemony or something of that sort. Put differently, the relation of conservative politics and liberalized markets is not one of logical entailment but of political efficaciousness. The present problem, then, may be usefully understood as engaging an entrenched coalition that manages to work in effective unison to block progressive critical practices. As Carey and others have noted with respect to the "mass society" debate, and as recent events involving the Federal Communications Commission have reminded us, conservative and radical voices are sometimes united on issues.[10] Or, to push the point further, the "neoliberal" coalition may itself only hold together *as a response* to the perceived threat each value system feels regarding the radical proposals for social transformation often advocated in progressive criticism. In fact, Samuel Huntington made this point five decades ago in his advocacy for precisely this coalition and presciently pointed to the manner of covering over its obvious fissures: the proliferation of concerns with security.[11]

All this *is* sad, of course, for it bespeaks the failures of cultural studies to render relevant in a practical sense a generation or so of work. A political economist might suggest with a barely contained smile that the problem of progressing beyond a "trade union consciousness" now faces a cultural studies project that has won concessions from a corporatized university. How, then, should one seek to reorient cultural studies in this situation, if at all? Can an institutionalized cultural studies project advance the goals Carey set for it? Can a positivistic orientation to knowledge be combated, historical work rendered relevant, and Dewey's "Public Socialism" made viable and useful?

Carey's Response

Given his increasing skepticism about the viability of cultural studies as a general intellectual movement, Carey has attempted to distinguish the French poststructuralist line of thought from his own "increasingly strange brand of that increasingly discordant project."[12] Sometimes called "the Dewey group," and other times "ethnocentric" or plain old American cultural studies, does Carey's apparently shaken faith extend to the resources found in Dewey's pragmatism or the Progressive movement? How might their recovery and contemporary transformation avoid or resolve the problems defeating earlier pragmatist and Progressive movement projects while responding to ours?[13]

At the core of Carey's "Dewey group" are John Dewey, William James, and Richard Rorty; in the "French group" are Jacques Derrida, Michel Foucault, and Louis Althusser.[14] This categorization raises a number of questions. Carey is enough of a pragmatist to know distinctions are made in particular contexts to serve specific ends or purposes. We know the failure of cultural studies to adequately forward its general task serves as the context. But to what end? What is the motivating purpose of these distinctions? Is Carey seeking "to jump-start an argument" with the French group over the direction of the cultural studies project?[15] Does he feel, as Rorty once put it, that James and Dewey are waiting ahead on the path that Foucault and Deleuze travel?[16] Or is Carey stylizing their significant differences into irreconcilable visions of cultural studies in order to cut the French group loose?

It is worth emphasizing that Carey is far from unreflective about the enterprise. Whereas one might plausibly claim his early theoretical reflections tend to see intellectual work through a Kuhnian prism as "the formation of broad communities of overlapping consensus,"[17] Carey's later work clearly and consistently notes the limitations of this view. In claiming that the encounter between British cultural studies and the French group is "a deeply deforming episode," Carey notes, "there are more relationships within academic life than consensual and antagonistic ones, a fact that the widespread influence of Thomas Kuhn's notion of a paradigm may have obscured."[18] An earlier suggestion that the "detour through theory," as Hall famously put it,[19] was a "fatally wrong move" comes moments after Carey has reflected on the purposes and warrants for characterizing intellectual conflict along a continuum of capitulation, reconciliation, divorce, and hostile estrangement.[20] Why, then, does Carey choose to address the French group in a polemical register? Why is "the encounter with Michel Foucault" singled out as a "particular misfortune" in an already deeply deforming episode?[21] Why the proposal of divorce if not hostile estrangement?

To be sure, Carey's most memorable contributions to the field have often had a combative tinge: the proposal for a cultural historical approach to displace Whig histories of journalism, the proposal for a ritual model of communication to displace the media effects codification of a transmission model, and the defense of a Deweyan-inspired public to displace the reliance on expertise inspired by Lippmann.[22] Has he exhausted these rhetorical resources? Does he feel the French can serve as an adequate foil for another attempt to reconstruct Dewey's vision of participatory democracy? Or does Carey feel there is competition within cultural studies for students and resources, and so he emphasizes the differences in order to more firmly distinguish and establish the institutional identity of the "Dewey group"? Does he feel, as a number of Foucault's advocates have suggested, "that proponents and critics of cultural studies have to address this Foucauldian influence"?[23] Or is instigating an ostensibly in-house feud intended to accentuate the "American" nature of the project done to deflect the damaging ridicule of conservative commentary to one branch of cultural studies? Are contemporary Foucauldians a farcical return of Marx's Young Hegelians, sheep in wolves' clothing, mistaking active reflection for reflective action? Is this Carey's impatience with certain conventions of Continental philosophical discourse, his distaste for the stylistic flourishes and temperament of French intellectuals, or simply his most effective mode of expression? Or is this path simply the best way of forwarding Carey's cultural studies project at present?

A Counterproposal

I want to propose another way, one complicating Carey's proposed strategy but by no means abandoning his project. Stated boldly, I think Carey needs Foucault. Dewey *and* Foucault, or, more specifically, Dewey's view of publics *and* contemporary Foucauldian work on governmentality and problematization can help reorient and revitalize a viable political project adequate to Carey's vision. At one time, Carey felt Foucault's voice had something of the right spirit in it.[24] More recently, Carey has seen Foucault as the epitome if not progenitor of a deeply flawed notion of power and domination, one severely distorting the progressive potentials of public discourse. Undoing this view of Foucault is no easy task, and undertaking it properly would require greater erudition and familiarity with tendencies in the politics of American cultural studies than I have at my disposal. Moreover, my interest is less in filing charges of libel on Foucault's behalf and more with what Foucault can do to advance Carey's project. To this end, I will simply register an interesting point of fact in hopes of securing the attention and interest requisite to this task. Joli Jensen and John Pauly draw on a familiar sentiment among those in Carey's "Dewey group" when they suggest too many intellectuals in the 1960s and 1970s were led "to a Paris café . . . as French intellectuals were transforming their disenchantment with the failed revolution of 1968 into cultural theory."[25] No doubt. Michel Foucault, however, was not in France in May 1968, and he was doing something different in the late 1960s. He was doing something those who take their pragmatism from Benjamin Barber, Robert Westbrook, Cornel West, Richard Bernstein, Chicago School sociology, and James Carey sometimes forget to do. Michel Foucault was reading John Dewey.

How does the fact that Foucault read some Dewey do anything to help advance a cultural studies project drawing on that tradition? Are there not significant differences here? Has Carey not long insisted on the importance of recognizing the distinctiveness of American social thought, in its core problems, conceptual vocabulary, traditions, and experience? As Carey claims, "American social thought both rejected and transformed the basic dichotomies between gemeinschaft and gesellschaft, status and contract, organic and mechanical solidarity, feudalism and capitalism—the distinctions that framed European social theory."[26] Yet, Foucault also worked outside of these distinctions. The important question, then, is what impact these contextual differences have for cultural criticism and political activity. For Carey's part, the main consequence of this is clearly and consistently embodied in one of the central concerns of his work: American versions of ideology critique, "were framed within an American language of democracy rather than a theory of mass society," and, as such, "were straightforward, descriptive, and aimed at provoking public action rather than theoretical reflection."[27]

How can Foucault advance this project? I address this question by quickly sketching Foucault's own relationship to one, positivist scientific discourse and two, history, before turning more substantively to the issues of "provoking public action" to stress both the consistency and productive possibilities of his work and Carey's Deweyan-inspired project. I contend that each of Foucault's critical operations are consistent with Dewey's and Carey's view of participatory democracy, that they forward the tasks and goals of cultural studies as outlined by Carey, and that they do not depend upon a commitment to those critical tools developed in European social theory, such as ideology critique or analyses of hegemony. Foucault also takes seriously and confronts the emergence of a strictly utilitarian economic rationality as both Dewey and Carey insist we must do. My main focus, however, will be how Foucault's notion of problematization advances the "core issue" and "aim of culture studies," which is to renew a public sphere and democratic dialogue.[28]

On Positivistic Scientific Discourse

Shortly after reading Dewey, Foucault published an interview containing some remarkable claims, a piece later republished as the lead essay in the first English-language collection of studies in governmentality.[29] He claimed three times to be a pluralist, explicitly renouncing structuralism. He then addressed the matter of progressive politics on issues of history and the conditions of the exercise, functioning and institutionalization of positivist scientific discourses. What followed in Foucault's discussion was an extended reflection on the relation of scientific discourse and political practice.[30] Though Foucault's concerns with scientific discourse clearly precede his reading of Dewey, it is at least of mild interest that he begins to investigate the determinations between expertise and politics, or power/knowledge, after reading Dewey's own similar attempts. Later formulated more starkly as a distinction between expert and subjugated knowledge, a perhaps overly dualistic formulation, Foucault's work on discourse consistently focuses reflection on how claims to scientificity work in specific instances to enable or exclude certain voices and claims.

It seems to me that Dewey was the first person to fully realize how these claims to scientificity were going to eviscerate public life. He realized that scientific knowledge and technical expertise would soon be central to all sorts of urgent sociopolitical issues and that our prevailing ways of coping with this fact—blind assimilation based on unwarranted faith or hurried rejection based on undisciplined skepticism—would distort if not destroy public life in its contribution to key problems and institutions affecting our lives. Our usual epistemological tendencies would not only reinforce each other, such that when celebratory faith in science and technology meets uncritical skepticism, each gain strength and confidence only through the weaknesses of the opposing position, but also paralyze our ability to participate and respond to pressing problems. When we consider that Dewey spent five decades or so trying to work out a reconceptualization of inquiry to enable us to deal with such problems and renew public life, you realize the extent and importance of the problem for him.

Whether Foucault's attempts to denaturalize progressive politics and to illustrate the contingencies of discourse are valuable or not in the present American context, it is not inconsistent with either Dewey's or Carey's attempts to resituate scientific inquiry as one among many other practices. I will examine briefly the relation between Dewey's view of inquiry and Foucault's view of power, but the viability of linking the approaches will rest on the usefulness of problematization in filling out their respective approaches to inquiry and the relevance of inquiry to political and policy issues in the public realm.

Two points that cannot be adequately fleshed out require note. First, it is important to realize that Dewey's political project is geared toward revising our view of values and ends, and so the means-ends relation, in contrast to positivistic and utilitarian views, and second, for Dewey, impoverished ways of thinking about causality encourage these positivistic and utilitarian views. This requires an engagement with these views over issues of causality and the formulation of a more adequate notion of responsibility.[31] In the next section, I focus on the understanding of history both Dewey and Foucault share and what, if anything, this entails or makes possible for progressive political practice before turning to the matter of how Foucault's scattered remarks on power and problematization help advance the reconstruction of Dewey's view of publics.

On a History of the Present

Randell Auxier provides a focused study of the relation of Dewey and Foucault in terms of, one, what Foucault read and knew of Dewey and, two, the concrete ideas in Foucault's life and work that might plausibly be traced to Dewey.[32] Auxier claims Foucault likely developed his image of the politically engaged intellectual from Dewey's example and almost certainly borrowed and elaborated Dewey's idea of a "history from the standpoint of the present." Perhaps the most interesting theoretical suggestion in Auxier's piece is that Dewey's take on a "history of the present" is more accommodating of an ethos of political engagement. "The difference between a history of the present and an ordinary history of the past," says Auxier, "is that the former can resist institutional inertia, while the latter either consciously or unconsciously capitulates to the discursive practices and institutional structures that give rise to it."[33]

Auxier develops the suggestion in two ways. First, he suggests that Foucault's early intellectual work and activities showed little inclination toward political engagement, a point agreed upon by all of Foucault's biographers. This is the decade or so in which Foucault developed his philosophical critique of the human sciences. Then Foucault took a job in Tunis and upon returning to France some years later developed and enacted his idea of the specific intellectual. What happened in Tunis? Auxier suggests three key events. First, there were student revolts and political unrest, activities in which Foucault seems to have been at least partly implicated if not directly engaged. Second, Foucault wrote his *Archaeology of Knowledge*, a reflection on his previous work and a rethinking of the role and possibilities of historical analysis. Third, there was Gerard Deledalle, who at the time was translating Dewey's *Logic: The Theory of Inquiry* and finishing up his magnum opus, *L'idée d'expérience dans la philosophie de John Dewey*.

Deledalle reports that Foucault read both of these books and "probably owes to Dewey his idea of a history of the present."[34] Aside from the manuscripts, there is the fact of Deledalle and Foucault's frequent interactions. As one of Foucault's biographers put it, "Foucault consulted with him as an expert on English and American philosophy, which he did not know well. Deledalle talked with him almost daily."[35] As Deledalle was working on both of these works at the time, one might speculate on the substance of their conversations. The content of the books, however, is more easily substantiated.

In Auxier's estimation, "Deledalle's book on Dewey is the most comprehensive treatment of his philosophical development ever written. There is nothing to rival it in English." This is no mere monograph, but a twenty-year project undertaken by a leading authority on American philosophy in France, one providing both a contextual and critical account of Dewey's philosophical development, his reading, his influences, and all of Dewey's own books and his significant articles. Not only did this provide an account of Dewey's turn to political engagement and his numerous and varied activities, but the central theme of Deledalle's book is Dewey's insistence on "active participation in the living struggles and issues of its own age and times." In fact, the relationship between Dewey's intellectual work and his political engagement is the core issue of the work: "This experiential nexus is the focal point of Deledalle's book."[36] But how does a particular view of history entail, accommodate, delimit, or rule out political engagement? To be sure, Carey has been vocal about how different images of journalism are empowering or distorting of democratic practice, but history? And, even if Foucault did take his point of departure from Dewey, what significance does this have for better advancing Dewey's own project?

Auxier's piece connects Foucault's philosophical development, his methodological reflections on history, and his political engagement to Dewey's history from the standpoint of the present. Drawing on Deledalle's recollections, Auxier establishes that Foucault knew Dewey's *Logic: The Theory of Inquiry*. He then draws particular attention to a fourteen-page selection in which Dewey develops his view of history from the standpoint of the present. Auxier notes the similarities between Dewey's work in this section and Foucault's own theoretical reflections on history in *Archaeology of Knowledge*, a book he wrote during the Tunis period. Foucault would later, if somewhat cryptically, describe his work as a "history of the present" in his 1975–1977 *Discipline and Punish*.[37] Auxier then elaborates on a number of political engagements Foucault took up upon returning to France and draws similarities between these activities and those political projects forwarded by Dewey in his time. The bulk of Auxier's essay strives to establish a specific intellectual link between Dewey and Foucault through this view of history, which, though highly speculative, is thought provoking.

It is beyond the boundaries of this chapter to elaborate this view of history and all its implications or to more fully investigate the similarities and differences between Dewey's and Foucault's usage of it to guide inquiry. Most reflection on Foucault's view of a "history of the present" has been pulled in either a philosophical or historical direction. The typical way of taking up Foucault's views is heuristically, as a new approach to historical analysis, prioritizing issues of engagement over matters of how to ground or justify its viewpoint philosophically. I think there is much to recommend this approach as it lends itself well to "a certain philosophical and pragmatic work on ourselves," as Rabinow and Rose conclude.[38] Although I do not think we should evade the philosophical criticisms of Foucault's approach or the relevance reading Foucault within the Western philosophical tradition might have for rethinking historical inquiry, my focus will remain on his elaboration of problematization as a mode of criticism intimately related to questions of political engagement.

A focus on problematization should illuminate several important points. One, it will emphasize the continuity of pragmatism and Foucault, as the problematic situation is the impetus to all forms of inquiry for Dewey, and Foucault's advocacy for an experimentalism in politics was terminology Dewey preferred even to pragmatism. Two, it will highlight the ignored work of Foucault and provide better grounds for raising questions about the relationship of problematization to a history of the present. Is problematization entailed by a history of the present or required to address pressing issues raised by it? Or does it disastrously redirect our attention away from phenomena Foucault's institutionally oriented genealogical work insisted upon, modeling political activity on narrowly available models of aesthetic self-fashioning? Three, it will bring questions of political engagement to the fore. Problematization, in this reading, is an insistence on framing cultural issues in ethical terms, rather than scientific, philosophical, or conventional historical terms, that redirects us toward practices having consequences for how we live our lives. It is not prior to science, philosophy, or history, and it typically draws on these materials for its substance, but it accords these modes of inquiry no priority and reshuffles their descriptions to illuminate the ethical element of cultural conflicts that require response in cultural and ethical terms if engagement is to be genuinely public and properly political.

What is worth immediately registering, however, is the unavoidability of selection in histories of the present. Historians are no different from journalists or lay people in this regard, and the issue is not so much the difference between impartial and biased work as a matter of the awareness with which one forwards or excludes certain ends. This is why Auxier suggests Dewey's notion of a history of the present will lead to a consideration of the ends for which histories are written and, in turn, the issue of how certain ends are selected and forwarded while others are excluded or forgotten. For Auxier, this leads to matters of power/knowledge as one is led to ask how this selection takes place and according to what interests and purposes. This requires a view on the formation of ends and motivations, their selection and exclusion, and it is not a stretch to rethink political engagement and public participation within a more adequate notion of responsibility in light of this understanding. This, in turn, requires avoiding prevailing individualist views on the subjective formation of ends and the mantras of personal empowerment, while also avoiding the temptation to slip back into naturalization stories. Perhaps the task is better understood if characterized as facilitating response-ability and improving its quality.

Dewey's generic sketch for publics is one prompted by reflection on the formation and direction of ends that tries to avoid capture by prevailing notions of causality and individualist discourses of responsibility. But what is that view and why should we expect it to be any more viable today than in Dewey's time? In what follows, I first revisit Dewey's view of the conditions required for the emergence of effective publics. Then I elaborate on the aspects of Foucault's view of power most relevant to this project before turning to Foucault's notion of problematization and its importance to Dewey's view of publics.

Dewey's View of Publics

"The very doctrine of "Sovereignty" is a complete denial of political responsibility."[39]

Dewey, much like Foucault, initiates his rethinking of power by breaking with Thomas Hobbes's theory of sovereignty. Dewey makes this point directly in his 1894 "Austin's Theory of Sovereignty," in which he rejects conceptions of sovereignty characterized by traits of independence and absolute power or, if these traits define any intelligible notion of sovereignty, by rejecting it altogether. Such views lead to two characteristic errors in thinking about power: one, they tend to confuse the organs or institutions of the exercise of sovereignty with sovereignty itself, and, two, they misconceive the matter of determinacy, which is the central matter and main criterion by which sovereign power is distinguished from public opinion. This leads Dewey to raise the following issue:

> Whether there is any alternative between a theory like Austin's, which, placing sovereignty in a part of society, makes the government an entity *per se*, whose operations are all commands, and a theory which finds the residence of sovereignty in the whole complex of social activities, thus making government an organ—an organ the more efficient, we may add, just in proportion as it is not

an entity *per se*, but is flexible and responsive to the social whole, or true sovereign.

Dewey is clearly pushing in the second direction and suggests further reflection on conceptions of sovereignty must be focused on three specific points: "force, or effectiveness; universality, or reference to interests and activities of society as a whole; and determinateness, or specific modes of operation—definite organs of expression."[40] But what does Dewey mean by this? Does he ever go on to develop this theory of sovereignty?

Dewey's 1894 reconsideration of Hobbes's influence on matters of power and sovereignty are a first hint at the project he states most directly in a 1946 "Afterword" to *The Public and Its Problems*. Dewey gives up the language of sovereignty as too implicated in preconceived and confused notions of the state to speak of publics. He insists the assumptions necessary for an effective public are a better characterization of our activities than the assumptions of state sovereignty. Hobbes's criteria of sovereignty, independence, and absolute force must be abandoned. They are inadequate to contemporary cultural circumstances and produce bad consequences when acted upon or when informing the self-understanding of those acting as state representatives. Interdependency and responsibility must be recognized as the starting point.

In advocating for recognition of interdependency, Dewey simply feels this is an empirically adequate characterization of the prevailing state of affairs.[41] Inquiry serves to determine the nature and consequences of these interdependencies, a requisite condition for intelligent response or responseability. Inquiry, as the movement from the indeterminate effects of actions toward a determinate characterization of the consequences of activity, would make clear that no group or state acts with complete independence or absolute force.[42]

Dewey is clear about the conditions and consequences of this point in chapter 5, "Search for the Great Community," of *The Public and Its Problems*. First, he attacks the belief that prevailing political forms and institutions are an expression of the idea of democracy. Prevailing forms of government are more the product of contingent circumstance than the march of the idea of democracy through history. If you want a democracy, you need a public. This requires a community, which, in turn, requires associated and interdependent activities.[43] In Dewey's view, this initial and minimal condition is widely met. Humans everywhere act in association and these relations are most adequately characterized as interdependent. In fact, we have interdependency in spades, and the bare fact of noting this achieves very little other than to highlight the absurdity of views predicated on independent and self-sufficient individuals or sovereign actors. It is worth noting that this is all

Foucault means by claiming power is everywhere and all that is accomplished in making this claim.

To move beyond mere interdependency requires communication. Further, Dewey suggests communication is the "only possible solution" to problems stemming from interdependency: "the perfecting of the means and ways of communication of meanings so that genuinely shared interest in the consequences of interdependent activities may inform desire and effort and thereby direct action."[44] Instead of a singular sovereign acting with impunity but not, in turn, acted upon, Dewey's substitution of the public makes power an inherently ethical or moral issue. The goal of this substitution, in fact, is the one denied by the doctrine of sovereignty: responsibility. But what does Dewey mean in claiming this is an ethical issue, one not of causality but response-ability, of values and criticism?

Perhaps the best clue is found in Dewey's definition of responsibility as a disposition: "the disposition to consider in advance the probable consequences of any projected step and deliberately to accept them: to accept them in the sense of taking them into account, acknowledging them in action, not yielding a mere verbal assent."[45] In Dewey's explicit political works, he addressed the problem historically. Although there has been a shift from individuals as the source of agency, however restricted or idealized that might have been in classical liberalism, to organized interests and corporations as dominant actors, there has not emerged a subsequent manner of attributing responsibility able to escape both notions of sovereignty and liberal mantras of "personal responsibility." In fact, these assertions of sovereignty and personal responsibility become all the more vocal and desperate in their ineffectiveness. Dewey's work on publics is set within this historical perspective, in a sense recommending a pragmatist perspective on publics over liberal ones as a response to this problem. In his view, the ability to become response-able requires inquiry into the consequences that a set of actions has on the actions of others; communication enables us to become responsive and thus response-able in light of such inquiries. Inquiry and communication must be mutually reconstructed in integral fashion.[46]

This provides an initial characterization of what might be called "Dewey's hypothesis," which, stated forthrightly in *The Public and Its Problems,* is that we need a new form of knowledge in order to have effective publics.[47] His hypothesis is stated in the following manner. First, our view and very conception of knowledge have been corrupted by an impoverished epistemology or view of science. Second, we have a historically unique situation in terms of compromised communicative relations, ones characterized not only by an increase in the production and circulation of knowledge but also of errors, half-truths, and opinions manufactured by public relations agents and propagandists to an unprecedented degree.[48] This has not resulted in a similar progression toward critical sensibilities or discriminating judgment.[49] Therefore, we must rethink both social inquiry and communication together to produce a new knowledge in order to more adequately characterize scientific inquiry, to rethink history in its relation to present events, and to address the problems of the public—in short, the three tasks articulated for cultural studies by James Carey.[50] The condition for successfully undertaking these tasks is the formation of an experimental disposition or a critical ethos.[51] The central question is how problematization relates to the formation of this disposition, how it facilitates a reconstruction of inquiry and communication, and how it thereby aids in the constitution of contemporary publics.

Foucault on Power

Whether or not Dewey's history of the present drove Foucault to reflect on the matter of values (ends) and their implication in power relations, as Auxier suggests, Foucault clearly reversed matters throughout the 1970s to introduce a different conception of power relations into matters of historical analysis. For Foucault, history is used not only as an instrument in political struggles but new forms of history are "actually forged in the struggles that took place around the workings of power—struggles within power and against power." In a shift from sovereign power to disciplinary power, there is a shift not only in forms of history but "a new mode of relationship between power and knowledge."[52] What, then, is this shift in modalities of power? What is Foucault's theory of power?

It is worth addressing a major point of contention at this point lest we too quickly marry Foucault and Dewey. In particular, John Stuhr has registered warnings, specifically suggesting Dewey's theory of inquiry works against attention to the contextual features of power relations for which Foucault is so valuable: "The *Logic* readily can seem to plaster a big yellow and black happy face on Foucault's genealogies of power."[53] Therefore, it seems useful to specify which aspects of Foucault's work on power can carry forward Dewey's view of inquiry. Put simply, the Foucault of the Nietzschean hypothesis is out. Foucault's approach to governmentality, as a regulatory power distinct from disciplinary and sovereign power, begins not from a postulate of war but a problem of governing. Foucault develops this work almost immediately after the 1975 publication of *Discipline and Punish* through his 1976 January–March Collège de France lecture series. Consider this early indication of his shifting approach to analyses of power:

> One might say this: It is as though power, which used to have sovereignty as its modality or organizing schema, found itself unable to govern the economic and political body of a society that was undergoing both a demographic explosion and industrialization. So much so that far too many things were escaping the old

mechanism of the power of sovereignty, both at the top and at the bottom, both at the level of detail and at the mass level.[54]

According to Foucault, this situation requires two different responses, each appropriate to the scale at which the difficulty is felt. At the micro level, or "the level of detail," Foucault refers to his now-famous analysis of disciplinary power and its attendant focus on the body, training, and surveillance. This is the Foucault of *Discipline and Punish*. But there is far more to it than that. On a broader scale, at "the mass level," Foucault begins to develop his analysis of a regulatory power, which cognizes "people" as a population in terms of demography, utilizing statistical tools and the analyses of experts working in departments of an administrative and regulatory state. The key document here is the "Governmentality" lecture of the 1978 lecture series, "Security, Territory, and Population," in which Foucault elaborates on the interrelations of these three ways of approaching power. Whereas in 1976 Foucault merely suggests normalization as the link between a disciplinary (micro level) and regulatory (mass level) approach to power, in 1978 Foucault suggests an even more historically specific and complex interrelationship among these modes of power in an attempt to refigure our understanding of the state. Although I would wager that it is discourses of safety and risk, both personal and institutional, that tend to mediate these different scales in America today, it is of more pressing importance to develop an alternative means of articulating these scales of activity.

When Foucault began lecturing on governmentality, his explicit focus was on a "history of the critical attitude," specifically the various sorts of critical operations a governmentalizing tendency provokes and the attitude such governmental-critical interrelations might engender. However, Foucault's broad concern with mapping the relation between the extension of regulatory power and the critical disposition it engenders seems to have been lost or de-emphasized. Perhaps this is due to the fact that only the single "Governmentality" lecture was widely available and used as the basis for much Anglo-American reflection on Foucault's work of this period. However, that lecture offers only the briefest snapshot of Foucault's thinking on the matter. In light of this, I want to draw attention to the critical practice Foucault develops alongside his conception of governmentality and the regulatory state: problematization.

Problematization

How can Foucault's examples and brief moments of reflection on problematization help to reformulate and advance Dewey's conception of publics? I want to suggest that problematization as a critical operation is Dewey's view of inquiry in a retooled vocabulary and run backward in order to facilitate the constitution of publics. It renders a previously determinate situation more indeterminate. It forces that which goes without saying into discourse. It attempts to resolve that which is self-evident into the process by which it became such. A given state of affairs is resolved into the conditions of its emergence to the effect that the self-evident is now viewed as a specific response to a problem taken to achieve particular ends. Perhaps no better characterization could be found than Williams's 1977 definition for structures of feeling: "social experiences *in solution.*"[55]

Foucault is brief in his comments on problematization, a style of criticism he only explicitly elaborates in the 1980s, shortly before his death in 1984. It must be noted that Foucault's characterizations are often quite broad to the point of being unqualified, usually poorly integrated with his previous work in an explicit way, and not historically contextualized. In fact, Foucault simply suggests thought is an activity of problematization. Thinking is the cognizing of an activity as an object, reflected on as a problem, or a process by which actions enter into reflection by becoming uncertain, unfamiliar, or suddenly difficult to continue as usual. Glossed even more minimally, thought is, in Foucault's own words, "an original or specific response."[56] A history of thought, then, if it is to understand what is going on in any particular cultural context, needs to recover the problem to which programs, proposals, or a specific characterization of the prevailing state of affairs are a response. "This development of the given into a question, this transformation of a group of obstacles and difficulties into problems to which the diverse solutions will attempt to produce a response, this is what constitutes the point of problematization and the specific work of thought."[57]

Through this critical operation, one resolves "solutions" into the process by which they became such, or holds "social experiences in solution," to return to Williams's 1977 phrase. One recovers the different responses that were posed for any particular problem and reexamines the basis on which one response prevailed over other responses. It allows for a reexamination and reevaluation of the principles and postulates and ends, or "objectives," that guided the formulation of the responses given.[58] This is what Dewey called a critique of prejudices, in which holding experience in solution meant understanding how present experience "is already overlaid and saturated with the products of reflection of past generations and bygone ages. It is filled with interpretations, classifications, due to sophisticated thought, which have been incorporated into what seems to be fresh naïve empirical materials."[59]

Throughout the 1980s, Foucault's work on problematization was consciously styled as a third prong to his research program, alongside and presumably complementing the archaeological and genealogical approaches to his historical ontology. During this time, Foucault made constant reference to not only a history of the present, an idea he located with reference to Kant's work, but also an experimental approach to political questions through problematization. Although it is impossible to quickly gloss the complexity of the internal economy of Foucault's work, one suggestive way of illuminating the link of genealogy and problematization might be West's distinction between demythologizing, in which genealogical work provides historical maps to render contingent what is considered necessary, and demystification, which seeks theoretical explanations for the role and persistence of specific social practices.[60] In this sense, problematization would view states of affairs or political logics as "solutions," which, viewed historically, were the prevailing responses to what were once problematic situations. Rethinking a state of affairs through problematization allows us to situate the "self-evident" as one response among many. This abstract formulation is hardly a sufficient basis on which to argue for a redirection of cultural studies. But I want to make the case for exploring it more fully by linking it more tightly to the problem of publics in the work of Foucault, Dewey, and Carey.

If one traces the emergence of Foucault's emphasis on a history of the present, one notices this work is almost always linked to Kant and that Foucault usually links Kant's text to brief reflections on journalism or public reasoning. Foucault's essay, "What Is Enlightenment,"[61] is exemplary in this respect and the most complex reflection on problematization as a critical practice in the context of his other work. First and foremost, Foucault strives to characterize the experimental attitude that accompanies problematizing as a critical practice, one that can then find expression in theoretically, methodologically, and practically sound inquiries. In fact, Foucault unites a number of intellectual components—theory, method, practice, relationship to history, informing intellectual traditions—*not* in a system of thought but through this critical attitude, and asks whether or not this requires a faith in the Enlightenment tradition.

Moreover, Foucault links and develops this line of thinking through reflection on the role of publics. Consider Foucault's opening words:

> Today when a periodical asks its readers a question, it does so in order to collect opinions on some subject about which everyone has an opinion already; there is not much likelihood of learning anything new. In the eighteenth century, editors preferred to question the public on problems that did not have solutions.[62]

We find similar references throughout Foucault's attempts to elaborate problematization alongside archaeology and genealogy, as a third aspect of his intellectual inquiries. To be sure, Foucault does not forward a conception of publics beyond marking the distance between views that represent a public as an aggregate of individual opinions and those inviting public discourse on problems not yet sufficiently resolved. But his views on problematization as a mode of criticism read against his continual references to public engagement suggest one. I want to recall and emphasize once more, Foucault developed this style of approaching issues alongside his investigations into governmentality and the operations of regulatory power, a condition in which demography replaces democracy, in which populations replace people, in which statistical analyses replace dialogue, and in which politics becomes a logic of administrative routine and crisis avoidance.

Governmentality, in short, is a condition where Walter Lippmann defeats Dewey. It eviscerates the public for the policy domain. Recall, however, that Herbert Croly and Lippmann's views of politics emerged during the high point of fairly effective muckraking journalism and posed a rather elitist alternative to that style of engaging publics. The muckraker's domain is not the policy circle but public discourse. It addresses not the presidential nominee but those affected by the conditions brought to public attention. It is not a matter of abstruse technical knowledge and mathematical models developed as means for ends, which are unexamined, unexplained, and taken for granted by experts themselves. It is concerned with the normative aspects of expert knowledge and specialized institutions, which it thematizes and forces to give account. In short, it is a means of forcing public reflection on ends and characterizing cultural conflicts in explicitly ethical terms. Does Foucault's work on problematization hold similar possibilities in our contemporary situation?

Foucault's view of problematization provides hints at a critical operation able to articulate Dewey's generic sketch for the constitution of publics in chapter 1 of *The Public and Its Problems*. There is still a widespread assumption that people are entitled to perceive, identify, thematize, and draw attention to intolerable conditions requiring political response. Dewey's view of the constitution of publics attempts to develop the conditions required to enable them to do so. In this view, social practices often impact those not specifically included in a particular practice, which Dewey characterizes as interdependency and which sets an initial condition for the formation of a public. Perception, inquiry into, and knowledge of these effects as consequences for one's activity set a further condition. However, as Dewey's theory of inquiry makes clear, it is an action toward the end of resolving a problematic situation. Therefore, the manner in which a situation is rendered problematic, or nonproblematic, is of primary importance and constitutes an initial condition for the constitution of publics. It is in response to a problem, to problematization, that inquiry and communication are linked together, as problem and response; it is this mode of criticism that reconstructs prevailing and proposed states of affairs *as* responses to problematic situations. To put the matter as Dewey might have, contemporary publics exist not only *by* problematization, by inquiry and communication, but *in* problematization.

In closing, I realize how inadequate this initial formulation of problematization remains if the critical standard of evaluation is anything other than suggestiveness or perhaps, at best, plausibility. Much work remains to be done. Nonetheless, it is worth reiterating the hunch informing this chapter. Dewey claimed that the emergence of a democratic public required a reconstruction of both inquiry and communication. Carey has admirably and fearlessly carried forward a Deweyan view of communication in advocating for genuinely democratic publics. However, Dewey's views on inquiry, a subject he published on over the course of five decades, have been largely ignored in communication. Those forwarding Dewey's theory of inquiry, specifically Robert Craig and Vernon Cronen, have not attempted to integrate their views with Carey's theory of communication. However, if I am correct in suggesting Dewey's view requires linking communication and inquiry in integral fashion, and if those in the "Dewey group" have taken up only one aspect of this task, and if Foucault is influenced by Dewey to take up the other half of this task through his study of Dewey's theory of inquiry, might not Foucault provide some of the tools of inquiry requisite to reconstructing contemporary publics?

Notes

1. James Carey, "Reflections on the Project of Cultural Studies," *Cultural Studies in Question* (London: Sage Publications, 1997), p. 3.
2. James Carey, "The Problem of Journalism History," *James Carey: A Critical Reader* (Minneapolis: University of Minnesota Press, 1997), p. 87.
3. James Carey, "A Cultural Approach to Communication," *Communication as Culture: Essays on Media and Society* (New York: Routledge, 1989), p. 23.
4. James Carey, "Reconceiving "Mass" and "Media," *Communication as Culture*, p. 83.
5. Carey, "The Communications Revolution and the Professional Communicator," *Critical Reader*, p. 141.
6. Carey, "Reflections on the Project of Cultural Studies," p.4.
7. Carey, "Reflections on the Project of Cultural Studies," p. 4.
8. Carey, "Reflections on the Project of Cultural Studies," pp. 1, 15.
9. Carey, "Reflections on the Project of Cultural Studies," p. 2.
10. I have in mind the "radical" response to the summer 2003 TV rule changes and the "conservative" response to the "indecency" of the 2004 Super Bowl halftime show. A better example is the coalition of radicals and conservatives united in response to the 2000–2004 Republican energy policy on shared grounds: the massive subsidies given to fossil fuel industries.
11. Samuel Huntington, "Conservatism as an Ideology," *American Political Science Review*, 51 (1957): 454. In addition to the national security trump card often played by conservatives, one might similarly investigate the actual articulations and effects of neoliberal concerns with discourses of personal safety.
12. Carey, "Afterword/The Culture in Question," in *Critical Reader*, p. 309.

13. I review Dewey's pragmatism below. On progressivism, see Carey, "Communications and the Progressives," *Critical Studies in Mass Communication,* 6 (1989), and "The Press, Public Opinion, and Public Discourse," in *Critical Reader,* pp. 242–243.

14. Carey, "Political Correctness and Cultural Studies," in *Critical Reader,* p. 270; also see Carey, "Reflections on the Project of Cultural Studies," p. 2, where Geertz is included with the good guys, and Deleuze and Guattari join the French.

15. See Carey, "Political Correctness and Cultural Studies," p. 270 for this phrase.

16. Richard Rorty, *Consequences of Pragmatism* (Minneapolis: University of Minnesota Press, 1982), p. xviii.

17. Carey, "Communications and the Progressives," p. 264

18. Carey, "Reflections on the Project of Cultural Studies," pp. 6, 15.

19. Stuart Hall, "Cultural Studies and Its Theoretical Legacies," *Cultural Studies* (New York: Routledge, 1992), pp. 277–294, see p. 283.

20. James Carey, "Abolishing the Old Spirit World," *Critical Studies in Mass Communication,* 12 (1995): p. 83.

21. Carey, "Reflections on the Project of Cultural Studies," p. 18.

22. On journalism, see Carey, "The Problem of Journalism History," on communication models, see Carey, "A Cultural Approach to Communication," on publics, see Carey "Reconceiving "Mass" and "Media," and "Reflections on the Project of Cultural Studies."

23. Jack Bratich, Jeremy Packer and Cameron McCarthy, eds., "Governing the Present," *Foucault, Governmentality, and Cultural Studies* (Albany: State University of New York Press, 2003), p. 3.

24. Carey, "Overcoming Resistance to Cultural Studies," in *Communication as Culture,* p. 97.

25. Joli Jensen and John J. Pauly, "Imagining the Audience: Losses and Gains in Cultural Studies," *Cultural Studies in Question,* p. 162.

26. Carey, "Communications and the Progressives," p. 269.

27. Carey, "Communications and the Progressives," pp. 269, 278.

28. Carey, "Abolishing the Old Spirit World," pp. 87–88.

29. Michel Foucault, "Politics and the Study of Discourse," *The Foucault Effect,* eds. Graham Burchell, Colin Gordon and Peter Miller (Chicago: University of Chicago Press, 1994).

30. See Foucault, "Politics and the Study of Discourse," pp. 65–70.

31. For Dewey, many of our problems are linked to flawed naturalistic or subjectivist theories of the formation of ends or values, an issue for which his view of inquiry is an answer. Usually Dewey introduces the issue by first attempting to disabuse us of the "causal force" notion of thinking. The first chapters of both *The Public and Its Problems* and *Freedom and Culture* are exemplary in this respect.

32. Randell Auxier, "Foucault, Dewey, and the History of the Present," *Journal of Speculative Philosophy,* 16(2002): 78.

33. Ibid., pp. 79–80, 92.

34. Ibid., p. 82, also note 48.

35. Eribon, p. 192, as cited by Auxier, p. 82.

36. Facts and quotations in this paragraph taken from Auxier, "Foucault, Dewey, and the History of the Present," p. 83.

37. Beatrice Han, author of an extensive philosophical study of Foucault's views of the "historical a priori," makes the surprising suggestion that *Discipline and Punish* is,

among other things, an implicit dialogue with William James on the nature of truth. See Han, "Reply to Gary Gutting's Review of *Foucault's Critical Project: Between the Transcendental and the Historical*" (2003) available at: http://private www.essex.ac.uk/~beatrice/

38. Paul Rabinow and Nikolas Rose, *The Essential Foucault* (New York: The New Press, 2003), p. xxxii

39. Dewey, "Afterword," *The Public and Its Problems* (Athens: Ohio University Press, 1997), p. 223.

40. Dewey, "Austin's Theory of Sovereignty," *Early Works*, vol. 4 (Carbondale and Edwardsville: Southern Illinois University Press, 1971) p. 90.

41. Dewey, "Afterword," p. 228.

42. I am unaware of work that links Dewey's mature and overly formalist definition of inquiry to his earlier advocacy for conceiving power in terms of determination. For the later definition, see Dewey, *Logic: The Theory of Inquiry, Later Works*, vol. 12 (Carbondale and Edwardsville: Southern Illinois University Press, 1986), p. 108: "Inquiry is the controlled or directed transformation of an indeterminate situation into one that is so determinate in its constituent distinctions and relations as to convert the elements of the original situation into a unified whole."

43. Dewey, *The Public and Its Problems*, pp. 143–149, 151.

44. Ibid., pp. 152, 155.

45. Dewey, *Democracy and Education, Middle Works, vol. 9* (Carbondale and Edwardsville: Southern Illinois University Press, 1980) p. 185.

46. Dewey, *The Public and Its Problems*, p. 184.

47. Ibid., p. 166. See p. 157 for the beginning of this statement of his hypothesis.

48. Ibid., pp. 162, 169, 181.

49. Ibid., p. 163.

50. Ibid., pp. 168–178 on science and p. 179 on history.

51. Dewey, in his 1939 *Freedom and Culture* (New York: Prometheus Books, 1989), calls this the "scientific attitude" and claims that substituting this attitude for prevailing dispositions is the "the sole guarantee against wholesale misleading by propaganda" and "the only assurance of a public opinion intelligent enough to meet present social problems" (p. 114). By "scientific," Dewey means experimental.

52. Foucault, *Society Must Be Defended* (New York: Picador, 2003), pp. 135, 185.

53. John Stuhr, "Power/Inquiry: The Logic of Pragmatism," in *Dewey's Logical Theory*, eds. F. T. Burke, D. M. Hester & R. B. Talisse (Nashville, TN: Vanderbilt University Press, 2002), p. 283.

54. Foucault, *Society Must Be Defended*, p. 249.

55. Raymond Williams, *Marxism and Literature* (Oxford, England: Oxford University Press, 1977), p. 133.

56. Michel Foucault, "Polemics, Politics, and Problematizations," *The Essential Works of Foucault, 1954–1984, Vol. 1: Ethics*, ed. Paul Rabinow (New York: The Free Press, 1997), pp. 117, 118.

57. Foucault, "Polemics, Politics, and Problematizations," p. 118.

58. Ibid., pp. 118–119.

59. John Dewey, *Experience and Nature, Later Works, Vol. 1* ((Carbondale and Edwardsville: Southern Illinois University Press, 1981), p. 40.

60. Cornel West, "Theory, Pragmatisms, and Politics," in *Consequences of Theory*, eds. Jonathan Arac and Barbara Johnson (Baltimore: Johns Hopkins University Press, 1991), pp. 22–38.

61. Foucault, "What Is Enlightenment," *The Foucault Reader* (New York: Pantheon Books, 1984), pp. 32–50.
62. Ibid., p. 32.

4. Rethinking Dependency: New Relations of Transportation and Communication

JEREMY PACKER

When I first proposed doing research on automobile transportation as a cultural activity, two wise men suggested I begin by seriously investigating the writings of James Carey.[1] This at first seemed like strange advice. I just didn't see the connection between the work of Carey and the project I envisioned, one located at the theoretical crossroads of Michel Foucault[2] and the British cultural studies tradition. Eventually I heeded the advice and, quite clearly, they were correct on far too many accounts for me to elaborate here. So it was in light of how to think about the relationships between transportation, culture, and communications (as a field and as a set of technologies and practices), that I first read James Carey's writings. This chapter begins to address these relationships in historical terms and through a set of theoretical frameworks that aren't often used in conjunction with each other; Foucauldian theories of governmentality and Carey-style American cultural studies. Most explicitly it asks that we rethink our notion of dependency, a classic explanation of the pre-telegraphic history of communications and transportation. Not in order to alter what Carey sees as being fundamentally marked by communication's independence from transportation but, rather, to ask if there is a not-so-new dependence that runs in the other direction. As transportation has become increasingly dependent upon communications, via apparatuses of control must we necessarily keep transportation in mind as part of our field of enquiry? As will be shown, it is not simply the technological processes by which such interconnections exist that matter, instead, as Carey has pointed out, it is the means for which technologies are imagined to be useful that is of greater intellectual and political import. One such force of articulation is the concern for safety and security.

Communication technologies insofar as they have been studied in relation to safety and security have typically been thought of in terms of secrecy—the secrets of the state and the corporation and the privacy of the individual—that is, ensuring that information is secure from prying eyes and ears.[3] But, an often overlooked duty of communications, the "promotion of safety through the use of radio, on land, water, and in the air," acknowledged even by the FCC, makes clear the rationalities addressed in this chapter are being enacted not simply to ensure privacy and secrecy.[4] And these rationalities have bound communication and transportation technologies in the minds of governmental officials for decades and corporate entities for centuries.[5] But, this promotion of transportation safety via communications predates the 1934 advent of the FCC, and the interconnection of the two technologies toward this goal is far more complex than the "use of radio" implies. Furthermore, the discourses of safety and security are often fused with either utopian or dystopian rhetoric in order to legitimize or delegitimize various uses of communication and transportation technologies. In fact, it is one of the primary logics through which transportation regulation is enacted. And, it shows no signs of abating, as it has become an even more prevalent means for legitimating the regulation of communications and transportation following the events of September 11, 2001.

James Carey seriously considered the issue of the relationship between communication and transportation most significantly in "Technology and Ideology."[6] The advent of the telegraph brought about many phenomenally important cultural, economic, and political changes, but the greatest of these according to Carey is that communication was freed from its dependence upon transportation.[7] In simple terms, messages could be transferred without the aid of transportation technologies such as trains, coaches, ships, and so on. Long-distance communication was no longer bound to print media nor to the vessels used to transport them. The less cited, but possibly equally important, shift that Carey notes is communications can now be used to "control physical processes actively." It's not insignificant that it is railroads, Carey's example, to which this active process of control is very quickly put to use.[8] A very different effect of this historical dependence and subsequent separation is the primary object of Carey's now-famous article, "A Cultural Approach to Communication." As he argues, the way in which we, as citizens, scholars, policy advocates, technicians, and others, think about or conceptualize communication technologies and communication in general affects not only how we study communication and upon what aspects of it we focus but also what we imagine communication can accomplish and what goals to which it will be articulated. Hence, Carey's investment in opposing the transmission (transport) model with the ritual (cultural) model is not simply an ontological or empirical claim, it is also teleological in the positive sense of the term. It forces us to ask, "What ends do we want communications to serve?"[9] This chapter will address the first assumption via a redirection of the second—which is to say, I will sketch out some preliminary ideas of how we might think about transportation and communication in terms of a changed relationship of dependence. Communications may not have been dependent upon transportation technologies for more than 150 years, but transportation has become increasingly dependent upon communication technologies, and this dependence *depends* upon a specific way of conceptualizing or rationalizing the uses and goals of mating transportation and communication. In other words, there is no technological determination guiding how communications and transportation technologies are brought together and used in conjunction with each other. As Carey rightly points out, it is in the political, economic, and cultural realms that these articulations are conceptualized, imagined, legitimized, and implemented. Furthermore, that fact should force us as scholars to recognize all technological conceptualizations in political terms, not as foregone conclusions.[10]

Thus, any conceptualization regarding the relation between communications and transportation should be brought under scrutiny and not merely treated as a natural outcome of technological progression. It is here that I want to begin to move in two theoretical trajectories somewhat simultaneously. On the one hand I would like to think a bit more about how through Carey, and vicariously through Innis, we might imagine this changed dependence in terms of the control of space. On the other, how, through Michel Foucault and his understanding of governmentality, we might think of this dependence in terms of a political rationality that attempts to use communications and transportation as a means for ensuring and expanding the possibilities of liberal governance. This second route is most actively pursued by Armand Mattelart, who argues that the very idea of communication has always been concerned with overcoming natural barriers to facilitate the movement of people, goods, and culture.[11] Carey makes much the same point, though he situates the articulation in thought as following from the articulation in practice.[12] Mattelart emphasized that the idea of communication in modern European societies was deeply about how to effect a rational, good, and open circulatory system (a system consonant with the aims of liberal government and capitalism). Whereas Carey makes it clear that in the American context a second analogical system—the nervous system[13]—structured thought on communications and transportation. This system, it was imagined, would create a utopian relationship between man (sic) and nature via freedoms of press and movement.[14]

I want to continue in this comparative spirit and add another concern to which communications and transportation were imagined to be vital; how to rule or govern a vast and mobile population, nation, or empire? Recent Foucauldian-derived scholarship has attempted to formulate a means for theorizing this formation of rule, which they call, following Foucault, governing at a distance.[15] The notion of governing at a distance can be understood in two different, yet interconnected fashions. First, it is through transportation and communications that the state is able to maintain its hold over the population and in some cases its empire, something Carey points out quite clearly in several places, sometimes through his own histories and also through the work of Innis.[16] In fact, it's no stretch to say that it is precisely through Innis's explanation of the spatial bias of such transportation technologies as writing, road building, the railroad, and so on, which leads to the control of space and the annihilation of time/ritual-based forms of culture that Carey is able to make such historical assertions. This use of communication to govern at a distance is not necessarily built upon any pretense of democratic or communitarian principles, in opposition to the rhetoric that Mattelart claims is foundational to European liberalism and which Carey and Innis posit is a principal potential outcome of time/ritual-biased communications forms. Yet the second notion of governing at a distance depends precisely upon using communications to activate subjects without being overly intrusive or coercive, which is to say, acting according to the most basic tenet of liberal government. It is through a combination of the press, freedom of speech, and the telegraph that Andrew Barry argues governing at a distance, in this sense, was initially ensured.[17] It is a form of governance built upon allowing and encouraging, one might say fostering, very particular forms of freedom that lead to, and are derived by, the maxim that the government is best which governs least. For Barry it is primarily the realm of communications through which this form of governance takes place. Innis has a different take on the role of freedom of speech, in that when the authority of free speech is institutionalized in the press through the First Amendment, there was a loss of public life, not an affirmation of democratic participation.[18]

These two theoretical concerns, when combined, provide a means for analyzing the subject of this chapter; the expansion of governing at a distance or controlling space, not via a freeing of communications from transportation but rather by *making transportation dependent upon communication* by conceptualizing the solution to problems associated with transportation as deriving from a lack or excess of information that produces unsafe conditions. Hence, it is a particular means of conceptualizing a technological linkage, for a specific purpose, as a type of problem to be overcome, through which the dependence of transportation upon communication must partially be understood. The conceptualization, or problematization,[19] that I'm suggesting here is that of safety and security, which is completely consonant with the aims of liberal governance and has been born out historically, most especially when the issues of controlling and overcoming the barriers of space are concerned.[20] The combination of these three political rationalities, (1) to overcome space (2) while ensuring the safety and security of goods and populations as they traverse and (3) are governed in and by that space, is often a rather difficult task. The discourse and techniques of safety and risk analysis are most often called upon to legitimate and facilitate these political rationalities where mobility is concerned.[21] Yet, it is only through the maintenance, indeed the expansion, of the communication/transportation couplet that mobility can be increasingly monitored, guided, regulated, made productive, expanded, and ultimately, in theory, guaranteed safe. There are two approaches to thinking about safety's relationship to communication/ transportation analogically. First, safety could be to communication/transportation as diet and exercise are to the circulatory system or adequate sleep and maintenance through mental exertion (unfortunately there is no antonym for atrophy) is to the nervous system. More legitimately, safety could be thought of in terms of a codependent grouping of systems in which it exists only when and insofar as it is grouped with other codependent systems, such as (neo)liberalism and modern capitalism. In the former, safety is more like preventive medicine, it keeps a preexisting system flowing smoothly. In the latter, we would need to think in terms of multiple overlapping and integrally productive systems that could not exist in their present form without the accompanying nourishment of other equally dependent systems. The importance of thinking in this fashion is to point out that we cannot separate out safety, or communications for that matter, from capital or liberal government, as if it is an addendum or reducible to another system.

Keeping the original two concerns in mind, dependence and how to approach communications, we could ask an empirical question, "How do communication and transportation remain dependent?" and we could further investigate how thought about communication as a means of ensuring the safety of transportation technologies then factors into decisions regarding the regulation of communication technologies and the continued desire to meld the two. I'd like to investigate both by touching upon moments in which the debate over how to govern communication technologies was organized and situated by the degree to which communication was seen as facilitating or hindering the safety of transportation. We might call this the *discourse of lack or excess*.[22] As in, a lack of communication leads to accidents and unsafe conditions and simultaneously the converse is also true; an excess of communication also leads to accidents and unsafe conditions. There is an assumed ideal balance between the two, an ideal communications equilibrium of sorts. However, this fine line between the two has over the past 150 years meandered according to an as-yet-not-understood calculus. No mathematician, but I'll try nonetheless to chart its changing coordinates.

As Carey notes, the use of communications to control transportation at the behest of safety occurred with the use of the telegraph in order to provide more trustworthy switching of train tracks. Carey is cited here at length in order to emphasize (1) the import Carey gives to this ability, (2) the role safety plays in the rationalities of its use, and (3) to begin questioning why this outcome of the "split" has received so little attention.

> The great theoretical significance of the technology lay not merely in the separation but also in the use of telegraph as both a model of and a mechanism for control of the physical movement of things, specifically for the railroad. That is the fundamental discovery: not only can information move independently of and faster than physical entities, but it can also be a simulation of and control mechanism for what has been left behind . . . It was of particular use on the long stretches of single-track road in the American West, where accidents were a serious problem.[23]

This in Carey's words foreshadows communication's role in the system—the ability to unify thought and action, often from afar, via the flow of information. For it is the dream of the systems analyst to *erase the human element* in the hope of ensuring efficiency and functionality that finds its way into the sphere of transportation as well. This point will be further addressed near the end of this chapter through the driverless automobile. In fact, it is the very thought of the systems analyst that perceives the driver as a component, not an autonomous subject, that alters how this dependency is being further changed.

What follows is a brief rundown of only a few of the significant communication technologies that are configured, understood, and governed, either partially or significantly, according to their adverse or beneficial effects upon transportation. Yet, no major transportation system over the past 150 years—since the advent of the telegraph—has been free from communications technologies. We need to keep in mind that we can think of a particular technology, say the bicycle, and make a claim that the bicycle itself has no communications component. To a degree and at a specific moment this could be said to be true. The bicycle is after all not attached to any telegraph cable, radio device, and certainly we've yet to see a DVD monitor as an option on our mountain bikes (though there is a consumer push toward the use of GPS units, often for safety purposes no less). However, once bicycles become part of a system of transportation, one that includes roads and pathways and rules of riding conduct, communication becomes an integral part of its efficiency, and safety becomes the mantra for its governance. Hand signals, reflectors, night lights, traffic lights, and traffic signs all become the means by which the system flows smoothly. The bicycle transportation system is impossibly dependent upon communications technologies. But this is a vague and ahistorical anecdote. What follows is a slightly more thorough account of how communications technologies have been mated with transportation technologies to create new assemblages, new machines. It often dwells on moments when new communications technologies were first mated

or crossed paths with various transportation technologies. This set of historical anecdotes is neither exhaustive nor all encompassing. Yet, it begins to
show just how dominant the notion of safety is as a means of justifying and
legitimizing modes of regulation and the enabling of the mating of communication and transportation technologies.

On Water and in the Air

> The real delay was the development of a system of communication that would
> allow space travel to be controlled from earth. As printing went with seagoing
> navigation and the telegraph with the railway, electronic and computer-based
> communication go with the space ship.[24]
>
> —James Carey

In many ways it is the advent of wireless communication that reorients the
possibilities for the interconnection of communications and transportation.
Telegraph was tied to the railroad, not just in terms of its routes, as Jonathan
Sterne ably describes in chapter 5, but also in terms of its ability to control
certain functions of trains and their tracks as noted earlier in the lengthy citation from Carey. As he suggested there is absolutely a historical and technological link between communications and transportation technologies, and it
radically altered the dominant question of what communication could do.[25]
Many of these uses can be accounted for in terms of their historical overlap,
at least to a degree. But, we still must take into account the reasons why they
were linked and to what aims they were put. It is with wireless, and eventually electronic and computer-based communication, that the nature of
dependency truly begins to change, as it opened up a much wider physical
space for interconnection that wasn't as spatially dependent on fixed routes,
at least in the abstract, as the telegraph lines and railroad tracks.

In Susan Douglas's[26] account of the early use and regulation of radio she
points out that one of the earliest selling points was the benefit it brought to
the safety of ships. This entailed providing warnings of inclement weather
(including storms and fog), helping out with navigation, relaying distress signals, aiding in the recognition of fellow ships, and so on. Amateur operators
played a role in this and were at first lionized for the part they played in rescue efforts following shipping disasters as well as the help they provided in
passing on important storm reports and helping in disaster relief. However,
with the sinking of the *Titanic* this all changed. Amateur operators in this
instance were blamed for clogging up the airwaves with false information that
hindered rescue efforts. Furthermore, prior to the sinking of the *Titanic*,
amateur operators were said to have either directly interfered in rescue efforts
or in fact caused other shipping disasters. Thus they were at first seen as
addressing a *lack* of information while later their *excessive* communication was

considered suspect or created static. It was this sort of rhetoric via an appeal to both national security—due to the navy's supposed vulnerability to misinformation—and the personal safety of shipboard passengers that ultimately led to radio regulation and the creation of greater government oversight and control.

The importance of amateur radio operators also influenced the growth of aircraft radio.[27] In fact, it was in relation to shipping that aircraft radio use was often compared. In 1928 the *New York Times* reported, "The research engineers point out that, whether it be passenger, mail or express plane, communication may be regarded as highly desirable if not as important and necessary as communication with ships at sea. The factor of safety is considerably increased."[28] One key connection was between air radio and the U.S. Post Office.[29] Seen in this light, the post office as a preexistent communications system first adds the airplane to its infrastructure and then further integrates radio into the mix. The post office was one of the major players in the early expansion and interconnection of radio and airplanes. The military also played a key role as did radio-linked air-adventurers who traveled great distances to otherwise hard-to-reach locales. In fact, much of the early public interest in radio-aided air travel concerned just how far wireless could reach. Making connections with air-adventurers was one of the earliest means for establishing, recording and breaking these distance records, and amateur operators were often the users to mark such records.[30] Three adventures in particular were greatly anticipated and covered by the press. The famous Lindbergh flight was not one of these, as Lindbergh chose against the added weight of radio. Rather, an earlier 1924 around-the-world flight by the U.S. Army, Commander Byrd's 1929 flight to Antarctica, and a dangerous fog-enshrouded Atlantic crossing to complete a circumnavigation of the globe were all something of a sensation, in part, because they were also about astonishing achievements in radio.[31] The 1924 flight was certainly not the U.S. military's first foray into radio-assisted flight. In 1919 they performed the first publicized flight-to-ground transmission, though the military claimed to have been perfecting its use for more than a year.[32] But the 1924 flight was unique in that the expansion of aircrafts' reach across space was being mirrored in real time through the use of in-flight radio transmission. These flights were made into daily news events as correspondence took place not just before and after but during such adventures. During a 1930 trans-Atlantic flight, "a running story of the happenings aboard the airplane was sent to anxious listeners ashore in America."[33] The transmissions were described as being equally astonishing as the flights.

It is also clearly the issue of safety by which radio transmission was evaluated, with cost a distant second.

The factor of safety is considerably increased when weather reports, flying conditions and landing field conditions are available to the pilot of an airplane. Surely, the additional weight of a reliable, compact and easily operated radio set is worth the insurance of the safety of the airplane not to mention the life of the pilot and perhaps the lives of the passengers. Such radio apparatus to be considered at all, becomes the wrist watch of the radio family, yet it must do what is expected of the cumbersome grandfather's clock. It may be the means of preventing serious if not fatal disaster.[34]

It is through this linking that air travel became an acceptable and actively advocated form of transport. Without wireless any number of specific activities were deemed too dangerous, such as blind flying and flying in inclement weather. Thanks to wireless the "Air Future [was] Now Bright" according to a 1935 *New York Times* headline. Yet "startling growth" could not occur until the safety of air travel was perceived to be comparable to rail and auto travel.[35] The linking then was not just an added form of insurance. It was integral for the very growth and establishment of what we would consider the airline industry. Various radio services had already been put in place well before this 1935 article appeared. The most important of which was the network of weather reporting stations and beacons that allowed for more blind flying. Radio-enhanced air travel was built upon much older routes of transport that produced a network of potential flight paths according to the overlapping radio signals strategically spaced so as to allow flights that would connect major cities. Thus, early flight paths mimicked those of train or auto travel, as the placement of beacons and radio towers limited radio-enhanced air travel.[36] Through a strange twist of interconnection, air travel was not only made safer by radio, but as radio's use determined the limits of acceptably safe travel for certain forms of flight, it also strictly limited travel to preexistent routes.

This relation between the production of greater mobility and forms of regulatory limits runs very often along the paths of communications-aided safety. It is also clear that, due to the nature of sea travel and even more so air travel, radio provides the means to turn it into a more open system that doesn't necessarily have to correspond to a set of previously existent travel coordinates. But, it is also precisely this ability that makes the promotion of safety and security of such import for governing at a distance. Tracking, regulating, and instituting economic initiatives such as tariffs, bans on certain imports, quarantines, and weapon delivery are just a few of the problematic tasks made more difficult by systems of transport that don't answer to fixable routes—versus for instance railroad's immobile tracks. Communications technologies are one such means by which such tasks have been accomplishable. Freedom of movement, which we have already recognized thanks to Carey as a long-standing fundamental notion for America's success, has been increasingly governed through communications, not just at the level of thought and expression via the First Amendment but also quite clearly at the level of physical tracking and routing. This regulatory use of communications technologies is often legitimized through the discourse of safety and security.

On the Road

The automobile provides a unique point of entry into this history. In 1930 the New York Times began a special section called "Automobiles, Radio, Aviation."[37] Though the *Times* may have recognized similarities across these three technologies, this section of my chapter will also examine some notable differences. For one, unlike trains, ships, and airplanes, automobile use is most often not for commercial but for personal private use. Granted, commercial trucking has been highly governed, but the attention paid to it, particularly as a public problem, is dwarfed by that paid to citizen motorists. Police and other rescue and response teams have also played a part in this history. Yet, they are governed by different concerns than the citizen motorist. More important, truckers and police are specifically working under the aegis of economic and institutional guidelines and goals. Their automotive conduct is governed first and foremost by the institutions of which they are an integral part. In contrast, personal driving in the United States is governed via individual state regulation, though the federal government through its judicious use of financial compensations is able to mandate pressing regulations. The following section will trace a number of uses of communications technologies within and through the automobile. When communications technologies are used in these capacities a very narrowly defined set of criteria determine acceptable use and legitimate purpose—lack and excess.

The lack and excess discourse regarding automotive communication appears in popular periodicals as early as the turn of the century. One concern is how drivers communicate with each other and pedestrians. A second is how rules, regulations, and guidance are to be communicated to drivers in a safe and efficient fashion. Various forms of signage and technologies were imagined and implemented within the short period during which the automobile was introduced into daily life. Horns, turn indicators (appearing first in the United States in 1926 as arrow-shaped lights attached to the rear license plate), traffic signals, traffic signs, headlights, windshields, windshield wipers, hand signals, license plates, and various other devices were all imagined to ensure the safety of drivers, pedestrians, and horse-drawn vehicles early in the twentieth century. Many of these are today not even thought of as communication technologies. This exclusion speaks to a high-tech bias and provides a means to investigate not so much the claims regarding the effectiveness of these technologies but rather how safety continues to legitimize the dependency of transportation upon communications.

Some of the devices were quite simple. For instance a series of hand signals were developed to indicate such things as "You have a flat shoe," "You had better stop and inspect your car," "Am I on the best and shortest road to next town?," and the all-important "Danger ahead."[38] This system was considered "an amplification of the one-arm semaphore."[39] It was then a means of overcoming a lack, amplifying the signal to clarify interdriver communication. A different form of amplification overcame another lack—limited vision at night. "How do you signal to other drivers at night?"; with an illuminated prosthetic hand that allowed "the motorist to signal at night in the same way as he does so naturally and unconsciously during the daytime."[40] The blind turn was better managed by imagining it as a deaf turn and applying a series of horn blasts to make one's presence known.[41] But, it was said, "the horn scares people instead of warning them, thus inducing nervous disorders of all kinds."[42] Such claims may have been overblown, but they do repeat the logic of lack or excess—blow-hard versus breathless. Elaborate mechanical contraptions were created that linked automobile-triggered lighting systems and warning signs. However, in 1920, an article in *Scientific American* warned that "When one runs over a road which is posted 'Danger Ahead,' 'Caution,' 'Run Slowly,' etc. at the summit of every slightest twist in the roadway, the best intentioned driver in the world cannot help acquiring a feeling of contempt and disregard."[43] The line between lack and excess is a fine one indeed.

With their 1929 introduction of a car radio the company Motorola was born. Originally they manufactured and sold after-market units installed by amateur radio enthusiasts. Over the next decade the inclusion of car radios was standardized, first by automotive dealers and then ultimately by manufacturers themselves, which, oddly, first installed antennas as standard, not radios. Radios were installed in 85 percent of cars by 1933.[44] In 1930, 34,500 car radio sets were sold, less than 1 percent of total radio set sales.[45] Growth of sales was rapid and, even though there was a slowdown in automotive production during the 1930s, as early as 1933 car radio sales were the stabilizing force in the radio market with sales totaling more than 300,000 units.[46] Before the complete standardization occurred and radio could look forward to safely "find itself speeding along the highways as it intercepts broadcasts from near and far,"[47] debates raged over whether car radio was safe. A number of municipalities, large and small, outlawed the use of car radios or strictly curtailed their use. While according to an Auto Club of New York poll in 1934, 56 percent felt radio use was a "dangerous distraction."[48] Too much radio was seen as being distracting to drivers who, possibly excited by the live broadcasts of air-adventurers in Antarctica, might fail to pay attention to the road. Yet radio could also be used to warn drivers of inclement weather and other dangerous road conditions. It was also said to keep potentially drowsy drivers awake. Lastly, it "proved of considerable service in broadcasting the gospel of safety on the highways."[49] It almost goes without saying that again the concern is lack or excess. Interestingly, the issue of car radio use raised serious questions regarding freedom of speech. Could state and local governing bodies pass laws that could de facto limit free expression and communication?[50] In 1933 this issue was being debated in a slightly different form regarding citizen's use of police radio, a use that foregrounds our continued interest in matters regarding surveillance, communications, and governing at a distance.

Indiana representative Louis Ludlow, before the Committee on Merchant Marine, Radio, and Fisheries in 1933, made this grand proclamation in defense of his police radio bill.

> These laws are intended to reach a very definite evil that is obstructing the law-enforcement officers in every city in the United States where there is a police-radio system, that is, the use of short-wave radio sets by law violators of all classes to evade arrest . . . no good citizen should object to it, because it is in the interest of the security of himself and his family, and is in the interest of the well-being and security of society in general.[51]

The great evil of which Ludlow spoke was the use of shortwave radio sets in the automobiles of everyday citizens, well, specifically the criminal element said to be listening in on the police to help plan getaways. One proviso of the bill framed access to information in terms of its ultimate use. Listening in on police transmissions, it was argued, should be made illegal if said information was to be used to violate or conspire to violate any laws. This logic of illegal application of information reappears with the advent of debates over police radar detection and citizen's band (CB) radio. For now though, I want to reframe this decades-old debate in terms of surveillance and countersurveillance. From this vantage, the control of information access is a means to protect the state's monopoly on technologies of surveillance, thereby protecting its ability to govern at a distance. The maintenance of this particular monopoly, listening to police transmissions, protected a significant application of the state's rapidly expanding communications-aided surveillance capabilities, which were increasingly aimed at and aided by the automobile. More generally, First Amendment protection and access to information are seen as vital concerns to democratically inclined thoughts and minds. It is possible that these concerns are also about the control of mobility, the control of movement through space and the freedom of that movement.

Briefly, there has long been a struggle over the use of surveillance technologies between state forces and private citizens. For one, the use of CB radio to monitor police tactics, to enact countersurveillance, was a hugely popular practice during CB's heyday in the 1970s.[52] This struggle over the definition of proper CB use recognizes that its intended use and its unintended use were legitimized or delegitimized according to the logic of safety. Furthermore, it was assumed that what CB could and should be used for was to aid in transportation. It was seen as an addendum to already existing transportation technologies and already existing safety and security agencies. The threat of CB was not so much what was said, "there is a Smoky under the I-80 overpass at mile marker 99," rather, the concern was over how that information was being integrated into transportation activities deemed safe or unsafe. The surveillance of mobility is a subset of practices that are justified by the logic of safety and tend to be associated with the lack or excess discourse. Police radio, radar detectors, black boxes, Global Positioning Systems, antitheft devices such as Lojac, GM's OnStar service, and a whole host of imagined and soon to be implemented technologies are used to survey, monitor, and regulate automobility.[53]

But the most extensive and far-reaching connection between communication and transportation has to do with the overarching desire to do away with the greatest threat to safety altogether—the human operator. We can witness this desire at least as early as James Carey's example of train switching devices. Once information can travel faster than transportation devices, that information can be used to help in the navigation and control of transportation. Communication technologies can act as warning devices and sending devices that act upon and in response to transportation technologies. Radio as stated earlier was used to pass on inclement weather reports and initiate rescue operations. But, this still involved human recognition of danger and then the use of communication devices to pass on vital information to other humans who would then respond. In this sense, communication technologies were aids used to make transportation more efficient and safe. Through the integration of Global Positioning Systems; video, infrared, and microwave monitoring devices; computer-monitored and controlled engines; car-to-car (not to a human in a car) "conversation"; smart roads; and a plethora of other internal and external communication technologies, the automatic automobile is currently a reality, though quite obviously not a publicly available one. In fact, over the past decade the U.S. government apportioned more than one billion dollars for research advocating an Intelligent Vehicle Highway System (IVHS), and numerous government organizations (in the United States, Europe, and Asia), research consortiums, and corporate bodies have invested heavily in attempts to create the fully automatic automobile. The backbone of all such attempts is communications.

More than a dozen years before GM's Geddes-designed Futurama at the 1939 New York World's Fair, often portrayed as the first real vision of automated cars, a prophetic experiment gone awry took place on the streets of Manhattan. A local New York radio specialist designed and built a radio-driven automobile that, as if by magic, traveled driverless up Broadway and back down Fifth Avenue. The car was ingeniously controlled by a combination of wireless radio and motorized actuators connected in order to start, stop, and steer the automobile. A cadre of motion picture cameramen were shooting footage from an adjacent car just in front of the radio-driven car that maneuvered "as if a phantom hand were at the wheel."[54] Like Frankenstein's monster, the machine lost control and crashed into the cameramen's car.

More recently, the driver is not simply seen as using communications to control a vehicle from afar, rather, the car itself gains autonomy; it has been made to think. In fact, the driver starts to become not the agent of control but a mere part of a cybernetic system. As Carey pointed out, "creating a 'new future,' modern technology invites the public to participate in a ritual of control in which fascination with technology masks the underlying factors of politics and power."[55] Two elements that need stressing are that the driver of the future becomes an unnecessary element, and this future is increasingly one consumed by national security as a discursive replacement of personal safety. For instance, the Pentagon is creating a communications and transportations system that depends upon much of the technology previously devoted to and envisioned for the IVHS for use in its "Combat Zones That See." Here is an Associated Press description:

> The Pentagon is developing an urban surveillance system that would use computers and thousands of cameras to track, record and analyze the movement of every vehicle in a foreign city. Dubbed "Combat Zones That See," the project is designed to help the U.S. military protect troops and fight in cities overseas. Police, scientists and privacy experts say the unclassified technology could easily be adapted to spy on Americans.[56]

The project's centerpiece is groundbreaking computer software capable of automatically identifying vehicles by size, color, shape, and license tag, or drivers and passengers by face.[57]

On the domestic front, cars are given subjectivity and they can be used to monitor and talk to drivers. There is currently a collaborative project between the Massachusetts Institute of Technology Media Lab, DaimlerChrysler, and Motorola to produce a car that will act as a "virtual driving coach—an electronic back-seat driver turned front-seat friend—to help reduce driver distraction."[58] It works through a network of cameras, sensors, and computer processors that work to not only understand and know the road conditions and act accordingly but also to understand drivers and their conditions. It looks for potential breakdowns in the driver's ability to manage the vehicle and then talks to them, warning of distractions and impending danger. The car is the ultimate communications mediator, negotiating the lack versus excess dynamic, as John Hanson, Toyota's national manager for product communications, explains.

What happens is that the vehicle begins to anticipate what you're going to want to do, what your priorities are, what your agendas are," he says, speaking into his own cellphone headset while driving through the Nevada desert. "It knows what kind of music you like. It knows where you live and how you usually drive home. It can say, 'John, I think you'd better take an alternate route 'cause there's a pileup on I-5.' So it thinks ahead. It begins to know you as a person the way a good friend would.[59]

What the rhetoric of both the journalistic and industry PR revolves around is the issue of whether these communications technologies will be safe. For instance, the most recent mobility-related safety scare, the distracted driver, appears. As drivers of the future, we will increasingly be imagined as a node in a communications network, "all of the car-to-car and car-to-driver chatter will be voice-activated and absolutely second nature, a safe and seamless give-and-take between metal and flesh."[60] Drivers are thought of merely as part of a difficult equation that recognizes human fallibility and semipredictable agency within a system in which the driver is an integral node—a transistor in transit. Drivers will act as capacitors, receiving and storing the system's power; as processors, one link in a systemic chain of actions; and as conductors. But here is where it gets interesting: will power pass through drivers or will they lead and guide? In other words, as the automobile becomes increasingly part of a communications network, does the driver become simply a necessary evil, there to handle the increasingly rare failure in the system. Of greater import, how is the driver imagined in this system? What are her goals? How are autonomy and freedom envisioned? Increasingly freedom is not the mobility that driving allows but rather being free from the obligation of driving, free to manage other communications-oriented activity—watching TV, talking on the phone, working via the Internet. (Didn't we learn something from HAL, the ultimate backseat driver?)

Once cars are fully automated, primarily via what we consider to be communications technologies, will the car continue to be considered a transportation technology? When each component will not only provide a mechanical function but also a communicative function, will each part itself be thought of as a communication device? When a tire senses changes in the adhesive character of the road and transmits that information to a central processor that then sends signals to the brakes, the accelerator, the shocks, the steering unit, the windshield wipers of the video monitoring lens, and so forth, is the tire a communications device? When cars provide links to all variety of communication networks that command one's full attention in transit, is it a venue, a workstation, a domestic or public sphere? Is it worthy of study?

HALlelujah for the Future of Communications?

When we think of the fully automatic automobile, in every possible sense of the term, what vision is brought to mind? Do we register a sense of relief as we imagine our newfound freedom from risk and the drudgery of driving? This would be consonant with Carey's claim that it is through a rhetoric of progressive liberation that new "computational gadgets" and communications technologies in general are legitimized.[61] Or do we think back to the control exerted by HAL in *2001*,[62] a dystopian narrative of a backseat driver mutiny? Clearly for Carey the reason to study communications is to assess what it might be able to do for our future. How can it be used and conceptualized in order to produce a more democratic world? How can it be used to generate community and not simply be thought of in terms of the gains in control and profit it might generate? And maybe, I'd argue, how can we overturn previously dominant frameworks for its study in order to bring to light aspects of communications that heretofore have been underevaluated to the detriment of not just our field but our future?

I want to argue that we need to rethink now, more so than before, how we conceptualize our object of study by at least acknowledging that this split in our thinking about communications and transportation has left a hole in our field. A hole that has been covered (in both senses of the term) by risk analysts, engineers, military specialists, insurance companies, and other invested parties. As Carey notes when speaking of policy analysts, "They will also fail to meet the minimal demand on scholarship: that it attach the life of the citizen and scholar to the fundamental currents of social change."[63] This type of scholarship always works within the assumption that the institution under examination is structurally acceptable. It cannot ask questions that fundamentally undermine the very social relations that have determined, to a degree, its importance. Carey makes clear policy work on TV can never ask whether TV should be abolished or its use severely cut back. It can only ask how to make it "operate more effectively and with less danger and abrasion."[64] And should it be of any surprise that reducing "danger" is precisely that which organizes the transportation history just sketched? Discussion of transportation's increased dependence on communications has remained free of much critical analysis by the field in part because the notion of safety is such an unexamined good that it might at first appear not to demand the scrutiny of critical analysis. But in an age that celebrates mobile communications, we need more critical histories of this term and its affiliated technologies and practices. As the means of exerting force, maintaining control, and enacting surveillance are increasingly done through mobile communication technologies, we have to seriously ask why it is that communications as a field predominantly seems to investigate mass media, whether through qualitative or quantitative work, whether as histories, textual analysis, or meaningful activity. When the field decides to study mobile communications, it looks at the new, the interpersonal, the subcultural, or the commercially profitable.

When Carey asked that we study the ritual aspects of communication, he began showing us how to connect daily communicative activities to larger structures of meaning production, greater frames of analysis, across a wider spectrum of contexts, through history. In other words, communication was to be approached as an integral part of the maintenance, management, and production of meanings; the forging of profound interconnections; and the hope for democratic possibility. Carey countered this optimism and claimed one must examine the deployment of communication forms and technologies to recognize "the elements of inauthenticity and domination in the very models of development and deployment of these media."[65] Media can be and are used to aid in the creation of very undemocratic systems of meaning and communities. But it is to the oral tradition that Carey, through Dewey and Innis, wants to turn as a possible antidote to the potential domination of space over time. However, when thinking in terms of transportation's increased dependency upon communications technologies, we need to engage not only and exclusively with issues of communication as a means of meaning production and community development. By taking the notion of governing at a distance as one starting point, we can look to how freedom of movement is organized in obedience to safety and security as a means to ensure control over space and time—and potentially subjectivities.

I would like to suggest that the split between communication and transportation has clearly never been a complete one. In fact, historically it may have been a bit of an anomaly, a brief moment when the two types of technologies were considered separate, when the activities of the mind and the body, of ideas and things were most explicitly torn apart and made to appear quite different from each other. I would further add, given current forms of political rationality, the justification for their connection will continue to be safety and security. Furthermore, as Carey, following Innis and others, has so forcefully argued, both communication and transportation networks have so very often been put in place to expand the reach of power. It is now those same networks that have become battlegrounds and means for battle, both culturally and physically. They were built with circulation as their ethos and this makes them exponentially far-reaching and exponentially open to invasion. Might we not reorganize at least one subset of our field, not in opposition to Carey and the cultural approach, nor obviously in terms simply of transmission but, rather, as a critical intervention and set of approaches that examine any communications technology, social, political, personal, or concrete, that is used to govern at a distance?

Notes

1. It is only in the interview reproduced in chapter 1 that Carey reveals which wise man suggested he begin his investigation with Dewey. In my case, Lawrence Grossberg and James Hay both provided me this truly useful advice.
2. In fact, Foucault is one of the key figures Carey includes in his list of those whose influence has been detrimental to the cultural studies tradition. Chris Russill examines this rift in chapter 3 of this volume.
3. For a historical overview of some of the communications technologies used for this, see Zbikowski and Dorte, "The Listening Ear: Phenomena of Acoustic Surveillance," in *ctrl[space]: Rhetorics of Surveillance from Bentham to Big Brother,* ed. Thomas Y. Levin, Ursula Frohne, and Peter Weibel (Cambridge, MA: MIT Press, 2002), pp. 33–49.
4. Federal Communications Commission. *Annual Report.* Washington, D.C.: Government Printing Office, 1934.
5. The early history of insurance provides on example of how the rationality of governing at a distance operated according to an economic logic devoted to insuring the safety and security of goods and crews on ocean-bound ships . Michel Foucault, "Governmentality" in *The Foucault Effect: Studies in Governmentality,* ed. Graham Burchell, Colin Gordon, and Peter Miller (Chicago: The University of Chicago Press, 1991) 93–94.
6. James Carey, *Communication as Culture: Essays on Media and Society* (Boston: Unwin Hyman, 1989).
7. "The simplest and most important point about the telegraph is that it marked the decisive separation of 'transportation' and 'communication.'" Carey, "Technology and Ideology," p. 213.
8. Carey makes clear that the telegraph was quickly put to use to switch tracks from afar and, as he states, "thereby multiplying the purposes and effectiveness of communication." "Technology and Ideology," p. 203.
9. "Models of communication are, then, not merely representations of communication but representations *for* communication: templates that guide, unavailing or not, concrete processes of human interaction, mass and interpersonal (italics in the original)." Carey, "A Cultural Approach to Communication," *Communication as Culture,* p. 32.
10. This is a theme that has remained important to Carey's work, but it is thoroughly dealt with in "The Politics of the Electronic Revolution: Further Notes on Marshall McCluhan," (Urbana: Institute of Communications Research, University of Illinois, 1972), particularly pp. 8–10.
11. Armand Mattelart, *The Invention of Communication* (Minneapolis: University of Minnesota Press, 1996).
12. "Before the telegraph, 'communication' was used to describe transportation as well as message transmittal for the simple reason that the movement of messages was dependent on their being carried by horseback or by rail." Carey, "Technology and Ideology," pp. 203–204.
13. "The relationship between communication and transportation that organicism suggested—the nerves and arteries of society—had been realized in the parallel growth of the telegraph and railroad." Carey, "Space, Time, and Communications: A Tribute to Harold Innis," *Communication as Culture,* p. 143.

14. James Carey, "The Politics of the Electronic Revolution: Further Notes on Marshall McLuhan," p. 12.

15. Foucault argues that future work regarding power should focus on "the three great variables—territory, communication, and speed" (*The Foucault Reader*, ed. Paul Rabinow [London: Penguin Books, 1984] p. 244).

16. "How was this continental union to be held together? . . . the answer was sought in the word and the wheel, in transportation and transmission, in the power of printing and civil engineering to bind a vast distance and a large population into cultural unity or, as the less optimistic would have it, into cultural hegemony." Carey, "Introduction," *Communication as Culture*, p. 5. "It was the cable and telegraph, backed, of course, by sea power, that turned colonialism into imperialism: a system in which the center of an empire could dictate rather than merely respond to the margin." Carey, "Technology and Ideology," p. 212. See also, "Space, Time, and Communications."]

17. Andrew Barry, "Lines of Communication and Spaces of Rule," in *Foucault and Political Reason: Liberalism, Neo-liberalism and Rationalities of Government*, eds. Barry, Osborne, and Rose (Chicago: University of Chicago Press, 1996).

18. Carey, *Communication as Culture*, pp. 163–166.

19. My description to this point of this political rationality is based upon a Foucauldian understanding of liberal political rationality that recognizes that governing agents, whether they be the state, corporations, or other institutions, have increasingly approached governing in terms of how something is made to appear as a problem. For a concise account see, "Ethics," in *Ethics: Essential Works of Foucault*, ed. Paul Rabinow, (New York: New Press, 1997) pp. 109–110.

20. Michel Foucault, "Governmentality," in *Foucault Effect*, pp. 93–94.

21. Packer, "Disciplining Mobility: Governing and Safety," in *Foucault, Cultural Studies, and Governmentality*, eds. Jack Bratich, Jeremy Packer, and Cameron McCarthy (Albany: State University of New York Press, 2003), pp. 135–161.

22. James Hay and I briefly address this in "Crossing the Media(-n): Auto-mobility, the Transported Self, and Technologies of Freedom," in *Media/Space: Scale and Culture in a Media Age*, eds. Nick Couldry and Anna McCarthy (New York: Routledge, 2004).

23. Carey, "Technology and Ideology," p. 215.

24. Carey, "Space, Time, and Communications," p. 171.

25. See the interview in chapter 10 of this volume in which Carey makes this very clear.

26. Susan Douglas, "Amateur Operators and American Broadcasting: Shaping the Future of Radio" in *Imagining Tomorrow: History, Technology, and the American Future*, ed. Joseph J. Corn (Cambridge, MA: MIT Press, 1986) pp. 35–55.

27. "'Amateurs' Standby Since 1915 Is Basis of Aircraft Radio," *New York Times* (4 March 1928), p. 154.

28. Ibid.

29. "Radio on Mail Planes Tested Successfully," *New York Times* (23 November 1923), p. 9.

30. "Amateurs Establish Records in Tests with Airplane," *New York Times* (6 November 1927), p. XX18.

31. "Radio to Aid World Fliers across Sea," *New York Times* (27 July 1924), p XX15; "Byrd Plane in Air over the Antarctic 'Talks' to New York," *New York Times* (26 January 1929), p. 1.

32. "Talks with Pilot in Air," *New York Times* (17 January 1919), p. 12.

33. "Plane's Radio Held Factor in Success," *New York Times* (26 June 1930), p. 2.

34. "'Amateurs' Standby Since 1915 Is Basis of Aircraft Radio," p. 154.

35. "Air Future Now Bright," *New York Times* (5 May 1935), p. X20.

'AIRPLANE WEATHER SERVICE SPREADS FAST

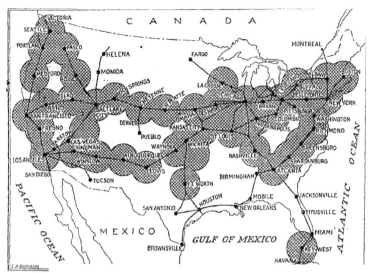

Planes Flying in the Shaded Areas Now Receive Half-Hourly Broadcasts of Weather Conditions. The
Other Named Cities Are Centres of Proposed Stations.

36. "Civil Airways Gain Rapidly in Aids Derived From Radio." *New York Times* (24 November, 1929), p. XX9.
37. "Automobiles, Radio, Aviation," *New York Times* (27 July 1930), p. 111.
38. R. Skerrett, "Finger Signals for the Motorist," *Scientific American* (20 March 1920) p. 305.
39. Ibid.
40. "An Illuminated Celluloid Hand for Automobile Signaling," *Scientific American* (8 July 1916), pp. 46–50.
41. C. Barrett, "The 'Blind Turn': Its Dangers and Various Methods of Solution," *Scientific American* (1 January 1916), pp. 24, 45.
42. "Ding to Beep to Boo-oom," *Fortune* (November 1936), pp. 36, 50.
43. B. G. Dacy, "Automobile Signals for Danger Spots," *Scientific American* (6 November 1920), p. 468.
44. "Auto-Radio Spurs Business," *New York Times* (9 July 1933), p. X7.
45. "A Year in the Radio Business" *New York Times,* (15 March 1931), p. 136.
46. "Auto-Radio Spurs Business," p. X7.
47. Ibid.
48. "Vote Shows Drivers Oppose Car Radios," *New York Times* (30 March 1934), p. 23.
49. E. L.Yordan, "At the Wheel," *New York Times* (13 November 1932), p. XX8.
50. "Radio on Motor Cars," *New York Times* (14 September 1930), p. 132.
51. "Police Radio: Hearings before the Committee on Merchant Marine, Radio, and Fisheries House of Representatives, Seventy-Third Congress, First Session on H.R. 1558 and H.R. 1559" (27 and 28 April 1933), p. 2.

52. I've provided a thorough description of the struggles over CBs use and regulation in "Mobile Communications and Governing the Mobile: CBs and Truckers," *The Communication Review* 5 (2002): 39–57.
53. Hay and Packer, "Crossing the Media(-n)."
54. "Radio Driven Auto Runs Down Escort" *New York Times* (28 July 1925), p. 28.
55. Carey, "The History of the Future," *Communication as Culture*, p. 195.
56. Michael J. Sniffen, "Pentagon Developing System to Track Every Vehicle in a City," (1 July 2003), available at http://www.thetruthseeker.co.uk/article.asp?ID=904
57. "Urban Spying System Would Eye Vehicles," *Los Angeles Times*, AP Report (2 July 2003).
58. Phil Patton, "Driving: Cars That Nudge You to Drive More Safely," *New York Times* (26 December 2003), available at http://www.nytimes.com/2003/12/ 26/automobiles/26AUTO.html?ex=1073542126&ei=1&en=3aa85b0bf33f3ef1
59. Bruce Grierson, "The Pod Car," *New York Times Magazine* (14 December 2003).
60. Ibid.
61. Carey, "Space, Time, and Communications," p. 148.
62. Stanley Kubrick, dir., *2001: A Space Odyssey* (Warner Brothers 1968).
63. James Carey, "The Ambiguity of Policy Research," *Journal of Communications*, 28, 2 (Spring. 1978), p. 119.
64. Ibid., p. 118.
65. James Carey, "Graduate Education in Mass Communication," *Communication Education* 28 (September 1979): 289.

5. Communication Scholarship as Ritual: An Examination of James Carey's Cultural Model of Communication

GRETCHEN SODERLUND

Between a systematized hallucination and the first impressions which gave it birth, the distance is often considerable. It is the same thing with religious thought. In proportion as it progresses in history, the causes which called it into existence, though remaining active, are no longer perceived, except across a vast scheme of interpretations which quite transform them. Popular mythologies and subtle theologies have done their work: they have superimposed upon the primitive sentiments others which are quite different, and which, though holding to the first, of which they are an elaborated form, only allow their true nature to appear very imperfectly.

—Emile Durkheim (1915)

James Carey's 1989 *Communication and Culture: Essays on Media and Society* begins with the proposition that communication is the very substance that enables social life. Far from merely allowing us to describe a preexisting reality to each other, language and symbols serve to create, maintain, and even overturn the social worlds in which we live. Symbols carry meanings that have the potential to draw us together or pull us apart. Carey emphasizes that the mass media are an increasingly important site of symbolic activity in the United States and elsewhere. Because they overcome earlier limitations of space and time, mass communications systems are perhaps the primary vehicles through which understandings circulate and are shared in late-modern societies. As expressive forms implicated in a "system of interacting symbols and interlocked meanings," mass media both shape and reflect the contours of social life (p. 55). The newspaper, for instance, does more than inform the public about topics or events of social import: it allows us to collectively partake in a social rite, enabling a collective dialogue to ensue.

Carey suggests that a careful interpreter—steeped in Weber, Durkheim, and more recent social scientists such as Clifford Geertz—can elicit from a television show or dance production a sense of the kinds of lives we lead, the meanings that hold us together, and the general social order that shapes our relations with one another. Whereas traditional U.S. communications research projected individual motivations, drives, and anxieties onto society, Carey posits a more embedded relationship between media texts, audiences, and the broader social world, one more far-reaching and profound than the previous programmatic formulas that media effects research maintain. Borrowing from Geertz's work on culture and ritual (who in the last instance borrows from Durkheim's work on religion), Carey recasts the modern mass media as a modern cultural form. He construes media producers and audience members as participants in complex cultural rituals through which social life and the central beliefs upon which it rests are produced, reproduced, and contested.

Carey's push for a thoroughgoing disciplinary paradigm shift in North American mass communications was both timely and important and served to reintroduce classic and current social thought into a field guided by administrative priorities. His interconnected essays painstakingly take traditional U.S. communications research to task for its limited definition of communication and externally driven research agendas. The importance of such an intervention cannot be overstated: as Carey suggests, the conceptual models to which we as communications scholars adhere are implicated in the types of social relationships we forge and, consequently, the kinds of societies we build. Armed with the mandate to create more humane models, Carey calls for a cultural science that "delves deeper into the empirical world" of symbolic forms and practices with the aim of unearthing and explaining cultural meanings and their connection to existing social relations (p. 56). Such a project entails focused investigations into "the creation, representation, and celebration of shared even if illusory beliefs" (p. 43).

While my intellectual sympathies and predilections lie with Carey, this chapter uses a case study to both identify and challenge his neo-Durkheimian understanding of representational practices and processes of meaning production elaborated in *Communication and Culture*. Given Carey's call for empirical research, I focus on the episodic public controversies that arise in the United States over trafficking in women to test an implicit argument that permeates Carey's book: that media texts ultimately signify a shared culture and that their primary referent is society itself. Like Durkheim, Carey treats symbolic forms as collective products that ultimately refer back to the social order in which we live. Each text therefore stands in synecdochic relationship to society, while the ultimate referent of all expressive forms becomes social life itself. In this sense, Durkheim echoes throughout Carey's work. Durkheim's understanding of collective representations is eloquently stated in this passage from *The Elementary Forms of the Religious Life:*

[R]eligion is something eminently social. Religious representations are collective representations which express collective realities; the rites are a manner of acting which take rise in the midst of the assembled groups and which are destined to excite, maintain or recreate certain mental states in these groups. So if the categories are of religious origin, they ought to participate in this nature common to all religious facts: they too should be social affairs and the product of collective thought.[1]

Both Carey and Durkheim understand representations as social products that reflect or stand in some kind of homologous relation to the social orders in which we live. In the broadest sense such an understanding of symbols conveys an important truth about the constitutive role of language in producing social realities. Yet when we hold many twentieth-century media texts to the standards of empirical observation and careful interpretive analysis for which Carey calls, we find that such overarching concepts as culture and ritual do not adequately capture much of the political and institutional work that mediated representations perform.

Furthermore, this analysis of modern and late-modern representations of trafficking in women serves to challenge Carey's underlying assumption that community is an intrinsic social good and a useful analytic sociocultural category. Likewise, it underscores some problems with structuralist models of communication predicated on exchange. As I soon describe, while Claude Levi-Strauss's framework might serve as an interesting counterpoint to Carey's purely symbolist one by highlighting the role of exchange as a binding force, it, too, ultimately downplays the ways in which social cohesion has in many contexts been advantageous to some social actors precisely because it subordinates or controls others. While both symbolic and structural anthropology offer analytic advantages over the positivism and functionalism of classic communications research, only a synthetic approach that seeks to identify and understand political and institutional communication, social conflict, and lines of force can fully capture the meanings attached to mass-mediated expressive forms and cultural rituals in a modern and late-modern North American context.

Communication, Structuralism, and Symbolism

In the first chapter of *Communication and Culture,* Carey introduces a central distinction that crops up throughout the book: the difference between the cultural and transmission models of communication. He argues that in North America two meanings of the term "communication" have evolved. One (he implies) is largely transhistorical and comes closest to capturing what Durkheim might call the "primitive sentiment" behind communication, while the other is grounded in the history and politics of North America circa the Industrial Revolution. Where the preindustrial use of the term denoted religious ritual, social solidarity, and community bonding, the newer meaning of communication emphasized the practice of transporting goods, people, and information across space, often for purposes of control. During the nineteenth century, the transportation metaphor achieved cultural dominance, eventually overshadowing communication's previous association with communal life. The result of this definitional shift is that communication—the term if not the act itself—lost its longstanding association with ritual and social bonding and came to be associated with the accurate transmission of information. It emphasized techniques of persuasion and social control over community formation and social rites.

Carey offers a compelling narrative of the ascendance of mass media and communications research in the United States. In his story, both uses of communication vie for dominance not only in the university, but in social life more generally. The transmission model ultimately reigns supreme, a rise to prominence that for Carey has ominous implications. Conceiving of communication in terms of a transmission model causes us to see society "as a network of power, administration, decision, and control—a political order" (p. 34). Conversely, the ritual model of communication captures aspects of existence rendered invisible by an instrumental transmission model, including "the sharing of aesthetic experience, religious ideas, personal values and sentiments, and intellectual notions" (p. 34).

While transmission and cultural forms of communication may coexist in any given time and place, for Carey, only the latter captures the broadest and most intrinsic role of language: the creation and continuation of social life. In the above epigraph, Durkheim describes how with religious thought an initial impression gave way to a "systematic hallucination" as time elapsed. The distortions occurred as various other meanings and interpretations attached themselves to the original pristine understanding of religion. If we substitute the word "communication" for "religion" in Durkheim's story we arrive at Carey's analysis: that much of the intervening thought on the topic of communication has merely obscured what was once available to us as a phenomenological truth. Thus the widespread awareness of communication as ritual (or as culture in current parlance) was lost once the transportation model/metaphor was superimposed on the concept of communication. Because symbols are an elemental feature of human society, the ritual function of communication will persist whether or not its existence is recognized. One implication of Carey's argument is that communication as ritual currently exists unnoticed and without deserved celebration, concealed by an earlier nineteenth-century social order that drew its central metaphors from the domains of science, technology, and commerce.

The father of structural anthropology, Claude Levi-Strauss, once claimed that we can trace the contours of societies by looking at those borderlands where communication begins to wane. His model of social cohesion is not predicated solely on shared symbolic systems like Carey's but instead views exchange itself as a group-sustaining process both rich in meaning and content. In this view, linguistic and expressive forms constitute one necessary aspect of communication. However, there are two other levels of communicative phenomena that play an equal role in creating and sustaining deep social relations:

> In any society, communication operates on three different levels: communication of women, communication of goods and services, communication of messages. Therefore, kinship studies, economics, and linguistics approach the same kinds of problems on different strategic levels and really pertain to the same field. . . . Therefore, it should be kept in mind that culture does not consist exclusively of forms of communication of its own, like language, but also (and perhaps mostly) of *rules* stating how the "games of communication" should be played both on the natural and on the cultural levels.[2]

Although he can be faulted for relying too heavily on an analogy to posit an isomorphism between society, economy, and language, Levi-Strauss offers a valuable contrast to Carey's understanding of society, which ignores the bonding function of material and familial exchange as well as the often-unstated rules that govern much social behavior and language use. Nonetheless, both theorists engage in acts of reification when they celebrate the production of social cohesion while ignoring or glossing over social conflict and struggle. Levi-Strauss reifies communication structures as exchange processes that take on lives of their own. Instead we might conceive of actions within institutions as being undertaken by social actors who do not always play by the rules and who must engage in acts of improvisation when circumstances mandate.[3]

In reducing communication to abstract rule-bound deep structures, Levi-Strauss also glosses over the oppressive potential of exchange, particularly for women. As anthropologist Gayle Rubin indicates, serving as objects of exchange has historically been an unfavorable arrangement for women who have assumed the largely thankless role of gifts given and received by men. If in many societies women have been the invisible media through which social linkages are formed, they have also been isolated from the cultural process of determining the meanings of this elemental society-building communicative exchange:

> If women are the gifts, then it is men who are the exchange partners. And it is the partners, not the presents, upon whom reciprocal exchange confers its quasi-mystical power of social linkage. The relations of such a system are such that

women are in no position to realize the benefits of their own circulation. As long
as the relations specify that men exchange women, it is men who are beneficiaries of the product of such exchanges—social organization.[4]

In Rubin's revised account of Levi-Strauss, the productive basis of culture
has been carried on the backs of women, who mediate communication
between men.[5] Thus, even fundamental forms of communication that exist in
every society and serve to reproduce social and cultural life—linguistic, economic, and kinship relations—are crosshatched with imbalances between
partners in the exchange. This is not to suggest that women are universally
oppressed or that all communication excludes along gender lines. It is to suggest that when we celebrate the fact of social bonding, we need to ask for
whom this social cohesion is salient and beneficial. In fact, many of our
North American social rites that exploit gender serve to deepen insidious race
and class divisions.

If Levi-Strauss reifies communication structures, Carey reifies the notion
of community. At the center of Carey's plea for resurrecting the ritual model
is the promise of a return to conditions in which "communal life," "community," and "shared experience" can flourish. Yet Carey's argument relies too
heavily and uncritically on the rhetorical weight of such concepts, which are
conceived of in commonsense terms as intrinsic social goods. Here Carey is
deeply influenced by John Dewey, whose early pragmatist conception of the
social good consciously attempted to avoid pitfalls associated with communities built on intolerance and exclusion. Yet, despite the positive valence of
terms such as community, solidarity, and bonding in both theorists' work,
each ultimately downplays the ways such conceptions have been used to
exclude and expel outside elements as well as encourage insular forms of
social control. Both assume that language, symbols, and the artistic realm
have the power to transcend materially grounded conflicts of interest. In
making this assumption, they ignore the ways in which the language of community can serve to unite as well as to divide people and neutralize potentially antagonistic relationships. Carey Nelson's work on modern wartime
poetry demonstrates that even such consecrated expressive forms as the poem
have been used within most major twentieth-century nations to persuade
working-class people to sacrifice their lives for empire.[6]

In *Democracy and Education* (1916), Dewey lists his criteria for a desirable society: it should be one in which interests are largely shared by all members of a group, and diverse groups interact with each other in a full and free
manner. Undesirable societies institute internal and external barriers that pre-
vent the free exchange and communication of experience. In this model, the
greatest good of the group is held up as the standard for assessing value.
Dewey and his acolytes tend toward a democratic pluralism that recognizes
the existence of multiple communities and places a high priority on main-

taining strong relations between them. This is certainly a noble vision and political goal, and therein lies the problem as I see it. It is unclear how such appeals to community actually advance social theory, our understanding of existing group formations, or our knowledge of how group identities are forged.

As Raymond Williams observes, despite its ubiquity in social life and scholarship, the term "community" is notoriously elusive and ambiguous. It can signify anything from a geographically bounded group of people to groups held together by common interests or proclivities. The primary defining feature of the term is that—in contrast to most other references to social collectives—"community" almost always carries positive connotations:

> Community can be the warmly persuasive word to describe an existing set of relationships, or the warmly persuasive word to describe an alternative set of relationships. What is most important perhaps, is that unlike all other terms of social organization (*state, nation, society*, etc.) it seems never to be used unfavorably, and never to be given any positive opposing or distinguishing term.[7]

While communication and political theorists make lavish use of this term, perhaps they should instead consider why it has come to index all that is desirable.

As I suggest in the following section, modern and late-modern invocations of community as the antidote to a real or perceived traffic in women obscure the ways in which community and family protections have been of dubious value to women. A sense of community and common purpose—bolstered by ritualized performances of national and community belonging as well as material facts of existence—may exist even where there are extreme structural inequalities among those sharing a similar group identification. Pragmatists tend to assume that community members share common problems and goals that allow them to reach similar visions of the social good. Such consensual views of community can cover up structural inequalities that deny some members access to the language of belonging while endowing others with the ability to actively represent the totality of group interests. The objective of placing the term "community" under analytic scrutiny, by asking what the concept obscures, serves to question its legitimacy as an analytical category, as well as to move outside the echo chamber in which the far right, the left, and everyone in between offers forth community as the antidote to social conflict, instrumentality (in Carey's case), and the problems of anomie in modern life.

While Carey's work offers us the potential of understanding how groups—be they entire nations or small communities—cohere around shared symbols, it pays insufficient heed to the conflicts that in fact may lay at the heart of communication. In this respect, models that begin with the assumption of disparities between groups, including the political economic, feminist, and sociological/institutional perspectives, serve as helpful correctives to neo-Durkheimian approaches that begin with assumptions of social unity and end with social fragmentation and breakdown. In what follows, I consider a phenomenon whose trajectory oddly parallels Carey's account of the definitional life of the term "communication." If Levi-Strauss is believed, this phenomenon—the traffic in women[8]—has been equally important as linguistic processes in fostering and reproducing social cohesion. The real or perceived traffic in women's bodies may once have functioned materially as a producer of social bonds. However, by the late nineteenth century trafficking in women became a potent signifier of social disorder and community breakdown.

Indeed, when we examine popular and activist representations of trafficking in women, the "global sex trade," or "virtual sex slavery," we find these productions contain several assumptions about not only gender and race but issues of community, communication, and technology. Public sphere discussions over trafficking often make rearguard claims about community and technology in the name of protecting women. A defining feature of trafficking is the transportation of (mainly women's) bodies across space for the purposes of control. Given that discussions of this practice were contemporaneous with a transformed understanding of communication, we can assert an analogy between trafficking and what Carey bleakly describes as the rise of a transmission model of communication. This issue is even more pertinent to our discussion if Levi-Strauss is correct that the circulation of language and of women should be viewed as parallel structures of exchange.

Trafficking, Community, and Technology

The traffic in women has gripped the U.S. public's imagination since the late nineteenth century, when stories of women kidnapped and sold into sexual slavery circulated in the era's mass-distribution print media. Triggered by a series of muckraker exposés, the moral panic over "white slavery" reached its crescendo between 1907 and 1911. During this period, the notion that women were forced into prostitution by organized vice syndicates became the chief cultural explanation for prostitution. Allegations that "white slavers" had extended their operations across the United States precipitated one of the first truly national moral panics. Driven by a large-scale mass media system and an easily reproducible narrative of innocent white victims and swarthy eastern European villains, localities across the United States began to perceive themselves as imperiled by a similar threat. Responding to the alleged increase in trafficking, social purity campaigns and citizens' groups pressured their towns and municipalities to take action against the illicit trade.

The unprecedented flow of people between U.S. cities after the 1880s made urban populations less pervious to local- and family-based forms of social control. Indeed, the potential such mobility and lack of supervision held for race, class, and gender mixing incited intensive efforts by moral reformers to domesticate and regulate urban space.[9] Certainly the most intensive middle-class reform efforts centered around curbing the alleged traffic in women. In cities and small towns across the United States, vice units to combat sexual trafficking and prostitution were established as permanent arms of local police forces. Meanwhile citizens voluntarily formed the first community watch groups to aid these formal policing efforts. Such local efforts to contain the traffic in women were matched on the national level with anti-trafficking legislation such as the Mann Act, which made the movement of unmarried women across state lines for "immoral purposes" punishable by jail.

In addition to newspaper and magazine reports of white slavery, spin-off productions and institutional responses were inspired by the initial exposés. These include commissioned studies of white slavery, notably the famous Chicago and New York vice commission reports, national and international Immigration and Naturalization Service investigations, popular novels, and a new literary/social scientific genre that combined case studies and "testimonials" with reports from social workers, church leaders, and physicians (the various competing sites of cultural authority at that historical conjuncture). A mass-mediated cultural phenomenon became a social fact that initiated investigative, legislative, punitive, and other forms of restrictive mechanisms aimed at managing it.

The specter of white slavery also spawned some of the first cinematic sexual exploitation crime dramas, including George Loane Tucker's immensely popular *Traffic in Souls*.[10] The film grossed half a million dollars when it debuted in 1913 and made Universal Pictures famous. *Traffic in Souls* contains swashbuckling and lurid action scenes: kidnappings, brawls, shootouts, and brothel raids. The film follows a large-scale hierarchically organized trafficking network that uses the latest technology—dictagraphs, Model Ts, and telephones—to manage an army of cadets whose job is to satisfy the sex industry's seemingly insatiable demand for young women. These villains deploy every strategy available to them, including seduction, knockout drugs, and physical force to ensnare their victims. In the film, as in other popular representations of white slavery, women who fall prey to traffickers share common social conditions: most are already in the workforce and lack male protectors. In popular representations of trafficking like *Traffic in Souls*, women's distance from family structures and lack of strong local communities render them easy targets for sex traffickers. For example, cadets fix their sights on stores with female employees as well as ice-cream shops, ports, and train stations. Immigrant women who arrive at Ellis Island without families are easy prey for the sex slavery rings, as is the tragic heroine forced to work in a candy store because her father, the kindly "invalid inventor," is confined to a wheelchair, Only two women successfully avoid the cadets in *Traffic in Souls:* a prominent well-loved and protected judge's daughter and a policeman's fiancée, both protected by men active in fighting the traffic in women. Indeed, Officer Burke ultimately carries out a successful military-style raid on the brothel where his fiancée's sister is held captive.

In addition to human heroes and villains, communications technologies and the early-twentieth-century print media figure prominently in representations of trafficking. In *Traffic in Souls,* traffickers are seen coordinating their trade with the dictagraph, transmitting instant messages such as "#03400832 No. $350" that numerically label and price each girl they procure. The ringleaders' more sophisticated point-to-point technology allows them to outwit civil servants and civic organizations, at least until massdistribution media step in to galvanize the public in an effort to stop the villains. Letters and daily newspapers prove instrumental in alerting New Yorkers of the trade's existence and coordinating citizen action against trafficking. Ultimately, Officer Burke and his fiancée devise a way to record the traffickers' discussions using another communication technology, the phonographic record, thereby obtaining a key brothel's location as well as "hard evidence" that the trade is real (always a question throughout these panics).

From the lurid magazine and newspaper exposés of "white slavery" in the 1900s to sensational televised disclosures featuring Russian, Filipino, and Thai trafficked women in the 1990s, the mass media has been the primary site where trafficking narratives are generated and reproduced. Although each trafficking exposé promises to reveal, seemingly for the first time, the truth about this unthinkable and invisible trade, most audiences do not need to read or view one of these productions to describe the basic plot of a trafficking story. The temporal and spatial vectors—the where and when of trafficking narratives—may vary, but the cast of characters as well as the solutions offered to combat the traffic in women typically remain the same.

For more than a century, antitrafficking discourses for both general and specific audiences have pointed toward the role of communication technologies in facilitating the traffic in women and dissolving community- and family-based forms of social control. Public debates over the exchange of women have been inextricably tied to cultural anxieties about the flow and distribution of information—words and images—across space.[11] Organized campaigns against the sex trade have focused on the technologies that enable trafficking and bring the phenomenon to public light nearly as much as they have concentrated on alleged sex slavery itself. The late-nineteenth- and early-twentieth-century social purity campaigns that organized vociferously against white slavery responded with equal parts horror and fascination to the proliferation of stories about trafficking in the era's mass media. Civic organizations concerned with urban vice alternated between lauding newspapers and monthly magazines for calling the public's attention to vast trafficking networks and castigating them for facilitating the trade by rendering it visible. In 1910, the growth in photography led American feminists attending the International White Slave Conference in Paris to lobby for the establishment of headquarters in every country to police against the use of "photographic publications used in the illicit traffic."[12]

In the 1980s, a number of feminists (such as Dworkin and MacKinnon) rose to both academic and public prominence with their powerful formulation that the circulation of pornography lay at the very center of women's oppression. Most recently, the end of the Cold War incited a proliferation of narratives of Eastern European lawlessness and social disruption, provoking a number of new anxieties surrounding the "global sex trade." In the mid-1990s, the Western media became fascinated with stories of women from the former Soviet Union now reduced to individual workers in the global economy. Many feminists, policymakers, and journalists in the United States responded by turning their attention away from pornography and toward trafficking. Both movements emphasized the illicit circulation of women's bodies.

This shift witnessed publications such as Donna Hughes' *Pimps and Predators on the Internet* (1999), which condemned digital communication networks for allegedly turning all men into pimps. This activist pamphlet claims the Internet has intensified the breakdown of community norms that once protected women. Hughes alleges that digital technologies have allowed the emergence of virtual male-oriented communities that override the surveillance associated with familial propinquity: "the Internet allows pimps and predators to create their own culture outside community standards or interference."[13] In this rendering, a new and frightening globalized world has emerged in which the actions associated with pimping—"stalking, buying, and exploiting"—occur over the Web rather than on city streets.

Further, the rise of the Internet allows traffickers to attain a new level of integration as well as unprecedented breadth of organization:

> Forums on the Internet have become meeting grounds for pimps selling women, predators buying women or stalking victims. Web sites and newsgroups have become showrooms and bragging spaces for every type of violence perpetrated against women and children. . . . With Internet technology and communications pimps and predators can access global markets and unsuspecting victims. Pimps can locate their computer servers in countries with the most libertarian laws and operate outside the reach of regulations in all other countries. (6–7)

Although the pamphlet suggests that the libertarian and anarchic nature of new technologies render cracking down on trafficking virtually impossible, it offers three possible remedies: the formation of vigilante groups that hack into sex sites to disrupt commercial activities, the establishment of hotlines for reporting illegal sites, and the strengthening of local communities to ensure that young women do not fall prey to men who stalk via the Internet.

From the white slavery panic to the antipornography movement of the 1980s to current concerns over global sex trafficking, it appears that the fact of circulation and migration (of images as well as material bodies) triggers much of the hype and concern around this sex-related social issue. Indeed, *Pimps and Predators on the Internet* has sections entitled "Interstate Travel by Predators" and "International Travel by Predators." There has been a shift in the material and social function of the exchange of women from the material function such traffic served in nonindustrial societies (forging group and community cohesion) to the symbolic role it has played in the capitalist West (as a potent sign of community disintegration and disorder). Even old controversies over trafficking illustrate in a clear and still politically vibrant way the problems with invocations of community and group cohesion. While the specter of sexual trafficking seems to crystallize anxieties over other mobile threats (especially the deployment of new communication technologies to facilitate international immigration), it also uses the figure of compromised femininity rhetorically to signal other fears about racial mixing and the ability of a community or entire nation to regulate the exchange of women and serves as an occasion for news institutions to configure themselves as social actors serving the public interest.

Conclusion

Over the last 150 years, the traffic in women has become a phrase denoting the (often forced) buying and selling of women's bodies in the context of prostitution, pornography, and the organized sex trade. Paralleling the definitional life of the term "communication," in many respects, traffic is no longer conceived as a symbolic or material force of social cohesion but has come instead to signify social disorder, community breakdown, and illegitimate control. The initial campaigns against a perceived international sex trade were contemporaneous with the conceptual fusion of communication and transportation, a metaphor that highlights the role of technology in facilitating the spread of information (or propaganda) for the purposes of social control. The process of shoring up local and state community borders through campaigns against trafficking contrasts starkly with the exogamous tendencies of nonindustrial societies, in which the prescribed exchange of women often forged intergroup connections.

In antitrafficking texts, family- and community-based social control is invoked nostalgically. Consequently, the legal measures established to curb trafficking tend ultimately to undermine women's ability to migrate.[14] Indeed, most efforts to curb trafficking are aimed at landing women back in family and community contexts where they are instinctively assumed to be safest.[15]

In a different domain altogether, an analysis of ritualized national panics over trafficking in women reveals some weaknesses inherent in Carey's understanding of language, symbols, and public ceremonies as unifying forces that function according to Durkheim's vision of collective representations. Carey's understanding of symbolic communication unduly celebrates its bonding function while downplaying the ways in which (1) symbolic systems—including those produced and reproduced by the North American mass media—are often political, promoting "illusory" or self-interested beliefs that exploit unity and division, promoting cohesion among some groups and division and fragmentation among others; (2) mass communication is often driven by institutional languages and logics that favor certain forms of representations and social rituals at the cost of others; and, (3) society and culture are not singular entities and, therefore, representations that occur in one institutional field or emphasize one phenomenon can refer to or be about something in an altogether different institutional and social field. Carey occasionally gestures toward the divisive uses to which language, ritual, and expressive forms can be put, but despite such acknowledgments he repeatedly falls back on a nearly religious belief in the sublime power of communication to facilitate social cohesion. In doing so, he overrides a sustained critique of these other functions, instead locating illegitimate power in a corrupted understanding of communication.

Ultimately, Carey wants others to partake in his quasi-religious awareness of the wonders of communication as that practice which allows social and cultural life to take place. If anything, *Communication and Culture* entreats us to hone our analytic sensibilities while simultaneously feeling awestruck before the vast sea of cultural texts and performances that daily reproduce our social and cultural lives. Quite surreptitiously the book casts a nostalgic eye toward a time before wide-ranging technological, economic, and social changes disrupted smaller bounded communities. With the onset of industrialization, the United States was increasingly envisioned as an interconnected landscape across which information, people, and things circulated from point to point, an incessant traffic linked to secular relations of control. By invoking nostalgia for an earlier time when the wonders of communication were more apparent, Carey gives short shrift to the exclusionary aspects of seemingly shared symbols, communities, and ideologies of group belonging that certainly persist in the present but also likely existed during the ritual under-standing of communication's heyday.

Since its inception as an institutionalized field of research, communica-tions has understood its object in largely utilitarian terms as a process whereby messages are transmitted and received with largely predictable effects. Carey has long entreated communications scholars to rethink their basic assumptions about communication as the transmission of information. Despite the critiques outlined above, his suggestion that we locate the repro-duction of social life in rites of passages and rituals that confer shared mean-ings to groups is an invaluable starting point in any study of mass media content. Far from being neutral carriers of information, mass media play a central role in constructing and imparting symbols through which social identities and social relations are both forged and understood. Carey deserves much credit for bringing this long-neglected insight back to the center of North American communications scholarship.

Notes

1. Emile Durkheim, *The Elementary Forms of the Religious Life*, 1915. Reprint (New York: The Free Press, 1965), p. 22.
2. Claude Levi-Strauss, *Structural Anthropology* (New York: Basic Books, 1963), p. 296.
3. Pierre Bourdieu and Loic Wacquant, *An Invitation to Reflexive Sociology* (Chicago: University of Chicago Press, 1992).
4. Gayle Rubin, "The Traffic in Women: Notes on the Political Economy of Sex," in ed. Rayna R. Reiter, *Toward an Anthropology of Women* (New York: Monthly Review Press, 1975), p. 174.
5. In a later essay, Rubin argues that this process does not hold true for modern indus-trialized societies. Kinship and exchange—and therefore the "traffic in women"—are not the means through which industrial societies cohere. She argues, along with Fou-cault [*History of Sexuality: An Introduction* (New York: Vintage, 1990)], that as sex-uality became loosened from kinship, taboos restricting and prescribing appropriate marital partners became prohibitions against particular sexual acts:

    > The old religious taboos . . . were meant to deter inappropriate unions and to provide proper kin. Sex laws derived from biblical pronouncements were aimed at preventing the acquisition of the wrong kinds of affinal partners. . . . When medicine and psychiatry acquired extensive powers over sexuality, they were less concerned with unsuitable mates than with unfit forms of desire . . . the shift to an emphasis on taboos against masturbation was more apposite to the newer systems organized around qualities of erotic experi-ence. ["Thinking Sex: Notes for a Radical Theory of the Politics of Sexual-ity," in eds. Henry Abelove, Michèle Aina Barale, and David M. Halperin, *The Gay and Lesbian Studies Reader* (New York: Routledge, 1993), p. 15].

    As the old marital taboos faded away, sexuality became the province of a number of social institutions, including medicine and law.

6. Cary Nelson, "Martial Lyrics: The Vexed History of the Wartime Poem Card," *American Literary History* 16:2 (2004) pp. 263–289.

7. Raymond Williams, *Keywords: A Vocabulary of Culture and Society* (New York: Oxford University Press , 1976), p. 76.

8. Despite the moral panics that periodically erupted over alleged sexual slavery over the course of the last century, trafficking has proven a thorny issue for feminists and reformers because the existence, scope, and scale of trafficking is notoriously difficult to prove. There currently exists no consensus among international feminist activists, human rights advocates, or policymakers as to the actual number of trafficked individuals in the world today (see Kamala Kempadoo and Jo Doezema (1998), *Global Sex Workers: Rights, Resistance, Redefinition* (New York: Routledge, 1998). Even if the existence of large-scale trafficking networks is taken as a social fact, there is significant disagreement over why women (and some men) end up working abroad in the sex industry. Do they willingly enter into debt-bondage agreements believing these arrangements offer them more security or money than they will find elsewhere or are they forced into such contracts against their will? NGOs, activists, and policymakers are currently fractured over such issues.

   This chapter does not engage the above question, but instead focuses on the way issues of community and media are invoked rhetorically in popular and activist productions that attempt to expose the dreadfulness of trafficking. Such a focus is in no way meant to circumvent a discussion of "real" sexual slavery. While few would go so far as to say trafficking does not exist and is merely a textual illusion, a figment of crusaders' imagination, literature on the phenomenon offers wildly diverging statistics on the true extent of the problem globally and within U.S. borders. A practice that is so hard to pin down using standard sociological methods deserves special inquiry into the terms used to describe and produce it. It also bears asking what other social concerns may be embedded within or hidden by controversies over trafficking. Indeed, the symbolic link between trafficking, communications technologies, and community breakdown is compelling precisely because the phenomenon raises such difficult epistemological questions.

9. See Kathy Peiss, *Cheap Amusements: Working Women and Leisure in Turn-of-the-Century New York* (Philadelphia: Temple University Press, 1987). See also Christine Stansell, *City of Women: Sex and Class in New York, 1798–1860* (New York: Knopf, 1986).

10. Tucker shot the film in New York City before permits were required; consequently, the bustling city streets, the streetcars, and the port where immigrants arrived from Ellis Island were not staged. A number of European immigrants are used as extras in the film, which was not only a blockbuster hit but also was shown at Ellis Island to warn the newly arrived of the dangers they may encounter in the United States.

11. See Penelope Saunders and Gretchen Soderlund, "Threat or Opportunity: Sexuality, Gender, and the Ebb and Flow of Traffic as Discourse," *Canadian Women's Studies/les cahiers de la femme* 22, 3/4 (2003), 16–25.

12. "Act against White Slavery," *The New York Times* (April 30, 1910), p. 1.

13. Donna M. Hughes, *Pimps and Predators on the Internet* (Coalition Against Trafficking in Women, 1999), 7.

14. See Kamala Kempadoo and Jo Doezema, *Global Sex Workers: Rights, Resistance, Redefinition* (New York, Routledge, 1998).

15. See Nicholas Kristof's series in the *New York Times* "Back to the Brothel" (22 January 2004), A15 for an example of the instinctive but often erroneous assumption that families and communities somehow automatically function to protect women and girls.

6. Transportation and Communication: Together as You've Always Wanted Them

JONATHAN STERNE

I.

For a long time now, people in communication studies have insisted on the irreducibly symbolic dimensions of the word "communication."[1] This symbolism thesis is accepted as doxa in several subfields of communication studies. A rich notion of communication as symbolic enterprise has not always been so dominant in the field. When James Carey's "symbolic construction of reality" thesis appeared in 1975, it was a necessary corrective to the methodological individualism and mechanism widespread in the field at that point.[2] Communication as symbolic action, analyzed as a ritual function, was the foundation for his cultural approach to communication. It has become a philosophical and ethical touchstone for many of us who study media, and it has allowed us useful and fruitful connections with scholars in literature, anthropology, philosophy, history, and other fields.

Today, it is time to question symbolic action as the foundation for our theories of communication. Communication is a social process with symbolic dimensions, to be sure, but it is not only symbolic action. I doubt that many scholars in any area of communication study would find that statement controversial. But, when we get down to the practicalities of it, the "nonsymbolic" dimensions of communication—for lack of a less clumsy term—often take a back seat to the symbolic dimensions. This is especially true at the definitional level, those moments when we consider the limits and boundaries of the term "communication." We usually distinguish our practices of communication from other practices by virtue of their symbolic functions. This chapter considers one such border territory: the distinction between communication and transportation in U.S. media history. For the purposes of social and historical description, I argue that communication is best conceptualized as organized movement and action. All movement has a symbolic dimension, to be sure, but movement is also a constitutive physical phenomenon. Without considering a specific instance of movement, we cannot *a priori* privilege the symbolic dimensions of communication because symbolic action may or may not be the most important action in our social analysis at any given moment.

To that end, this chapter considers a specific form of organized movement—transportation—and offers a reading of the relationship between train travel and telegraphy in the mid- and late-nineteenth-century United States. Carey's famous "Technology and Ideology" essay told an interconnected story of trains and telegraphs that argued telegraphy essentially severed the historical connection between transportation and communication.[3] My story is somewhat different: by considering both as forms of communication, I will demonstrate the possibility of understanding communication as a process that is sometimes symbolic and sometimes not. For Carey, the move to a symbolic theory of communication accompanied his departure from the "transmission" model of communication, where a message moves from a sender to a receiver. Carey's ritual model is certainly much richer in placing communication as the means by which social reality is symbolically constructed. But social reality is made not only at the level of symbols. It is also built and organized, a world of motion and action. This is why the shared history of technologies that we usually separate into nonsymbolic "transportation" and symbolic "communication" can help us build a richer sense of communication.

There are good reasons to use transportation as a foil to our symbolic model of communication. For most of human history, any definition of communication that separates symbolic action from movement is nothing more than an anachronism. Writers interested in the history of the idea of communication have often noted the associational connections between transportation and communication that held sway until late in the nineteenth century. As both Carey and John Durham Peters point out, in previous moments, communication meant—among other things—transportation, movement, connection, and linkage. "Steam communication" was travel by train, and a door could form a "communication" between a house and the outdoors.[4] At some point in the nineteenth century, the words "intercourse" and "communication" also traded connotation with one another. Lest we think this a distinctly North American orientation, there are other historical precedents, such as the Greeks for instance. Even our central terms for symbolic action gesture toward a concept of communication as a subspecies of movement. "Metaphor" comes from the Greek for "to transfer" or "to carry."[5] "The word *metaphoros . . .* is written on all the moving vans in Greece," writes Bruno Latour.[6]

Perhaps this seems more like an exploration of philological esoterica than a theoretical argument about communication. A critic might point out that even if transportation is at the roots of many of our concepts of communication those roots are so forgotten and so mediated, how could they possibly have an effect? More to the point, for the last century at least, it has been common parlance to separate communication and transportation. So perhaps the best route to take would be to examine two contenders for the cause of that conceptual separation: one that is explained via the history of ideas about communication and another that is explained via the history of technology—specifically, trains and telegraphs. Is it possible to analyze the interaction of trains and telegraphs as a particular social complex of communication, rather than as two separate things? What would it mean to consider them from the normative scale of the entire system, rather than from the normative scale of an individual? My goal is to explore some of the issues raised by thinking about communication and transportation as a combined, intertwined process—as a massive assemblage of organized movement in space.

II.

One explanation of the conceptual separation of transportation and communication is intellectual-historical: this perspective argues that we see communication and transportation as separate things because of intellectual traditions that emerged in the early twentieth century. John Durham Peters writes that by the 1920s, the meaning of communication had consolidated around five centers: "management of mass opinion, the elimination of semantic fog, vain sallies from the citadel of the self, the disclosure of otherness, and the orchestration of action."[7] Out of the five definitional centers—which are relatively close to the ones in common use today—only one relates in any significant way to movement: orchestrated action. For Peters, shifts in the meaning of communication are part of changing currents in intellectual history in the early twentieth century. They are a result of the influence of the pragmatists, new approaches to social science, and continental thinkers such as Martin Heidegger. In this way, Peters is in the good company of Carey and Dan Czitrom (and more recently Armand and Michèle Mattelart), who all argue that the idea of "communication" first gained intellectual significance through the Chicago School of sociology.[8] This to me seems like a robust account of *how* the two terms came to be separated, and how it came to be that communication was understood as a primarily symbolic form of action. However, it does not directly address the question of *why* this change occurred.

Carey points to another set of developments outside the sphere of intellectuals to explain the separation of transportation and communication. His explanation provides an intellectual justification for separating the two terms by arguing that they were separated in actual social practice. If we want to dispute the separation between transportation and communication in social description, this is where we would have to begin. Carey offers us a definitive breaking point. This story has become part of the canon of media history, and so it is to his account that I will attend most carefully. He writes that

> [T]he telegraph [and by this he means Morse's electrical telegraph and code] provided the decisive and cumulative break of the identity of communication and transportation. The great theoretical significance of the technology lay not merely in the separation but also in the use of the telegraph as both a model of and mechanism for control of the physical movement of things, specifically for the railroad. That is the fundamental discovery: not only can information move independently of and faster than physical entities, but it can also be a simulation of and control mechanism for what was left behind.[9]

Ironically—and all of this is according to Carey—this separation allowed for an "integrated system of transport and communication," where faster moving communication controls and regulates faster transportation. The integrated system requires transportation and communication to be separated so that one can regulate the other. This would become the basis for all modern forms of electrical control, organicism in nineteenth-century thought, the commodities market, and standard time.[10] A whole series of scholars such as Dan Czitrom, Menachem Blondheim, and Jeff Sconce have repeated Carey's assertion.[11] Carey tells a convincing story. But let's look more closely at what happens in this moment.

The argument that telegraphy separated transportation and communication hinges on Carey's claim that information could move faster than physical entities. This claim is, in turn, based on the hypothesized experience of a single individual standing in a single place. If we imagine a single person standing at a single point on a telegraph line that runs alongside train tracks, Carey's argument makes intuitive sense: our imaginary friend can send a message by telegraph that arrives faster than the train running alongside it, because electricity moves faster than trains. It is therefore true that in *use* the early telegraph governed the movement of the trains, because the electrical signals contained instructions for the movement of trains. But it is also true that in material form—in infrastructure—the physicality of the train tracks governed the geographic movement of telegraph signals. To control the trains, the telegraphic wires had to follow the same path as the tracks. So the circuits of telegraphy followed the circuits of the train before the train could follow the telegraph. Carey calls this a "painful" process, but it seems to me perfectly reasonable. There is a long and intertwined history of transportation and communication infrastructure in the United States. It starts with postal roads, seaways, and riverways in the eighteenth century and continues and transmogrifies in a series of cobbled-together forms over the next two centuries: trains and telegraph lines, radio and phone lines, a confluence of coaxial cables, for increased telephone traffic and network television, combined with interstate highways and, later, satellites. The physical infrastructure of the Internet continues to retrace this intertwined history as plans for Internet 2 infrastructure make use of abandoned railroad rights of way.

Interestingly, Carey's formulation has been so powerful that it has also set the terms for disagreement. In a stroke of classic historicist argument ("No, it actually happened *earlier* than we originally thought"), Richard John contests electrical telegraphy as the historical precedent for separation of transportation and communication. "Long before the electric telegraph was credited with having 'annihilated' time and space, the postal system had been described in precisely the same way. 'Distance is thus reduced almost to contiguity; and the ink is scarcely dry, or the wax cold on the paper, before we find in our hands, even at a distance of hundreds of miles, a transcript of our dearest friend's mind.'"[12] One could imagine a similar argument for semaphoric telegraphy, or other now-forgotten modes of communication.

Given this longer history, why even tell a story where the telegraph separates transportation and communication? Why try to explain electrical telegraphy through reference to the imagined experience of a single person standing somewhere along the line? After all, telegraphy required massive infrastructure, coordinated action across many states at once, an institutionalized and patented code, and vast organizations to manage it. Here is the terrain upon which we encounter the question of *scale* in our social theories of communication. A net effect of Carey's speculative phenomenology of telegraphy is to orient our theory of communication around the scale of the individual.

The scale of the individual person dominates our key cultural theories of communication, from Plato to Jurgen Habermas and beyond. It is well known that Derrida has derided the idea of a self-consistent, presocial human subject at the core of communication theory as "the metaphysics of presence." A host of other writers have followed in his wake to argue for rethinking the primacy of the individual, self-knowing, and self-enclosed subject in communication theory.[13] One could easily object that at a formal philosophical level it doesn't matter that much whether or not our social theory starts with individuals. It is possible to develop perfectly adequate, robust, and convincing accounts of communication that take as their starting point the single individual. But such accounts carry with them a political and philosophical hostility to large-scale society. In models that theoretically privilege the interpersonal, any large-scale event is defined negatively, as lacking a quality present in the interpersonal interaction. Such an approach assumes a certain homology or identity among small-scale phenomena. Writing becomes modified speech, recording becomes a modified form of writing, and so forth. If we take individuals as our base unit of analysis, all media are fundamentally "mediations" of a more primary, fundamental speech relationship between two people. Scale matters because it is a major political fault line in social theories of communication.

On this point, Carey would later be unequivocal: he claims that his ritual model of communication "forces one to begin with the analysis of communication not with technological forms of transmission, but to privilege the oral formulation of culture and its secondary displacement in mass-mediated forms." For him, it is an ethical as well as a descriptive matter: "Communication understood as a metaphor of ritual and conversation encourages, even requires a primitive form of equality because conversation must leave room for response as a condition of its continuance. Conversation enforces recognition of others in the fullness of their presence." Carey goes on to say that while critics might call this view naïve, it is just as possible to locate power relations in the conversational model as it is in any other: "the trick is to locate the mechanisms by which differentials of power and intractable conflict are buried, deflected, resolved, exercised, and aggregated into interests." Indeed, for Carey, the most basic unit of communication is two bodies in conversation. For him, the ritual model has its material basis in bodily action.[14] Though his position is clearly in line with both a long history traced by Derrida and Peters, as well as a shorter history that includes John Dewey, Marshall McLuhan, Walter Ong, and others, his major innovation is to situate the conversational model within his larger account of communication as ritual, which connects the bodily act of communication with larger movements of both social reproduction and social transformation.

The conversational model has problems both as a descriptive and as a normative formulation. McLuhan and Carey's other sources, who argue that conversation and language predate the use of technology for communication, are simply wrong on the historical facts. Archaeologists have found examples of musical instruments, sculptures, and paintings that even predate the existence of *Homo sapiens,* to the best of our knowledge. In other words, insofar as the capacity for speech goes all the way back to the beginnings of humanity so does the capacity to use tools for communication. Thus, while bodies are important, the connections between bodies and tools are as fundamental to the human condition as the bodies themselves. There is no such thing as a "human" body that is not already implicated in some form of techné. Or to put it another way, if we want to consider technology a force of mediation (and I do not), it is *no more* a mediation than speech or language. In fact, another of Carey's favorite writers, Lewis Mumford, has argued that language itself is best conceptualized as a form of techné. For Mumford, language is not prior to technological communication. It is one technology of communication among many.[15]

If the descriptive dimension is off, this also raises questions about using conversation as the normative basis for a theory of communication. The conversational model suggests that simpler societies are more equal, and the simpler parts of large societies are more equal. Again, this claim has little in the way of historical or anthropological evidence to back it up. It is true that large-scale societies are riddled with inequalities, but so are smaller societies. The advantage of a large society is simply that the life chances of any one individual are much more varied and variable than the life chances of a person born into a smaller society. It is an advantage of potential liberty, which is a necessary building block (though not a guarantor) of equality. Therefore, we cannot simply denigrate large social institutions as cheapened, mediated versions of face-to-face relations. We need to examine and critique them in their positivity so that we may build better ones. Vico, in one of the founding texts of the human sciences, points precisely to the human-made dimensions of reality as the most important for analysis: if we make them, he says, we can transform them.[16]

By now it should be clear that my disagreement with Carey is not so much about purpose (we both seem to subscribe to those old Enlightenment goals of liberty and equality) but about object construction and method. By changing the analytical scale we use to describe communication, we may in fact wind up with a better and more robust means to describe the qualities of a society necessary for enhancing the lives of diverse individuals.

By now, we may seem far afield of trains and telegraphs. But the story of communication and transportation is intimately linked to the scale of our social theories and to a preference for treating communication as a symbolic enterprise. It works like this: In order to tell the story in which trains and telegraphs separate communication and transportation, we must describe that history from the vantage point of a single individual, who observes that the train moves more slowly than the electricity on the wires of the telegraph. In the wake of writers such as Hayden White and Dominick LaCapra, nobody should be surprised to find an ethical and political preference (in this case, for individual scale) at the core of a descriptive history. Carey, as I have shown, is clear about this. So, a sharp division between individual and society (with moral preference for the individual) undergirds the transportation/communication dyad. The separation of communication and transportation that this account requires in turn allows for a separation of the symbolic and nonsymbolic aspects of communication. The symbolic dimensions of communication now carry the day in guises such as "ideas," "information," "memory," "consciousness," and so forth, while the nonsymbolic aspects fade into the background as "communication*s*," "infrastructure," and "enabling conditions."

III.

Even as contemporary theories of communication and society acknowledge that communication has not always been separable from transportation, they almost to the one express a preference for the symbolic notion of communication enabled by that separation. In fact, many scholars have used the phrase "transportation model of communication" to deride conceptualizations of communication as nothing more than a means to an end. This is an interesting slip of the pen, so to speak, from Carey's critique of the "transmission model" of communication in his "Cultural Approach to Communication" essay. He says that the transmission model casts communication as an instrumental process whereby a message is transmitted from a sender to a receiver. The goal, of course, is for the message's journey to have as little effect on it as possible. The transmission model casts communication largely as a process that gets in the way of shared meaning. The goal of communication in this model is to separate meaning out from the world in which it circulates, like Wolfgang Schivelbusch's train traveler, who is separated from the landscape through which she traverses.[17] Carey rightly criticized the transmission model for misrecognizing the fundamental purpose of communication, which is shared social action and not some bizarre conservation of ideas. Yet we must be careful not to confuse a specific model of communication, the transmission model, with all possible configurations of transportation. To treat transportation as a mere instrumentality, as nothing more than a means to an end, is to misunderstand the meaning of transportation for most of its history. Unbeknownst to many people in both camps, communication scholars have been trading insults with geographers for decades: we deride transportation as a mere instrumentality, and we elevate communication as a constitutive social process. Not surprisingly, a whole string of geographers have cast the problem the other way around: communication is a mere instrumentality; transportation and movement are constitutive social processes. The truth is obviously somewhere in between the two caricatures: there are instrumental and constitutive dimensions to communication and transportation, and I am interested in their shared constitutive qualities.

Today, many people—most, I imagine—understand that freedom of movement and the spaces of possible movement and action are a major part of social and political life. This is one of the classic points of contrast between democratic and totalitarian states—citizens of democracies can go where they want and live where they want. To discover the limits of this understanding, one need look no further than a classic feminist critique of urban planning: women are less free than men to move about urban space, and their movement is fraught with a greater degree of physical danger because of the threat of male violence and specifically sexual violence.[18] We can find a related argument in writings that document the attack on outdoor, public life in poor and nonwhite sections of U.S. cities.[19] In other words, the city is both a place of tremendous possibility and a place of fear and danger, depending on who you are and what you're doing. If we extrapolate back in time and talk about the movements of African Americans across states, the same could be said for the space of a whole country. Back in 1844, when communication and transportation were ostensibly separated, let us not forget that in the United States manifest destiny was at a fever pitch, the underground railroad was up and running, and the ship at sea symbolized freedom, power, and opportunity for free men and captivity, terror, and death for slaves.[20] Transportation was *intensely* meaningful and intensely constitutive. It formed a condition of possibility for social action as well as the substance of that social action in some cases.

That telegraphs and trains should go together should not surprise us: every claim made for telegraphy was made for trains beforehand. Let us compare some of the claims: the "annihilation of time and space" was a phrase applied to both train and telegraph. Faster travel meant that it was possible to cover greater distances in a shorter time. Schivelbusch writes that in the 1830s the average train traveled at about thirty miles an hour, or about three times the maximum speed of a stagecoach. He quotes a British writer in the 1839 *Quarterly Review* who speaks of "the gradual annihilation, approaching almost to the final extinction, of that space and of those distances which have hitherto been supposed unalterably to separate the various nations of the globe." The writer goes on to assert that for England "the surface of our country would, as it were, shrivel in size until it became not much bigger than one immense city."[21] The language remains the same today in writings on information technology from Jean Baudrillard, Paul Virilio, Anthony Giddens, or Manuel Castells. Castells's information city is our Londoner's England of 1840: new technologies are said to annihilate time and space.[22] A whole other set of writers, ranging from Marshall Berman to Stephen Kern to David Harvey, take the "compression" of time and space as an axiomatic dimension of modernity and/or capitalism, depending upon who you ask. Carey's account of an imaginary friend standing aside the telegraph wires partakes of the same logic—speed annihilates time and space.

As any of these writers would point out if questioned, time-space compression is more a question of degree than kind. As Blondheim argues in his study of news, it is true that the telegraph "had the [technical] potential of making information available simultaneously throughout the country" in the same time-space compression effect that we see with the railway. But he also argues that, because of changes in transportation practice, there had already been an ongoing "acceleration of news" for a few decades when the telegraph arrived on the scene. For instance, the average time lag between an event happening in Washington and its being published in Boston had dropped from 18 days in 1790 to 2.8 days in 1841. If we're talking newspapers, you need at least half a day to publish something in a print edition: this meant with the aid of the telegraph, time of event to time of publication could be further reduced to 0.5 from 2.8. That's a much smaller difference, Blondheim argues, than the shift from 1790 to 1841.[23]

A careful reader might note that Blondheim substitutes one type of technological determinism for another: whereas Carey wants to attribute time-space compression to electrical communication, Blondheim wants to attribute it to the "transportation revolution"—better seaways, faster ships, burgeoning railroads, and better roads—that comes right before the invention of the telegraph.[24] But even if we argue that contemporaries and the historians who cite them attribute too much significance to the device itself, the essential point is that *transportation and communication seem to be doing the same thing at this moment.* If we suspend temporarily the question of what communication and transportation *are* and instead look at what they *do* in this context, they're clearly doing some of the same things.

Beyond "annihilation of time and space" there are a range of other shared attributes between telegraphy and railroading. Rather than cataloguing all of them, let me focus on one other feature that's particularly interesting for this argument. Schivelbusch argues that for most travelers, especially regular travelers, railway journeys gradually became identified with their destinations. After an initial period of fascination, the railway journey was monotonous, boring, and disorienting. Even as they wrote of the rail system as annihilating space and time—and as creating new fields of experience from the extraordinary panoramic views and "shocks," to the mundane activities of reading while traveling—rail passengers came to treat the train and the tracks as nothing more than a "mere" instrumentality to get from one destination to another. Reading, for instance, was an activity that "passed" the time of travel. Schivelbusch contrasts this with stagecoach and wagon journeys, which were much more arduous and which therefore required more attention to the specific landscapes through which travelers passed on their journeys. Passengers did not pass the time of a stagecoach journey. They "got through it."[25]

Around the time of the telegraph, we can see a similar tendency emerging in discussions of communication, where the means and the infrastructure fall into the background as mere instrumentality, and the supposed symbolic substance of communication becomes separated from its supposed conduit. Even in accounts of telegraph offices, the network of wires outside almost disappears; we are left with stories of virtuosic telegraph operators listening to sounds of the apparatus in their cubicles and relaying information with fleet fingers. In stories such as the biography of James Francis Leonard, "world's fastest telegrapher," the speed of the network is entirely in the hands and ears of the telegraph operators and not at all in the wires or electricity that travels through them.[26] Today, this tendency is so pervasive that communication theorists rarely comment upon it, and when they do it is to bracket questions of means.

Sure, "infrastructure" probably sounds stale and inert: too big for an individual to traverse and too boring to bother. Perhaps this is so, but then perhaps we are looking at things on the wrong scale. To talk about communication as a social phenomenon or to talk about communication in terms of a society, one needs to move beyond the perspective of a single individual or pair of individuals. It is not that interpersonal contacts become insignificant but rather that they do not in any simple way graph, organize, or govern larger social processes of communication embodied in and facilitated by massive infrastructures such as rail and wire. This, of course, signals a long-term debate in social theory. Yet social theorists have for a long time now acknowledged that so-called micro and macro practices are not simply homologous with one another. Rather, we may have to use completely different schemas to explain them.[27] It is surprising how little impact this debate has had to date on our theories of communication. Infrastructure is by definition a massive undertaking. Like any other artifact of human activity—including the building in which I sit as I type these words—it transcends the temporal and spatial capacities of a single human being: infrastructures are usually built to outlast any particular human body, and they are usually large enough that no single human being traverses the infrastructure in its entirety. More to the point, none of us would want to.

Armand Mattelart's recent attempts to rewrite the history of communications (and I use the plural deliberately) group trains and telegraphs together as part of a whole technological complex. This seems only right, as countless theorists and technologists point out that the proper object of technological history is not the single instrument but the entire system. For Mattelart, trains and telegraphs are part of a massive apparatus of the Industrial Revolution, and trains and telegraphs together help to reorganize social time. Mattelart's telegraph story includes Chappe's semaphoric telegraph, which traversed the French landscape in the first half of the nineteenth century prior to railroads and which operated on the principle of vision at a distance, not simultaneity through electrical transmission. Chappe's system was only later supplemented by Cook and Wheatstone's version of the electrical telegraph. Mattelart's perspective on trains and electrical telegraphy is perhaps best summed up by a quote he takes from Fernand Braudel: "Inventions tend to come in clusters, groups or series, as if they all drew strength from each other, or rather as if certain societies provided simultaneous impetus for them all."[28]

Our theoretical language mimics the terminology that emerged along-side telegraphs and trains, and probably postal roads before that. We simultaneously fetishize the means of communication and pretend that they are absent. But communication is unthinkable without communications, and they are both constitutive and instrumental. When a family received news of a relative's death by telegram, or stock prices moved in a moment from New York City to Chicago, the telegraph *was* a means, but it was a constitutive means. The telegraph did not simply mediate already existing links among people; instead, it was the shape of the link among them. (Though, as Thoreau pointed out, it is one thing to make an instantaneous long distance communication possible and another to make it desirable.) Communication is impossible without communications, and while for intellectual histories it may make a good deal of sense to create an analytical distinction, we should be wary of simply mapping our intellectual abstractions back onto social activity: so it is for communication and communications.

IV.

There are a number of major twentieth-century thinkers who have teased out aspects of the significance of the connection between transportation and communication: Lewis Mumford and Harold Innis come to mind, as do Charles Cooley and C. L. R. James and, more recently, Gilles Deleuze and Felix Guattari, Paul Gilroy, and Friedrich Kittler.[29] But for my purposes, Raymond Williams's widely cited notion of "mobile privitization" is most suggestive because he picks up more or less where Carey leaves off. Williams sums it up thus:

> By the end of the 1920s, the radio industry had become a major sector of industrial production, within a rapid general expansion of the new kinds of machines which were eventually to be called "consumer durables." This complex of developments included the motorcycle and motorcar, the box camera and its successors, home electrical appliances, and radio sets. Socially, this complex is characterized by the two apparently paradoxical yet deeply connected tendencies of modern urban industrial living: on the one hand mobility, on the other hand the more apparently self-sufficient family home. The earlier period of public technology, best exemplified by the railways and city lighting, was being replaced by a kind of technology for which no satisfactory name has yet been found: that which served an at once mobile and home-centered way of living: a form of *mobile privatization*.[30]

For Williams, "mobile privatization" is a *context* for the history of television. This is how it has been read in subsequent cultural accounts of television. But if we move backward from television into radio and before, mobile privatization *becomes* the history of communication. Mobile privatization is useful for my present argument because it does not, a priori, distinguish between communication, transportation, and host of other practices. For Williams, cars, cameras, appliances, wires, waves, buildings, messages, movements, images, ideas, and sounds make up a whole social complex of practices. He smartly grouped practices by their domain—by what things did, made, or enabled, rather than what they might have meant. It was for Williams as it was for Braudel: inventions came in clusters.

If we take Williams's description as a reasonable generalization about what was happening to communication and transportation around 1920, then it contradicts Carey's interpretation of telegraph history from the vantage point of a single individual. If we accept that the unity of transportation and communication was shattered in the 1840s, it makes it more difficult to explain their confluence in the 1920s. Far from being a moment of separation, the train-telegraph articulation is a moment of greater interconnection, intensity, and reflexivity. It is a nourishing moment in a process that flowers in different forms throughout American history: for Williams, it is the automobile, fridge, and radio in the 1920s. But moving backward, we find the electric light, the trolley, the subway, and vaudeville theater in the 1890s.[31] These four technical and cultural systems worked together to build a cultural milieu for the emergent urban middle class of that decade. If we go further back, there is the train-telegraph confluence.[32] And before that, the intertwined histories of newspapers, letters, ships, and postal roads all indicate a deep, fundamental and functional connection between the phenomena we now separate as transportation and communication. As Williams suggests, it is almost impossible to separate the social organization of activity and the social organization of experience.

Carey, later in his career, follows suit on this question. He also casts the technological complex of trains and telegraphs as the condition of possibility for an emergent national consciousness in the United States: "[O]n the backbone of that system, a national community of politics and commerce could be constructed. No longer would people live in isolated island communities, exclusively attuned to local rhythms and customs, dimly aware of a nation beyond local border except as news irregularly arrived or national emergencies precipitated a heightened consciousness of the nation."[33] In this way, Carey, Williams, and other writers converge on the 1890s as a key decade, where systems sown earlier in the century come to their fruition and occasion a qualitative change in American culture.

There is another effect of this massive shift as well. The figures of the isolated individual and the small community come into relief as objects of nostalgia. This is clear in the mass society theories that were being developed at once by sociologists on two continents. Gustave Le Bon's *The Crowd*, Georg Simmel's reflections on the metropolis and mental life (as well as his writings on money), the community studies at the University of Chicago, all this work indicated a new awareness of society as a massive undertaking, at once disconnected and different from the individuals who made their way through it. Of course, mass society had been an issue for social theory before, but in this moment of increasing urbanization, its career follows in a certain way Walter Benjamin's claim for aura. The individual became "that which whithers" in the age of mass society for European and American scholars who aimed to diagnose the massive cultural changes at the turn of the twentieth century.[34]

At this moment in intellectual history, it also becomes more difficult to sustain an account of the individual and society that treats them as analogous or harmonious. Since Plato's *Republic*, social theorists had thrived on an analogy between the human subject and the state. Locke, Hobbes and Hegel, to name three major modern figures, all depend on the model of the individual for their account of the state. What happens at the turn of the twentieth century is that this approach shifts from a positive comparison ("roads are like capillaries") to a negative comparison; large social institutions are defined by the fact that they lack certain qualities inherent in the individual.

Although modern communication theory still often claims to speak the language of Plato because of its expressed preference for dialogue,[35] we are most likely to hear that talk through ears tuned to the din of modern life. The longing for an individual at the core of communication theory is the flip side of Simmel's assertion that "the deepest problems of modern life derive from the claim of the individual to preserve the autonomy and individuality of his existence in the face of overwhelming social forces, of historical heritage, of external culture, and of the technique of life."[36] The social theory of communication becomes a story about the individual's fight for the self.

So, in a way, the assemblage of trains and telegraphs inflected, or, to use a musical term, "treated" the normative basis of modern communication theory. Here is where we return to the question of how and whether communication and transportation were separated. We need a story of separation to long for a lost, unified subject. Once that subject is lost, or disturbed by larger social forces, communication is given a certain moral and ethical weight; its job is to repair the break, to overcome difference and distance. And this in turn leads to a preference for symbols, as they can be conceptually separated from things. Communication, as a symbolic practice, is supposed to ameliorate the damage caused to the subject by mass society. But even though it is rooted in a very specific response to developments at the turn of the twentieth century, our symbolic theories of communication carry with them some older baggage as well.

The symbolic definition of communication sustains a resolute and unyielding split between mind and body, and in that way it is a very seventeenth-century notion. We certainly live in a Cartesian culture. As John

Durham Peters, Friedrich Kittler, and Jeff Sconce all point out, the concept of communication as a ghostly and disembodied enterprise has been with us for a long time. But even as we grant that Cartesianism undergirds a certain kind of common sense, we need not adapt commonsensical notions of subjectivity as the basis for our own social theories.

The symbolic definition of communication sustains a resolute and unyielding split between mental and physical labor, and in that way it is a very eighteenth-century notion. This is another iteration of mind and body, I suppose, but it is pernicious in a different way. By defining communication as a fundamentally symbolic thing, we focus on the mind and its products, and we relegate the human body to "mere" means. By defining communication as mental labor, we forget that mental and physical labor always go together. Condensed into a telegraph key, a train wheel, a radio, a computer keyboard, and the paper on which this chapter is printed, we find a mix of those many incredible human capacities to shape the world around us, both through our abilities to speculate, imagine, and represent, and our abilities to make, to do, and to build. This is an old argument: Adam Smith and Karl Marx argued that labor was the defining value-giving activity of human life. Hannah Arendt denigrated "necessary" labor in *The Human Condition* but valorized a concept of work as the conscious creation of artifice. More recently, Ruth Schwartz Cowan has criticized the eighteenth-century taxonomists for choosing to describe people as *Homo sapiens* (primates who think) to the exclusion of *Homo faber* (primates who make things), and Dan Schiller has argued that communication theorists have abstracted communication from labor to the detriment of our theories.[37] Read from the perspective of a social theory of communication, all these authors argue that it is impossible to separate the mental and the physical. Their inflections are different, but their basic point is the same. After all, the sheet of paper on which these words will appear was abstracted from a tree—probably several trees—which is no small mental or physical feat. To presumptively privilege communication as a symbolic form is to denigrate the human and nonhuman physical forces at work in our social world, and to treat the physical world as an inert arena where our symbolic forms go to work.

The symbolic definition of communication sustains a resolute and unyielding split between content and means, and in that way it is a very nineteenth-century notion. Nothing could seem more natural to us than to talk about telegraph messages without a telegraph network, to talk about rail destinations without talking about the journey in between, to talk about films without the apparatus of cinema, to talk about speech without bodies. But these abstractions are artifacts of a particular social moment and of a particular sensibility. It is not that we should never separate content and means in description: my argument is simply that we can't assume such a separation before the fact.

By linking communication to movement, we leave open the relationship between mind and body, mental and physical labor, and content and means. These become questions we have to answer in each particular case that we study. We also restore communication to its proper sociality—as a process certainly undertaken and experienced by individuals but not by definition or function *limited* to the domain of the single mind or body.

So what starts as a small historical quibble—whether trains and telegraphs really did separate transportation and communication—turns out to trouble some of the central social-theoretical questions for communication studies. A split between individual and social scales makes possible the story about communication and transportation as separate things. The story about the separation of communication and transportation, in turn, bolsters the theoretical privilege of the symbolic over the nonsymbolic dimensions of communication. In the process of rethinking the relationship between trains and telegraphs in communication history, I have argued for a social theory of communication that is truly social, that does not take the individual or dyad as its normative base, and that does not automatically privilege symbolic over nonsymbolic action. Perhaps this chapter will be read as simply a defense of that American predilection for all things big. But communication is an undeniably large matter. Like a building, like a system, or even like language, communication exists on a scale much larger than a single person: it has existed before us and with some care and maintenance it will outlive us. It feels intimate and personal, but it is bigger than all of us together.

Notes

1. Many thanks to Carrie Rentschler, Jeremy Packer, and Craig Robertson for their reading and suggestions. Earlier versions of this essay were presented at the National Communication Association in November 2001 and the University of Pittsburgh Department of Communication's colloquium in February 2002. Additional thanks go to both audiences for their comments.
2. James Carey, *Communication as Culture* (Boston: Unwin Hyman, 1989), pp. 23–35.
3. Ibid, 201–230.
4. John Durham Peters, *Speaking into the Air: A History of the Idea of Communication* (Chicago: University of Chicago Press, 1999), pp. 7–8.
5. *Oxford English Dictionary*, s.v., "metaphor."
6. Bruno Latour, *Aramis, or the Love of Technology* (Cambridge, MA: Harvard University Press, 1996), p. 59.
7. Peters, *Speaking into the Air*, p. 19.
8. Carey, *Communication as Culture*; Daniel Czitrom, *Media and the American Mind: From Morse to McLuhan* (Chapel Hill: University of North Carolina Press, 1982); Armand Mattelart and Michèle Mattelart, *Theories of Communication: A Short Introduction* (Thousand Oaks, CA: Sage, 1998).
9. Carey, *Communication as Culture*, p. 215.

10. Ibid.

11. Menachem Blondheim, *News over the Wires: The Telegraph and the Flow of Public Information in America, 1844–1897* (Cambridge, MA: Harvard University Press, 1994); Czitrom, *Media and the American Mind;* Jeffrey Sconce, *Haunted Media: Electronic Presence from Telegraphy to Television* (Durham, NC: Duke University Press, 2000). For an earlier version of Carey's argument, see Allen Pred, *The Spatial Dynamics of U.S. Urban Industrial Growth* (Cambridge, MA: MIT Press, 1966).

12. Richard John, *Spreading the News: The American Postal System from Franklin to Morse* (Cambridge, MA: Harvard University Press, 1995), p. 10.

13. Briankle Chang, *Deconstructing Communication: Representation, Subject, and Economies of Discourse* (Minneapolis: University of Minnesota Press, 1996); Jacques Derrida, *Of Grammatology*, trans. Gayatri Chakravorty Spivak (Baltimore: Johns Hopkins University Press, 1976); Jurgen Habermas, *The Structural Transformation of the Public Sphere: An Inquiry into a Category of Bourgeois Society*, trans. Thomas Burger with the assistance of Frederick Lawrence (Cambridge, MA: MIT Press, 1989); Peters, *Speaking into the Air;* Plato, "Phaedrus," in *The Collected Dialogues of Plato*, ed. Edith Hamilton and Huntington Cairns (Princeton, NJ: Princeton University Press, 1961).

14. James Carey, "Afterword," in *James Carey: A Critical Reader*, ed. Eve Stryker Munson and Catherine Warren (Minneapolis: University of Minnesota Press, 1997), p. 314.

15. See Lewis Mumford, *The Myth of the Machine: Technics and Human Development*, vol. 1 (New York: Harcourt, Brace and World, 1966).

16. Giambattista Vico, *The New Science of Giambattista Vico*, trans. Thomas Bergin and Max Fisch (Ithaca, NY: Cornell University Press, 1984).

17. Wolfgang Schivelbusch, *The Railway Journey: The Industrialization of Time and Space in the 19th Century* (Berkeley: University of California Press, 1986), pp. 37–38.

18. Mona Domosh and Joni K. Seager, *Putting Women in Place: Feminist Geographers Make Sense of the World* (New York: Guilford, 2001); Women and Geography Study Group of the Institute of British Geographers, *Geography and Gender: An Introduction to Feminist Geography* (Dover, England: Hutchinson in association with the Explorations in Feminism Collective, 1984); Margaret T. Gordon and Stephanie Riger, *The Female Fear: The Social Cost of Rape* (Urbana: University of Illinois Press, 1998); Doreen Massey, *Space, Place, and Gender* (Minneapolis: University of Minnesota Press, 1994); Rachel Pain, "Space, Sexual Violence, and Social Control: Integrating Geographical and Feminist Analysis of Women's Fear of Crime," *Progress in Human Geography* 15, no. 4 (1991); Gill Valentine, "Geography of Women's Fear," *Area* 21, no. 4 (1989); Gill Valentine, "Women's Fear and the Design of Public Space," *Built Environment* 16, no. 4 (1990).

19. A classic statement of the argument can be found in the essays collected in Robert Gooding-Williams, ed., *Reading Rodney King, Reading Urban Uprising* (New York: Routledge, 1993). More recently, scholars interested in rap music have noted the connection between changes in musical practice and the collapse of possibilities for large, collective gatherings in urban neighborhoods. While Greg Dimitriadis argues that rap moved from outdoor parties to studios that fed bedrooms and cars, Murray Forman documents the collapse of urban space as a theme in hip-hop. See Greg Dimitriadis, *Performing Identity/Performing Culture: Hip-Hop as Text, Pedagogy, and Lived Practice* (New York: Peter Lang, 2001), pp. 15–34; Murray Forman, *The 'Hood*

Comes First: Race, Space, and Place in Rap and Hip-Hop (Hanover, NH: Wesleyan University Press, 2002), pp. 252–277.

20. Carey, *Communication as Culture*, p. 16; Sally Hadden, *Slave Patrols: Law and Violence in Virginia and the Carolinas* (Cambridge, MA: Harvard University Press, 2001). See also Paul Gilroy, *The Black Atlantic: Modernity and Double Consciousness* (Cambridge, MA: Harvard University Press, 1994).

21. Wolfgang Schivelbusch, *The Railway Journey: The Industrialization of Time and Space in the 19th Century*, p. 34.

22. Jean Baudrillard, *Simulations*, trans. Paul Patton Paul Foss and Philip Beitchman (New York: Semiotext(e), 1983); Marshall Berman, *All That Is Solid Melts into Air: The Experience of Modernity* (New York: Penguin, 1992); Manuel Castells, *The Information City: Information Technology, Economic Restructuring, and the Urban-Regional Process* (Cambridge, England: Blackwell, 1989); Manuel Castells, *Rise of the Network Society* (Malden, England: Basil Blackwell, 2000); Anthony Giddens, *The Constitution of Society: Outline of a Theory of Structuration* (Berkeley: University of California Press, 1990); David Harvey, *The Condition of Postmodernity: An Enquiry into the Origins of Cultural Change* (Cambridge, England: Blackwell, 1989); Stephen Kern, *The Culture of Time and Space 1880–1918* (Cambridge, MA: Harvard University Press, 1983), Paul Virilio, *The Information Bomb*, trans. Chris Turner (New York: Verso: 2001); Paul Virilio, *War and Cinema: The Logistics of Perception* (New York: Verso, 1989).

23. Blondheim, *News over the Wires*, pp. 11–17.

24. This is a dangerous game in history, where moments keep getting pushed back. There is a slippery slope of *historio ad absurdum*, where all of a sudden all the communicative power of digital and satellite technology was directly anticipated by the telegraph at the beginning of Aeschylus's *Agamemnon*. At the same time, debates over periodization are some of the most important historiographic debates because they help set the criteria for the "historical significance" for any specific event, they help to shape what counts as a legitimate object of historical study, and they define the terms on which we describe the relationship between the past and the present.

25. Schivelbusch, *The Railway Journey*, pp. 37–38.

26. Jonathan Sterne, *The Audible Past: Cultural Origins of Sound Reproduction* (Durham, NC: Duke University Press, 2003), pp. 147–148; John Wilson Townsend, *The Life of James Francis Leonard, the First Practical Sound-Reader of the Morse Telegraph* (Louisville: John. P. Morton, 1909).

27. Writers from a wide range of approaches to social theory have made this argument. See, e.g., Paul Baran and Paul Sweezy, *Monopoly Capital: An Essay on the American Social and Economic Order* (New York: Monthly Review Press, 1966); Fernand Braudel, "History and Social Science," in *Economy and Society in Early Modern Europe*, ed. Peter Burke (London: Routledge and Kegan Paul, 1972); Gilles Deleuze and Felix Guattari, *A Thousand Plateaus: Capitalism and Schizophrenia, Volume 2*, trans. Brian Massumi (Minneapolis: University of Minnesota Press, 1987); Giddens, *The Constitution of Society;*, C. Wright Mills, *The Sociological Imagination* (New York: Oxford University Press, 1959); Roberto Mangabeira Unger, *Social Theory: Its Situation and Task* (New York: Cambridge University Press, 1987).

28. Armand Mattelart, *The Invention of Communication*, trans. Susan Emmanuel (Minneapolis: University of Minnesota Press, 1996), pp. 48–49, Armand Mattelart, *Networking the World: 1794–2000*, trans. Liz Carey-Libbrecht and James A. Cohen

(Minneapolis: University of Minnesota Press, 2000), pp. 6–10. Original quote from Fernand Braudel, *Civilization and Capitalism: 15th–18th Century*, vol. 3, *The Perspective of the World*, trans. Sian Reynolds (New York: Harper and Row, 1981–1984), p. 543.

29. Charles H. Cooley, *Social Organization: A Study of the Larger Mind* (Glencoe, IL: Free Press, 1909); Deleuze and Guattari, *A Thousand Plateaus;* Gilroy, *The Black Atlantic;* Harold Innis, *The Bias of Communication* (Toronto: University of Toronto Press, 1951); C. L. R. James, *American Civilization* (Cambridge, England: Blackwell, 1993); Friedrich Kittler, *Gramophone-Film-Typewriter*, trans. Geoffrey Winthrop-Young and Michael Wutz (Stanford, CA: Stanford University Press, 1999).

30. Raymond Williams, *Television: Technology and Cultural Form* (Hanover, NH: Wesleyan University Press, 1974/1992), p. 20. Emphasis in original.

31. Carolyn Marvin, *When Old Technologies Were New: Thinking about Electrical Communication in the Nineteenth Century* (New York: Oxford University Press, 1988), pp. 63–108; David Nasaw, *Going Out: The Rise and Fall of Public Amusements* (New York: Basic, 1993).

32. It is also possible to read the telegraph as part of another transportation-communication network: bikes, roadways, and telegraphs go together as well as telegraphs and trains. In fact, Greg Downey has argued that the telegraph messenger boy was central to the function of the telegraph as a social system. As the telegraph messenger disappeared, so did the telegraph. See Gregory Downey, *Telegraph Messenger Boys* (New York: Routledge, 2002).

33. Carey, "Afterword," p. 322. This is to leave aside the contentious question of what constitutes a "national culture."

34. Walter Benjamin, *Illuminations*, trans. Harry Zohn (New York: Schocken, 1968), p. 221. In the notes to the "Work of Art" essay, Benjamin rightly points out that prior to mechanical reproduction, "aura" did not exist, as it is defined only by its absence. We might be inclined to make the same argument for the individual subject of conversational theory, but that would be an entirely different essay.

35. Peters, *Speaking into the Air.*

36. Georg Simmel, "The Metropolis and Mental Life," in *The Sociology of Georg Simmel*, ed. Kurt Wolff (New York: Free Press, 1950), p. 409.

37. Hannah Arendt, *The Human Condition* (Garden City, NY: Doubleday, 1958); Ruth Schwartz Cowan, *A Social History of American Technology* (New York: Oxford University Press, 1997); Karl Marx, *Capital, Volume I: A Critique of Political Economy* (New York: Penguin Classics, 1992); Dan Schiller, *Theorizing Communication: A History* (New York: Oxford University Press, 1996); Adam Smith, *An Inquiry into the Nature and Causes of the Wealth of Nations* (New York: Oxford University Press, 1993).

7. Technology and Ideology: The Case of the Telegraph Revisited

John Durham Peters

In this essay, I revisit James W. Carey's classic article on the telegraph.[1] His piece is a tour de force, an exemplar of what interesting communications history could be. Focusing on the United States, his piece treats the transformation of time, space, ideology, language, markets, journalism, and the sabbath in supple and elegant ways. It knocked my socks off when I first read it in a typescript draft in 1983—which Dean Carey, with characteristic generosity, had copied to give to a green young graduate student on a summer pilgrimage to Illinois—and there was a point when I had almost memorized it from teaching it so often. The telegraph, in his story, is the first full-blown instance of monopoly capitalism. It reorganizes the nature of the "commodity" as well as of business strategies and destroys the forms of journalistic storytelling that depend on incomplete verification, such as the tall tale and hoax (though the Internet brings the latter back in full force), as well as economic practices that depend on radically diverse pricing structures in local markets. Its separation of communication from transportation foreshadows the divorce of signifier and signified that is sometimes taken to be the mark of our age. The telegraph motivates the creation of standardized time. Carey's telegraph, though shrouded by flowery religious rhetoric at first, is an agent of the modern secular order, whose logic of space and time is homogeneous and whose empire is the grid. The notion of a sabbatical time-out, one day of seven, starts to wane with the Sunday paper (though its advertising sponsor, the department store, had something to do with that as well) as does the notion of temporal frontiers (such as nighttime) untouched by the reach of capitalism. Carey's essay is an implicit tribute to Harold Innis's analysis of the ways that technologies bias (push or pull) social, economic, political, cultural, and ultimately spatial and temporal organization, only with more supple prose and insight. The piece all but single-handedly rescued the telegraph

from scholarly neglect, raising it to its current status as the canonical foun-
tainhead of electronic media.

No one can do everything, even in an essay so chock-full of suggestion
that it deftly anticipates and outmaneuvers most criticisms one might want to
make of it, but there are many more stories to be told about the telegraph as
the intersection of ideology and technology. Electrical telegraphy sat at the
heart of the nineteenth-century revolution in the means of inscription. Its
practice of writing at a distance belongs to a family of new graphing machines
that sketched hitherto unrepresentable physiological and temporal processes.
Telegraphy shaped not only the outer world of culture and society, but the
inner engineering of media themselves. Telegraphy played a central role in
giving birth to new kinds of scientific instruments, in subdividing time, in
anticipating the processing (switching) infrastructure of the modern computer, and in inspiring Einstein's special theory of relativity. Telegraphy
helped redraw the map of the recordable and the transmittable. It put inner
and outer space, the human nervous system and the cosmos, into communication. This story becomes clearer by looking beyond Carey's focus on the
United States to Europe—and beyond his analytic preference for the human
world to the world of machines.

I proceed point by point, taking themes, arguments, or elements from
Carey's original essay. I draw on research done on media history in the past
two decades by German scholars inspired by the work of Friedrich Kittler,
especially the recent magisterial book by Bernhard Siegert on the history of
digital processing, *Passage des Digitalen* (2003).[2] This emerging body of
research completely rewrites the canon of media history in revolutionary
ways, and scholars in North America who share Carey's project, as I do, of
understanding how media technologies shape our times can find no more
illuminating and challenging sources. If Carey once nudged media history in
a Canadian direction, I would like to nudge it in a German one.

The Telegraph?

What Carey says about "technology"—that it is "too abstract a category to
support any precise analysis" (p. 205)—may also hold for "the telegraph."
Carey uses "the telegraph" as a wonderfully evocative net for catching lots of
cultural history fish. Rather like Wolfgang Schivelbusch's marvelous *Railway
Journey,* a book that, in turn, owes methodological inspiration to Walter Benjamin, the telegraph serves Carey as an analytic prism through which to
refract much of what we have learned to see as distinct in nineteenth-century
culture.[3] Carey uses the theoretical interests of his own moment as portals to
the past, as principles of selection for sorting his material. Carey, in this a
faithful disciple of John Dewey, regards the task of the historian as the clari-

fication of what in the past is alive in the present. The risk of this essentially Hegelian tactic is that the peculiarities and quirks of the past—what precisely does not survive the passage of time—can be lost from view. Such potential attrition is clearest in Carey's encompassing term, "the telegraph." He focuses on the electrical telegraph and mentions the Chappe brothers' optical telegraph from Napoleonic France, but the variety of telegraphic apparatuses in the nineteenth century quite overwhelms any single category. His essay is not deeply immersed in the technical discourses and practices of the age.[4] The abstraction in Carey's "telegraph" prematurely unifies a family of diverse devices and practices for sending intelligence at a distance. Optical, galvanic, magnetic, physiological, chemical, acoustic, and, of course, electromagnetic telegraphs abounded. Telegraphic devices sat at the center of a confused technical nexus: their designers understood them variously as extensions of the nervous system, clocks, compasses, musical instruments, the post, or writing machines, or, to be anachronistic, as telephones, phonographs, typewriters, and fax machines. Their readout could be dials, paper scrolls, or sounds. Their cargo could be signal, sound, text, voice, number, or random oscillation. They could be attached to frog-legs, fingertips, flames, guns, alarms, or pens. They could write and relay automatically or require the attention of human operators.[5]

Here it is wise to remember Lewis Mumford's advice to look for common uses behind technical diversity. The clepsydra, sundial, hourglass, wristwatch, and digital clock share little in common as machines and yet they share a crucial human need: the keeping and marking of time. (Hence my preference in what follows for the term "telegraphy" to mark a cluster of practices of distance writing over Carey's "the telegraph.") Further, it is an easy sport to move the level of magnification up or down a notch in order to accuse another scholar of either narrow focus or blurriness. Pragmatism and fractal geometry among other things have taught us that starting points and metrics are always contingent: any level of analysis obscures something and reveals something. The degree of abstraction is always a strategic choice and Carey's atmospheric take on the telegraph gives us a stunning landscape of nineteenth-century culture in general, but it doesn't tell us much about the era's machines or their ties to real bodies. There is more "ideology" than "technology" in Carey's mix, with consequences we shall explore.

"Our"

Carey's opening sentence refers to *The Education of Henry Adams* as "our most famous autobiography" (p. 201). I have often wondered who this "our," so generous, so inclusive, refers to. (I also rather like the inadvertent suggestion of a collective autobiography.) The essay, along with Carey's other work, makes clear that he means Americans. Fair enough, the essay was first written for an American studies annual, but Carey has always had a strong Americanist streak. His Americanism, he plausibly claims, is a "useful ethnocentrism" derived from the conviction that the United States is a privileged spot for seeing the modern world in action.[8] Whatever one thinks about an openly national(ist) focus, with its trace of a no longer fashionable American exceptionalism, telegraphy clearly had a different role, both in practice and theoretical imagination, in other parts of the world.[9] There is a tendency of Americanists to see capitalism as emerging in the nineteenth century rather than, say, the thirteenth and fourteenth, as it did in the city-states of northern Italy. Carey rightly insists that the United States has always been an experiment in communications, in the control of space and time, but he misses that this was true of the New World in general and well before 1776.[10] In sixteenth-century Spanish bureaucracy, for instance, maps, chronicles, and tables were the media by which "America," as part of the Spanish Empire, was simultaneously controlled and imagined.[11] The separation of paper and object for purposes of distant control is much older than the Morse code, and the European experience, at least, scrambles some of Carey's key claims, as I will show. To make a claim he doubtless would endorse, any future history of communications must be global and comparative, as difficult as that is in practice to achieve.

Historical Method

Carey generally deploys his "telegraph" as a point in a constellation, a Benjaminian monad through which a historical moment or field can be seen, rather than as a bald mover of history. Does he flirt with technological determinism? This has been a standard complaint of some of my graduate students. Technological determinism, like positivism, is a term of abuse. It is much easier to accuse other scholars of either "ism" than to figure out the precise role machines play in history or facts play in arguments. That both machines and facts play some kind of determinative role is a proposition no one seems ready to abandon, but watch out for the insults if you try to show how! Carey is too subtle a thinker to be tarred with any such label, though centering the story on "the telegraph" does superficially present the device as a prime mover. Though the essay treads lightly around causal attribution, preferring arguments from juxtaposition or affinity, there are occasional spots where "the telegraph" figures as a direct agent of historical rupture. "Before the telegraph, business relations were personal." After the telegraph, railroad, and similar innovations, the volume and complexity of business transactions required a new layer of impersonal managers (p. 205). Here we might rewrite one of Carey's sentences concerning the telegraph into a general maxim: "It is easy to overemphasize revolutionary consequences" (p. 203). That the transformations of nineteenth-century capitalism brought into being a new kind of managerial class is certainly true, but business has had an impersonal face as long as trading diasporas, shipping, and bookkeeping have existed. Indeed, as Max Weber argued, markets have always tended to foster open and impersonal relationships. Even if Carey means "face-to-face" by "personal," it is certainly not true that trade was always thus if we reflect on the historic economics of land or sea empires or even great cities. Impersonality is not exclusively modern, and it is not exclusively something to regret.

Here, briefly, Carey doesn't keep the facts from getting in the way of a good story, but otherwise one part of the genius of his method is linking historical particulars to larger scholarly arguments. The essay neatly invokes Innis on the penetration of the price system, E. P. Thompson on clock time and industrial capitalism, Benjamin on the decline of the aura, Marx on commodity fetishism, Chandler on the rise of the managed economy, the post-modernist horror (or thrill) that signifiers are empty, and the culturalist pathos that numbers are in the saddle and ride mankind (p. 222), among others. Carey shows how a long-forgotten relic can be made to speak to the pressing concerns of our own time.

Another strength of Carey's method is the rich use he gets out of economics, the topic of his dissertation and an ever-present strain in his thought. In light of some of the more frivolous boulevards cultural studies has promenaded down in the last two decades, the essay's grounding in the history of economic practices is most uncommon: we learn about commodity trading, futures, warrants, grading, arbitrage, pricing, and much more. (If only more cultural studies had gone this route!) Carey's work has always been an implicit refutation of the rather pointless tussle between cultural studies and political economy.[12] This essay is not at all the "idealist cultural studies" that some of his critics at Illinois and elsewhere liked to accuse him of at the time, though it is also clearly not Marxist political economy (which he lightly criticizes in turn on p. 205). In the heyday of ultrasophisticated neo-Marxist theorizing on ideology, hegemony, and other ways of seeing consciousness and culture as complicit with power, Carey's definition of "ideology" as "ordinary ideas" (p. 210) constituted almost fighting words. He bypasses ideology's theoretical thicket—and more power to him—and produces some real results, though he occasionally leaves "ideas" free of historical anchorage or agency, something bound to offend his more structuralist readers.

Organic Metaphors

The essay takes pains to refute the notion that the organicism in nineteenth-century U.S. social thought was a German import: "It was the telegraph and the railroad—the actual, painful construction of an integrated system—that provided the entrance gate for the organic metaphors that dominated nineteenth-century thought" (p. 215). Earlier he claims that "organic metaphors, so easily attributed to German philosophy, floated into American thought as means to describe how the telegraph would change life" (p. 207). The story is more complicated, and also more German, than Carey's floatation allows. One need not gesture to clouds of metaphors when there is so much evidence at hand about the cultural context in which telegraphic practices were received and developed.

Ever since the eighteenth century, electricity was connected closely to the human soul and body. Medical doctors such as Luigi Galvani understood electricity to be the body's vital principle, its means of animation, a notion that inspired Mary Shelley's *Frankenstein* (1818) and several stories by Edgar Allan Poe. Since Volta, physiological research and electrical innovation went hand in hand. Physiology and thermodynamics were two of the nineteenth-century's most innovative sciences, and both had intimate ties with telegraphic practices.[13] The notion that nerves are telegraphs, or better, that telegraphs are nerves, and that the body communicates with itself by electrical signals, prevailed in physiological thinking from the late eighteenth century through the early twentieth century, when the discovery of hormones gave another model for the body's self-regulation. The German physiologist and telegraph inventor Samuel Thomas Soemmering noted around 1809 that electrical telegraph wires are "a rough concrete (*sinnlich*) analogy for a nerve-cord."[14] Alfred Smee, a British polymath who, among other things, investigated the potato plant, founded modern first-aid practices, and developed counterfeit-resistant techniques for printing banknotes, noted in his popular treatise, *Instinct and Reason: Deduced from Electro-Biology* (1850): "In animal bodies we really have electro-telegraphic communication in the nervous system. That which is seen, or felt, or heard, is telegraphed to the brain *instanter*."[15] The great German scientist Hermann von Helmholtz, who measured the speed of signal propagation in frogs' nerves and studied the physiology of sensation as a media problem, likewise compared nerves to telegraph wires.[16] It is almost incorrect to say that these are metaphors, as it is utterly unclear what is literal and what is figurative. The body was not *like* a telegraph: it *was* an electrical system of signals and messages. The telegraph network was not like a body: it simply exhibited a homologous structure. The telegraph did not introduce physiological metaphors solo; physiology imported telegraph metaphors as well. Electrical telegraphy was a figure, a device for conjuring physical bodies and bodies politic, and it was born twins with physiological efforts to master electricity and harness the transmission of intelligence—whether we understand "intelligence" in the safe sense of information or the more daring sense of the human soul. There is even reason to claim Immanuel Kant as the inventor of the telegraph: he was the first to philosophize a world in which the transcendental conditions for human intelligence could be made physical. A promise that his disciple, the Danish philosopher-physicist Hans Christian Oersted, fulfilled in 1820 when he discovered electromagnetism.[17]

Marshall McLuhan claimed that media are extensions of human physiology, but when he said this, he unwittingly, as far as I can tell, built on a century and a half's worth of medical research on precisely the inverse: the human nervous system as an extension of media. As Stanford historian of science Timothy Lenoir remarks of Helmholtz, one of the greatest physiologists of the nineteenth century, "Telegraphic devices were not only important as means for representation and experiment; telegraphy embodied a system of signification that was central to Helmholtz's views about mental representations and their relationship to the world."[18] McLuhan was right to link media and physiology—all media are clearly designed as interfaces with human sensory organs—but he settled for poetic montage instead of historical knowledge. What later devolved into dead metaphors were once living connections. Nerves are not only metaphors; they are media. Physiologists were among the earliest telegraph inventors, and, even today, the connection persists in electrophysiology. Humans, like jellyfish, are electrical organisms, as nineteenth-century physicians, physicists, quacks, and inventors all insisted. Today, modern people are wired, inside and out. Carey is right to see the telegraph as a source of organic metaphors, but he misses that the organic was a source for telegraph metaphors.

Forms of Writing

In the wake of the telegraph, "older forms of language and writing declined" (p. 204). Let us consider writing first. Carey intends literary and journalistic genres of writing, but I want to suggest something more basic: that telegraphy helped inaugurate a new kind of writing, the tracing of fleeting processes. Telegraphs catch signals as well as throw them. Already in the two component parts of the name, "tele" and "graph," the communication innovations of the past two centuries are prefigured, the so-called conquest of distance and the explosion of new modes of inscription. We have "telescope," "telephone," "telepathy," "television" on the one hand; "phonograph," "seismograph," "electrocardiograph," "myograph" (muscle tension), "kymograph" (blood pressure), "polygraph," and "photograph" on the other. The "tele-" group transmits; the "-graph" group records. (Carey is more interested in the "tele" than the "graph.") These new graphic devices, which all arose from telegraphic experimentation, made it possible to record processes—such as voices, physiological events, the weather, and geological tremors—that hitherto escaped inscription or even notice. The writing these machines produced did not refer to a preexisting symbolic code (as of language). They were rather tracings ("translations" was the word preferred by the great French physiologist Etienne Jules Marey) written by the body itself without the superintendence of a human author or intervention of a doctor's scalpel. As Siegert notes, "A new analog inscription system coaxes bodies to confess the life-processes that occur in them. The graphic method as the handwriting of life, as language, in which the body itself betrays its secrets, constitutes the discipline of physiology as a science just as a scarce hundred years before the intimate diary, the autobiography and the private letter constituted psychology."[19]

Marey, who held a chair at the Collège de France in the exquisitely named field "the natural history of organized bodies," dubbed the tracing of breath, blood pressure, muscle twitches, and other physiological events "the graphic method" in 1878, the same year that Edison invented the phonograph.[20] We sometimes forget that Edison was a telegraphist as a youth and nicknamed his son and daughter Dot and Dash: telegraphy was the seedbed of his inventions. The phonograph was first intended as an improvement of the telegraph. By making a device that would store and not only send messages, he wanted to solve the problem of signal dissipation: "repeaters," whether human or electromechanical, were needed to reinforce the signal at intervals along the line. The urge to get signals to survive the transit across space inspired a device that preserves them across time. Edison saw the reversibility of transmission and recording: to send a message across a distance required some means of preserving it from decay. A phonograph is a telegraph inside out, a sender that keeps on sending, an infinite repeater. Transmission implies recording. Similarly, a telegraph can be understood as a very fast phonograph whose playback occurs only once. Recording implies transmission. Edison's phonograph belongs very much to the family of physiological tracers. It allowed the direct capture of sound waves without regard for their intelligibility or obedience to a linguistic system of meaning. Snorts, sighs, sobs, and any other vocalization could be bottled up in full fidelity, as could the peculiar contingencies of the voice (breathing, pitch, prosody, and accent). Sound in general, intelligible or not, became writable.[21]

The telegraph is a writing machine, a modality of inscription, that aids the diversification, radicalization, and multiplication of writing as a medium of recording. It enabled a whole series of graphing machines that could measure minute electrical and temporal variations of bodies of various sorts. Processes whose traces were hitherto confined to the live action of the event, the dead letter of written language, or the faint afterglow of a witness's memory became textual or at least graphic. Galileo famously compared nature to a book and discovery to the reading of the characters that God had written there. Telegraphy enabled the universe of bodies and processes to write itself in unprecedented ways. Those scrolls of paper that record our EKG (heart) and EEG (brain) processes, program player pianos, fill adding machines and cash registers, and inspired Turing's dream of a universal discrete machine, originate in telegraphy. From its beginnings, writing has been a means of both numerical calculation and diagrammatic illustration and not only a storehouse for speech.[22] Telegraphy helped writing recover an older possibility, the analog recording of nonlinguistic patterns. The graphic method escaped "the needle's eye of the signifier."[23] The new kinds of tele-graphing transcended the human nexus, the limitations of speed and fatigue imposed by hand, ear, mouth, and brain. Telegraphy made clear the discrepancy between the processing speed of the human nervous system and the speed of electrical signals: there were upper limits, neurophysiological in nature, to the speed by which operators, like electrical secretaries, could take down telegraphic dictations.

Phonography, like other automatic writing devices connected to telegraphs, was an effort to compensate for human finitude. For reasons of profit and efficiency alone, telegraph designers were in the business of seeking forms of automatic writing from the very beginning. The telegraph was always a writing machine and never only a transmitting machine: Edison's phonograph is the telegraph's Siamese twin, a telegraph capable of time-axis manipulation.[24] Quite like the camera, telegraphic devices were part of a writing/graphing revolution in which inscription of intelligence became possible apart from a human consciousness. Cameras, phonographs, and seismographs catch whatever comes their way, whether it makes sense to humans or not. Artificial intelligence is much older than the computer as we know it, and telegraphy inaugurated a world of lively writing-machines, alertly watching the world, tracing weather, stars, and the stock market in scribbles, patterns, and languages—and in quantities and speeds—not directly designed for human intelligibility. The order of the universe is not necessary located in human intelligence.

Forms of Language

Carey briefly notes that telegraphy inspired "a digital model of language" (p. 229), but says little more. In fact, telegraphic practices were central to the constitution of the phoneme, perhaps the key concept in the formation of the modern science of linguistics. As Harvard historian of science Robert Brain shows, telegraphy was a key thing to think with for such linguists as Michel Bréal, the foremost institutional figure in late-nineteenth-century French philology. "Articulate sounds, elementary phonemes, or entire words, thereby became analogies to the dots and dashes transmitted by cable throughout the French Empire. 'Words . . . are like telegraphic signals,' wrote Bréal." The phonograph was also important, as Bréal sent his colleagues into the provinces armed with phonographs to harvest the vowel sounds made in regional dialects. Working directly with Marey, Bréal's associates sought to overturn the preference for textual study and auto-experiment in German linguistics and instead attempted to capture speech as a physical-acoustic process. The graphic method went on the road; the physiological laboratory went into the field to study voices, tongues, and throats as it had blood and breath. "This inscriptive apparatus, then, rendered the hitherto fleeting phenomena of speech into materialized scientific objects: the phonemes." The phoneme was constituted as an object, and first named, in the process of being graphically inscribed in 1870s and 1880s France.[25]

For Ferdinand de Saussure, who time has treated more kindly than Bréal thanks to his seminal influence on French structuralism, telegraphy helped to model language. As he wrote in his famous *Cours de linguistique générale,* a posthumous edition of his lectures from the 1910s, "The vocal organs are just as external to language as the electrical means that serve to transcribe the Morse alphabet are strangers to this alphabet." Electrical telegraphy—with its break between mechanism and message—served Saussure as a model for the distinction between sound and sense, phonation and meaning—that is, the signifier and the signified. Saussure's circuit model of communication likewise owes something to telegraphy, though it seems even more like a telephone. Saussure's conception of the phoneme as the "sum of acoustic impressions" suggests the signal-shaving that telegraphy trafficked in.[26] Telecommunications machines and phonology have the same presupposition: that sound serves intelligibility of signals, not richness of aesthetic quality. Saussure, from his 1879 dissertation on ancient Indo-European vowel structure through his lectures on general linguistics, was essentially a theorist of sound and its articulations. His phonology belongs to a world of telegraphs, telephones, and phonographs.

Here it is important to remind ourselves that telegraphy, from its beginnings as the "singing wire," was an acoustic as well as graphic device. Anthony Trollope's story "The Telegraph Girl" (1877) treats the transition in British telegraphy from using the eye to the ear for recording messages: young women had to move from reading paper spools to hearing tinkling sound signals.[27] Charles Wheatstone, one of several men who can lay claim to being the father of telegraphy, was a musician by training who invented the concertina and got interested in telegraphy through his experiments with acoustics. Helmholtz used telegraphic apparatus in the 1840s and 1850s to produce vowel sounds and musical pitches. The electrical telegraph was a vibrating wire and not only a pipe for electrical pulses. The telegraph was a sound articulator and not just signal carrier, an intermediate link in a line of speech machines from Wolfgang von Kempelen's artificial voice to the phonograph. Saussure's conception of sound as signal may be part of what Carey meant by a digital model of language.

The Constraints of Geography

Central to Carey's argument is the idea that the telegraph ended the identity of "communication" and "transportation" and freed the former from "the constraints of geography" (p. 204). Symbols could now move quickly and independently of bodies. This is not merely a metaphysical break, in which lightning is harnessed for human purposes, but a new option in political-economic management as well: "not only can information move independently of and faster than physical entities, but it can also be a simulation of and control mechanism for what has been left behind." He calls this the "fundamental discovery" of the telegraph" (p. 215). Though Carey clearly knows of carrier pigeons, line-of-sight signaling, and other pre-electrical forms of distant signaling, he overloads the telegraph with a historical burden. Accountants had figured out similar techniques of control and simulation at a distance centuries earlier. Writing of nascent merchant capitalism in thirteenth- and fourteenth-century Europe, Siegert uses language uncannily close to Carey's (without knowing his work):

> Double-entry bookkeeping makes it possible for the merchant to substitute control of a large area with control of calculating operations on paper. The transportation of numbers replaces the transportation of goods. The actual business takes place on paper, and the real transportation of real goods in extended trade becomes increasingly separated—temporally, spatially, and semiotically—from the business operations in the bureau. The sphere of the signifier becomes deterritorialized from that of the signified.[28]

Granted, electrical telegraphy is a quantum leap in terms of speed of feedback, but the separation of receipt from product and the steering of business operations over expanses of time and space is as old as capitalism and may well be older. That "the buying and selling is not of goods but of receipts" (p. 220) might be said of Babylonian granaries as well as the Chicago commodity exchange.

In history writing one has to balance a preference for breaks or continuities. Carey's story about the telegraph emphasizes its historical ruptures; I would rather emphasize its long prehistory.

The Economy of a Signal

In his thesis of a separation between communication and transportation

Carey flirts with a "fantasy of friction-less transmission."[29] To some extent he does so simply as a student of the rhetoric of the technological sublime in which communication is an ethereal affair, the swift spirit sundered from the solid flesh. At other points in the essay, he does seem to believe in the essential spirituality of the signal: "The telegraph puts everyone in the same place for purposes of trade; it makes geography irrelevant" (p. 217). His "everyone" riles the Marxist and feminist conscience, and geography, as Carey has since emphasized, has not vanished as a decisive factor in social life.[30] He seems to hold to the theoretical possibility at least of symbols without a material anchor besides electricity, of communication free of transportation. I would argue instead that communication always has friction, however infinitesimal. Obviously, there is the issue of expense: telegraphy subdivided letters and words into units of price. Throughout most of the nineteenth century, access to telegraphic transmission was restricted to the middle class and especially the business class. Though, as Menachem Blondheim discovered, the American wire services, coupling electrical telegraphy with newspapers, enabled the first national news network in the late nineteenth century, decades before the conventional wisdom that radio provided the first up-to-date nationwide grid for integrated communication.[31] (Thus, telegraphy was a medium of broadcasting as well as point-to-point communication.) There is also the more subtle point that communication always has attention or surveillance costs, something that Charles Babbage, the forefather of the computer, noted in his 1820s work on manufacturing. He anticipated a principle that became a cornerstone of modern physics from Maxwell's demon to Heisenberg's uncertainty principle: there is no observation without perturbation. Babbage is the true prophet of the control revolution, of cybernetic command and control in industry. Information never lacks a body: there is always entropic drag. The friction of transporting information may be infinitesimally small compared to transporting cargo, but all kinds of mischief can happen inside of infinitesimally small things.

Changing Concepts of Time

Time is one of Carey's distinctive preoccupations, including his latest fascination with Internet time. For him the telegraph made standard time possible. Whereas each municipality had once set its own clock, making noon the moment of the shortest shadow, the telegraph enabled nation-states to synchronize and coordinate time on a national scale. He focuses on the railroad, the chief mover for North America, but in England, the Netherlands, and elsewhere, maritime coordination was equally important. England's Greenwich Observatory had been trying to coordinate time for much of the nineteenth century across sky, land, and sea. Electrical telegraphy helped signals leap the miles so that a slave clock (as the terminology had it) in Bristol, say, could be ruled by the master clock in Greenwich. Restating Carey, the telegraph allowed the apparent possibility of simultaneity. Point A and point B could be in communicative contact at the very same time. The circumference of local time could be expanded to include the entire world, as the world eventually came to use one standard clock (with a few significant deviations).

Telegraphy not only led to the standardization of time it provided the technical and imaginative means for exploring huge and tiny units of time. Telegraphic devices helped change the way we think about microcosmic and macrocosmic time. Early on, people realized that telegraphy offered ways to measure both extremely fast speeds and extremely small intervals of time. As Carey remarks, "Time has been redefined as an ecological niche to be filled down to the microsecond, nanosecond, and picosecond" (p. 228). An interval of time is also a measurement of speed—the shutter speed of a camera or the observation speed of a process. Helmholtz's circle in the 1840s and 1850s was fascinated by telegraphy's ability not only to provide graphic representations of fast processes but also to mark minute intervals of time; Helmholtz aptly called this project "the microscopy of time."[32] (Werner Siemens, the founder of the huge electrical concern by the same name and the chief introducer of electrical telegraphy into Germany, was a colleague of Helmholtz.) Modernity is marked by an interest in small units of time. Walter Benjamin famously wrote that the camera exploded reality with "the dynamite of a tenth of a second," a relatively modest interval.[33] Roget, of thesaurus fame, measured in the 1820s the temporal acuity of the retina, the famous 1/24 of a second that is still exploited when we watch a movie. Helmholtz, using his great array of devices, found that the ear is enormously faster than the eye in its time perception, something astronomers already knew: the ear's acuity ranges from 1/100 to 1/1,000 of a second (the latter is an interval that trained studio engineers can reportedly hear). Neurons may process in microseconds. Nanoseconds (10^{-9}, one billionth) are the standard unit for RAM speed, logical operations in digital circuits. Laser scientists use femtoseconds (10^{-15}) and photon researchers use attoseconds (10^{-18}). As George Dyson remarks, there is plenty of room at the bottom.[34] We can now represent and intervene in processes that occur in those intervals (which is to say, at those speeds). Curiously, there seems to be a lower limit, the so-called Planck time, 1.38 x 10^{-43} seconds, beyond which temporal subdivision cannot pass. We no longer live in the continuous, analog, infinitesimal universe dreamed of by nineteenth-century luminaries such as Laplace, Babbage, Marey, or Peirce. Ours is one of quanta, bits, and digits, a world jagged and fractally stepwise at the lowest—at all—levels of analysis.

In its automation of fast switching in small temporal intervals, electrical telegraphy was the forerunner of the modern computer, as Carey notes (p.

229). Edison invented the most successful version of quadriplexing, which separated telegraph signals into distinct parts that can be dispersed across wires and then be reassembled again. Packet switching, as we now call it, took early forms in telegraph nodes, the places where signal and text were turned into each other briefly. As Dyson says in *Darwin among the Machines*, an astonishing book that I recommend to anyone interested in pondering the large meaning of computers, "High-speed automatic telegraph instruments were ancestors of modern computers . . . the code itself and the protocols that regulate its flow [in computers] remain directly descended from the first strings of telegraphic bits."[35] A computer chip is something like a shrunken version of the nationwide or worldwide network of telegraphy, without the vulnerability of wires and the fallibilities (and slowness) of human operators. The high-speed signal processing of telegraphic devices contributed not only, again, to the spanning of space but the subdivision of time. Today processor speed is the measure of the power (and sexiness) of personal computers: people brag about their computer's ability to work at the smallest possible intervals of time.

Relativity: Communication and Transportation Again

The illusion that no time elapsed between sending and receiving was central to the fantasy of frictionless transmission, as in Alfred Smee's idea that nerves could carry messages from limb to brain instantly. In the 1830s, Charles Wheatstone tested the speed of electrical propagation. In a sense, he was measuring the possibility of simultaneity. Using a spinning mirror apparatus that allowed him to see electrical sparks (which he sent both through the air and along a prototelegraph wire) at intervals as small as $1/152,000$ of a second, he found that there was a lapse of time, however small, in electrical transmission. One can hardly overestimate the importance of his discovery: all communication, even electrical, takes time, however slight. Electrical signals may be relatively free of the burdens of transportation across space, but they are not free of the cost of transportation across time. All messages must pay a toll to time.

Someone who thought more deeply than anyone about the cost of transportation across time was a young patent clerk in Bern, Switzerland, named Albert Einstein. Relativity theory, like Wheatstone's experiments, turns on the minute slivers of time that lie between supposed simultaneities. Einstein faced the problem that the universe can communicate with itself only at finite speeds. Information can move no faster than the speed of light. On a cosmic scale, this is not very fast. The standard story of Einstein's discovery of special relativity in 1905—a story he himself actively spread—has him as a lonely, bored genius dreaming away of space and time in the patent office in Bern,

Switzerland, his talent being wasted, like that of Kafka, in the service of middle-European bureaucracy. In fact, as Peter Galison convincingly shows, Einstein was not a solitary brain thinking great thoughts but an expert situated at the heart of modern media and machines. Though trained as a physicist, Einstein achieved a high degree of competence as an electrical engineer. Einstein was working in the great homeland of clocks, Switzerland; his specific assignment was the review of patent applications involving the nexus of the clock and the telegraph. Einstein reviewed proposals for signal amplifiers and switching relays that linked clocks into national and international grids—devices that, transfigured to a higher level of abstraction, provided the imaginative context for relativity theory. The question of "distant simultaneity"—for example, how can two remote clocks be synchronized given that it takes time for light or any other signal to communicate between the two—was not only the founding question of relativity theory; it was the question that kept Einstein busy on a daily basis. The Bern patent office was no backwater; it was, as Galison says, "a grandstand seat for the great parade of modern technologies."[36]

One can hardly imagine relativity theory, or its mathematical ancilla, non-Euclidean geometry, without telegraphy and other nineteenth-century revolutions in space and time. The examples that inform relativity theory—elevators, train schedules, flashlights, synchronized watches, space travel—do not simply offer good things to think with but point to the theory's very transportational conditions of possibility. Einstein was a modern man living in a plastic world of space and time. His great discovery was, as he put it in a 1905 note to a friend, that "there is an inseparable relation between time and signal velocity."[37] This impossibly brilliant insight makes metaphysical profit out of telegraphic engineering. Time can move no faster than communication. For Newton, gravity operated instantaneously, irrespective of distance. He allowed, essentially, for division by zero (velocity is distance divided by time elapsed, and an instantaneous movement would take no time at all). For Einstein, gravity is not an action at distance but a warping of the time-space field; information from a massive object's movement can travel no faster than the speed of light. Information and gravity—message and medium—move inseparably. Relativity is a theory of communication, more specifically, of the universe's difficulty of communicating with itself. There is no cosmic telegraph to synchronize clocks at distant spots.

Einstein's universe, curiously enough, looks more like the old order of clock time before railroad time, when every town had its own local time, than like the Newtonian regime of Greenwich mean time, by which the whole planet is centrally coordinated in a single grid. There is no possibility of a single "now" that pervades the universe. Every now has a radius of dissipation. Time perhaps has a broadcast "footprint" like a satellite. "Now" can stretch only as far as signals can carry. The universe is bounded by the speed of its transmissions. Any signal has a velocity and its transmission costs time. Signal and being always travel in tandem.

Sociologically, electrical telegraphy might have separated communication and transportation, but cosmologically, it married them. Any signal drags across time. Clocks and telegraphs, in short, taught Einstein not the decisive separation of communication and transportation but their eternal fusion.

Conclusion

Carey has had an enormous influence in shaping the canon of communication studies, both in the ways we think about the cultural history of media and the intellectual history of media studies. He was a key mover in the theoretical renaissance of the 1970s and 1980s in media studies. His own idiosyncratic, humane brand of what he still bravely, doggedly calls cultural studies was for many of us like oxygen in a stale intellectual space. His democratic politics and sinuously ambivalent treatment of modernity have permanently benefited the field. Though I hesitate to criticize a friend and mentor who has done so much in so many ways to advance my own thinking and career, the only proper tribute for a street-fighter and democrat, both of which Carey fiercely is, is a direct confrontation.

Carey taught us (there's that generous we again—here I mean media scholars) to see the names McLuhan and Innis as markers of tendencies in media history. One focused on psychic and sensory integration, the other on social and political organization. McLuhan was frivolous, and Innis had gravitas, and it is easy to prefer the latter for reasons of scholarly soundness.[38] But an Innis-style approach has its limits. Like Innis, Carey invests a deep moral pathos in forms of communication that makes him vulnerable to a certain kind of yearning or wistfulness about modern science and technology. Carey's telegraph never gets under our skins: it remains safely external—social, economic, and infrastructural. Its challenge to the human soul is not grasped except as degradation or loss. The doctor and physiologist William James, whom I much prefer to Carey's choice of John Dewey as a pragmatist hero, recognized that the human body and even the human mind are machines to some degree. Dewey hardly touched the world of machines except to lament the social disruptions of steam and electricity. James directly grasped the nettle of the new psychophysical universe in which nerves were wires and wires were nerves, in which the human soul could be plugged into electrical outlets. He did not wish away the fact that modern electrical media engineer the sensorium and brought Hugo Münsterberg, the inventor of the perfect coinage "psychotechnik" (technologies of the psyche) to join him at Harvard. Of Helmholtz's measurement of speed of nervous signals, James wrote: "The phrase 'quick as thought' had from time immemorial signified all that was wonderful and elusive of determination in the line of speed, and the way in which Science laid her doomful hand upon this mystery reminded people of the day when Franklin first 'eripuit caelo fulmen' [pulled fire from heaven], foreshadowing the reign of a newer and colder race of gods."[39] James found ways to be both a tough-minded and tender-minded human being in the company of this colder race of gods. To probe the guts of electrical machines is, in some way, also to examine the circuits of our own psyches. The burning questions about telegraphy and modern electrical media in general cannot be answered by social and economic history alone: we need some mathematics, medicine, physics, and engineering to grasp what happened to the body, the soul, and the cosmos.

Notes

1. The essay was published in two rounds. First in *Prospects,* vol. 8, ed. Jack Saltzman (1983): 303–325, and then in a revised and expanded version in *Communication as Culture: Essays on Media and Society* (Boston: Unwin Hyman, 1989), pp. 201–230, which incorporated parts of an earlier essay of his on Innis. Parenthetical citations in the text refer to the latter source.

2. Bernhard Siegert, *Passage des Digitalen: Zeichenpraktiken der neuzeitlichen Wissenschaften, 1500–1900* (Berlin: Brinkmann und Bose, 2003).

3. *The Railway Journey: The Industrialization of Space and Time in the 19th Century* (1977; Berkeley: University of California Press, 1986).

4. This fault is even more extreme in my own brief, inadequate treatment of telegraphy in *Speaking into the Air* (Chicago: University of Chicago Press, 1999), pp. 94–95, 138–140. The present essay is partial penance.

5. For a survey, see Volker Aschoff, *Geschichte der Nachrichtentechnik,* vol. 2, *Nachrichtentechnische Entwicklungen in der ersten Hälfte des 19. Jahrhunderts* (Berlin: Springer, 1989).

6. Lewis Mumford, *The Pentagon of Power* (New York: Harcourt Brace, 1970), pp. 89–90.

7. A point Carey makes eloquently in "Reconceiving 'Mass' and 'Media,'" *Communication as Culture,* pp. 70–74.

8. "Introduction," *Communication as Culture,* p. 1. See also James W. Carey, "The Communications Revolution and the Professional Communicator," *The Sociological Review,* no. 13 (1969): 23; *Communication as Culture,* pp. 96–97.

9. Carey gives us an American exceptionalism "shorn of hubris." See Kenneth Cmiel, "Review of 'Communication as Culture,'" *Theory and Society* 21 (1992): 285–290.

10. "Introduction," *Communication as Culture,* pp. 2–9.

11. Siegert, *Passage des Digitalen,* pp. 65–120.

12. Carey's attempt to play umpire can be seen in "Abolishing the Old Spirit World," *Critical Studies in Mass Communication* 12 (1995): 82–89.

13. On physiology, see Siegert, *Passage des Digitalen,* pp. 267–304, 350–369; on thermodynamics, see Crosbie Smith and M. Norton Wise, *Energy and Empire: A Bio-*

graphical Study of Lord Kelvin (Cambridge, England: Cambridge University Press, 1989), esp. chs. 13, 19, and 20.

14. Quoted in Siegert, *Passage des Digitalen,* p. 363.

15. Alfred Smee, FRS, *Instinct and Reason: Deduced from Electro-Biology* (London: Reeve, Benham, and Reeve, 1850), 97. See also George Dyson, *Darwin among the Machines* (Cambridge, MA: Perseus, 1997), pp. 45–48.

16. Hermann von Helmholtz, *On the Sensations of Tone as a Physiological Basis for the Theory of Music* (1877; New York: Dover, 1954), p. 149. On Helmholtz as a media theorist, see my "Helmholtz, Edison, and Sound History," *Memory Bytes,* ed. Lauren Rabinovitz and Abraham Geil (Durham, NC: Duke University Press, 2004), pp. 177–198; Siegert, *Passage des Digitalen,* pp. 363–368; and Timothy Lenoir, "Helmholtz and the Materialities of Communication," *Osiris* 9 (1994): 185–207.

17. Siegert, *Passage des Digitalen,* p. 292.

18. Lenoir, "Helmholtz and the Materialities of Communication," 206–207.

19. Bernhard Siegert, "Schein versus Simulation, Kritik versus Dekonstruktion," *Die Experimentalisierung des Lebens: Experimentalsysteme in den biologischen Wissenschaften 1850/1950,* ed. Hans-Jörg Rheinberger and Michael Hagner (Berlin: Akademie, 1993), p. 232.

20. Etienne J. Marey, *La méthode graphique dans les sciences experimentales et principalement en physiologie et en médecine* (Paris: G. Masson, 1878).

21. See Friedrich A. Kittler, *Gramophone, Film, Typewriter,* trans. Geoffrey Winthrop-Young and Michael Wutz (1986; Stanford, CA: Stanford University Press, 1999), esp. pp. 26–29, 44–45, 83–87.

22. Siegert, *Passage des Digitalen,* pp. 32–41.

23. Winthrop-Young and Wutz, "Translators' Introduction," *Gramophone, Film, Typewriter.*

24. Kittler, *Gramophone, Film, Typewriter,* pp. 35–36.

25. Robert Brain, "Standards and Semiotics," *Inscribing Science: Scientific Texts and the Materiality of Communication,* ed. Timothy Lenoir (Stanford, CA: Stanford University Press, 1998), pp. 249–284, at 252, 261.

26. Ferdinand de Saussure, *Cours de linguistic générale* (Paris: Payot, 1972), pp. 36, 65. See especially the two figures on pp. 27 and 28.

27. Anthony Trollope, "The Telegraph Girl" (1877), *Why Frau Frohmann Raised Her Prices and Other Stories* (1882; New York: Arno, 1981), pp. 263–319.

28. Siegert, *Passage des Digitalen,* p. 43.

29. Siegert, *Passage des Digitalen,* p. 360.

30. The persistence of geographically based social inequality was a theme of his keynote address to the American Studies Association in Tampere, Finland, April 1999.

31. Menachem Blondheim, *News over the Wires: The Telegraph and the Flow of Public Information in America, 1844–1897* (Cambridge, MA: Harvard University Press, 1994).

32. Timothy Lenoir, "Farbensehen, Tonempfindung und der Telegraph: Helmholtz und die Materialität der Kommunikation," *Die Experimentalisierung des Lebens*p. 53.

33. Walter Benjamin, "The Work of Art in the Age of Mechanical Reproduction," *Illuminations* (1936; New York: Schocken, 1968), p. 236.

34. Dyson, *Darwin among the Machines,* ch. 10.

35. Dyson, *Darwin among the Machines,* pp. 143, 144.

36. Peter Galison, "Einstein's Clocks: The Place of Time," *Critical Inquiry* 26 (2000): 355–389. See also his *Einstein's Clocks, Poincaré's Maps* (New York: Norton, 2003). This and the next paragraph I have taken the liberty of reworking from my "Time, Space, and Communication Theory," *Canadian Journal of Communication 28* (2003): 397–411. With apologies to and in tribute of Carey's own self-borrowing at the end of the telegraph essay.
37. Galison, "Einstein's Clocks," 375.
38. James W. Carey, "Harold Adams Innis and Marshall McLuhan," *Antioch Review,* 27 (Spring 1967): 5–39.
39. William James, *The Principles of Psychology,* Vol. 1. (1890; New York: Dover, 1950), pp. 85–6.

8. The Public and the Party Period

JOHN NERONE

The decline of public life is a recurring theme in James Carey's work. A convivial democratic culture has succumbed to professionalization and mobile privatization; the mangled body of journalism is the corpus delicti. Carey summarizes this account best in his 1979 presidential address to the Association for Education in Journalism, "A Plea for the University Tradition."[1] Invoking Harold Adam Innis, he suggests that transmission technologies (both communication and transportation) have reconstructed public space and public discourse, undermining the hope of Dewey and others in the ability of free communities to build institutions of rational and democratic public life. Instead, increasing efficiencies threaten the oral habits and traditions upon which democracy depends. The professionalization of journalism is a symptom of this disease.

Carey's account moves from a convivial eighteenth-century urbanism to a privatized twentieth-century suburbanism. In Revolutionary-era cities such as Philadelphia, a dense network of public spaces—taverns and coffeehouses, public meeting houses and commercial exchanges, churches and civic groups—allowed for the civic engagement that republican governance presupposes. Then came a series of technological innovations, culminating in the domestic technologies interwoven into ordinary suburban homes by the end of World War II. Each of these technologies appropriated a piece of public space. The automobile brought the trolley into the garage; the telephone brought the town square in the living room; the refrigerator brought the market into the kitchen; the television brought the movie theater into the living room. These new necessities allowed people to stay ensconced in private life, leaving only sporadically to fill a specific need from an increasingly specialized service sector.

Carey suggests that communication technologies and practices anchored this transformation. New transmission tools made former ritual practices less viable. In another influential essay, Carey interrogated the cultural impact of the telegraph, arguing, along with Wolfgang Schivelbusch and in a frame suggested by Innis, that the railroad and telegraph system understood together had reshaped the spatial and temporal matrix of national life.[2] Again, the argument moved from technology to journalism. The telegraph revolutionized the culture of journalism by introducing costs and scarcities, producing a particular economy of words and a uniquely spare and staccato writing style that drove a fact-based and finally objective news discourse.

Carey proposes a history of the nexus of communication and transportation technologies, the public sphere, and journalism. It is not a very happy history. Improvements in transmission capacity eclipse the abilities of local communities and finally the national political community to ritually recreate themselves. The most painful site of this pathology is in the news discourse that had grown up around print media. Carey's work describes the death of the newspaper. In the modern space of mobile privatization, newspapers resisted the fragmentation of civic space—helped ironically by conditions rendering them local monopolies—but eventually ceased to generate citizen identities and instead became an appliance. It is suitable that Carey found himself among the Committee of Concerned Journalists—one of the few members of that group who lacked working-press credentials—pleading for a movement to rescue journalism from "the media."[3]

Carey's history dwells on the gulf between eighteenth-century ideals and twentieth-century social facts. When these collided, obviously, was in the nineteenth century. Public discourse walked healthy into the nineteenth century and staggered out crippled—eyes gouged out, tongue ripped loose, backbone neatly removed. Work in the history of the public sphere in the past generation has assembled a host of suspects accused of committing this mutilation. In this essay, I'll focus on the party press that flourished from the 1820s to the 1890s in the United States.

In the years since the translation of Jurgen Habermas's *Structural Transformation of the Public Sphere* (1989), an idealized version of the party period has often been conflated with an idealized version of a popularized public sphere. Scholars see the parties inviting citizens to vote through entertaining spectacles and also enticing them to participate continuously in the affairs of party through membership on committees and attendance at conventions and caucuses. In these wistful accounts, the party period produced high voter turnout because the parties and the political system as a whole were more open and more responsive, and therefore genuinely more popular, than later systems.[4] Not that Habermas suggests this to be the case. In his account, the arrival of mass politics meant the erosion of the wall of separation between civil society and the public sphere, turning the public sphere into a political marketplace. But among practicing historians, Habermas's sense of decline has been negated by admiration for the attack on privilege in the party system. These historians emphasize the ways party politics freed individuals from class restrictions, encouraged economic mobility and dynamism, and sparked movements to eliminate racial and gender restrictions—all elements of a "liberal" politics, as opposed to the "republican" vision often attributed to earlier politics, which emphasized virtue and the communal nature of freedom and thereby endorsed some forms of privilege. The Habermasian version of the public sphere, though, is more at home with republicanism. Rational public discourse requires that all points of view be responsibly debated, not that every individual citizen be free to grind one's axe.[5]

The rapid spread of a popular press supports the current admiration of the party period. In earlier "progressive" journalism histories, the party press played the villain's role, retarding the realization of the true potential of independent journalism.[6] In key works of the 1970s, the pivotal role of market-oriented newspapers, especially penny papers, continued to be understood as liberating journalism from parties.[7] But historians have reevaluated the work of the party press and find it more enduring, popular, and democratic than journalism historians have acknowledged[8] and have challenged the neat opposition between party and penny press.

This trinity of party, press, and public sphere makes for a nifty target. Like contemporary criticisms of the decline of civic culture, the scholarship on the party period can easily seem to share the romanticism and chauvinism of pleadings for "social capital."[9] Surely the antebellum Democratic Party is as scoffable as the post–World War II Lion's Club or American Legion, the prior vitality of which commands our nostalgia not so much because we want to join them but because we'd be so much happier if we still had them to piss on. The American Legion was no more a facilitator of the public sphere than the party of James Buchanan. Both displayed and encouraged extreme intolerance for the activists most admired by public sphere theorists—abolitionists and socialists, who laid the groundwork for twentieth-century notions of free speech.[10] Not to mention how they treated women and people of color, who were lavish in their condemnations of the party press.

Recently a counternarrative of the party period has appeared. Two works in particular offer round refutations of what they take as the new orthodoxy: Michael Schudson's *The Good Citizen* and Glenn Altschuler and Stuart Blumin's *Rude Republic*. Both are the work of senior scholars, both have percolated for quite some time through the grounds of the civic culture–public sphere discourse, and both offer, along with their historical rebuttals, more than a whiff of a counterpolitics. Schudson's is the distillation of a career's work in the history of the news media, combining an update of his earlier narrative in *Discovering the News* (still the default cite for a master narrative of the history of U.S. journalism) with a reprise of his engagement in the Jurgen-fest of the 1990s. Altschuler and Blumin, by contrast, bludgeon the party period to death with the blunt instrument of content analysis. Despite their differences, the two books seem to work in tandem.[11] Together they dismantle the image of the party period as an exemplar of grassroots democracy. Both note that it took the urgent ministrations of party professionals to make the system appear to work from the bottom up; both note that ordinary people as well as elites found much humbuggery and deceit in the workings of the electoral system. So the counternarrative they suggest is a story of the relationship between a disengaged populace and a manipulated spectacle of public engagement. The counterpolitics they insinuate is more disengagement. Knowing that our nineteenth-century predecessors were skeptical of politics should make us less concerned about the cynicism and disillusionment of our own generation. The political system is designed for people concerned with their own individual and familial welfare. Don't worry, Jurgen, be happy.

The antithesis between party period romanticization and its counternarrative hasn't done much to advance our understanding of the nineteenth-century public sphere. It discourages a more nuanced appreciation of the working of the party press. It also diverts attention from the very real structural transformation of the mainstream press in the years generally covered by the term "party period." And it drives out, as by a kind of ideological Gresham's law, all but the most simplistic lessons of this history for latter-day politics.

This essay suggests some adjustments to this argument. The party period straddled vast changes in the news system—particularly the shift from a press-post system to a telegraphic one—and the readjustment of the relationship between the news and editorial functions of the newspaper. These changes disturbed ideological expectations and suggest changes in the public sphere that resonate with Carey's account of communication, transportation, journalism, and public space. I want to complicate his account with an exploration of the dimension of representation, an aspect of public space that both apologists for and critics of the party period tend to disregard.

Transformation in the public sphere does not mean simply change in the terms of access to the public sphere. Critics of a romanticized party period imply that their task is accomplished when they show that ordinary people did not have access.[12] But participation in the public sphere always depends on a system of representation. The media are there to mediate, after all. So what we should be looking for are shifts in the public sphere as a system of representation. Newspapers were the crucial means of representing public discussion and representing public opinion throughout the nineteenth century. Changing the means of producing and distributing newspaper content would entail changing the system of representing public opinion.

The Party System and the Public Sphere

The Revolutionary generation did not envision party politics. The Constitution nowhere mentions party; the Federalist Papers devote considerable attention to explaining how the federal system will make party politics insignificant. The framers anticipated a system in which public opinion would form naturally and influence national politics by expressing itself to elected representatives. The newspaper system was supposed to support a national public sphere that would allow public opinion to form naturally. Newspapers were expected to operate as virtual town meetings; the press system would be governed by norms of "rational liberty," including impartiality and impersonality.

The Postal Act of 1792 institutionalized this notion of a national public sphere. Designed to subsidize newspaper growth by subsidizing distribution and newsgathering by local printers, the act demonstrated the shared belief that the press system was necessary to forming the consent that national government needed for legitimacy. In back of this consensus was the ideological impulse of the Revolution. A colonial press that was socially and culturally conservative, produced by artisans for use by gentlemen,[13] was recruited by the Revolutionary movement and assigned the task of supporting a national public sphere. The result was a commonly accepted notion that newspapers should run as virtual town meetings and that the entire newspaper system would provide the national equivalent of face-to-face local governance. The ideal inhabitant of this public sphere would be *Publius*, the pseudonymous author of the Federalist Papers, whose name referred to a hero of the Roman republic but would be translated literally as "public man" and who spoke in the voice of disinterested reason.

This was a fantasy. Although influential—vide the form of the Federalist Papers and the endless claims by printers to be open to all parties—it conveniently ignored the actual history of the Revolutionary press. Printers were propagandists. The Revolutionary movement assigned newspapers the task of representing public opinion both to citizens and to a "candid world"; this task required printers to depict the people as unanimous.[14] Printers developed techniques of advocacy to accomplish this but at the same time pretended to be passively representing the people. After the Revolution, when national politics commenced, these habits came into conflict. On the one hand, newspapers were imagined as neutral passive forums for public debate; on the other, newspapers were the tools available for party conflict. Understanding this contradiction helps unravel the ambivalence of the party press in the career of the public sphere.

In its first generation—from the Revolution to the 1820s—contemporaries viewed press partisanship with alarm. Partisan newspapering began with a few national papers and then spread outward as local newspapers clipped and reprinted the more flamboyant content. Because the Postal Act allowed editors to exchange copies of their newspapers free through the mails, an essay from a Philadelphia newspaper would be reprinted elsewhere, often with the context removed. In the 1790s, the system developed and distributed an ongoing spectacle of partisan warfare. High-profile partisan editors became the public faces of the federal parties, surrogate warriors for political chieftains.[15] But citizens found this kind of conflict revolting and hoped it would stop. Many practical printers agreed: as late as the 1830s, Hezekiah Niles could remark without fear of contradiction that to ask a printer about his politics was simply not done.[16]

This contradiction between practices and norms was dissolved with the rise of a mature party press, which, in turn, came from the rise of mass politics. For Habermas, this marked a decline of classical norms of public discourse. Earlier discourse achieved the appearance of rationality in part because it was restricted to propertied white men. It's easy to speak disinterestedly of the public good when it's only us at the table. But practical politics led to an expansion of the franchise, substituting voting for public debate as the key mechanism for representing public opinion. As elections came to drive politics, public deliberation was colonized by appeals to self-interest, eroding the bright line between public and private and the rationality of debate. To Habermas this story is tragic; to others it's happier. *Publius* never was everyone, and with the breakdown in the barrier between state and civil society urgent inequalities came into focus, leading to the enfranchisement of the working class, the abolition of slavery, and the emancipation of women.

A second cause of change in public discourse was the expansion of the press system. National information policy, expressed through the postal system, stimulated tremendous growth. As newspapers grew in number, they were hailed into and helped construct the system of mass politics. Subsidies were crucial to this development. National partisan papers relied on the informational subsidy of news and pseudonymous commentary from party chieftains, which, in turn, ensured that they would be widely copied. State papers relied on winning state printing contracts, a financial subsidy that became far more important later. They could also sometimes get an informational subsidy through the assistance of an editor, a member of a political organization who undertook the task of selecting and authoring material for the paper. This had traditionally been a printer's task but was not necessarily highly valued.[17] Professional editors remained ideologically suspect. The newspapers of the early republic are full of criticisms of "hireling editors."[18]

Squeamishness about partisanism eased after the election of 1800 but did not disappear. Newspapers mobilized for that election in an unprecedented fashion,[19] and in the years following there appeared a new sort of partisan "attack" newspaper, usually Federalist, and often titled *Bee, Wasp, Hornet,* or *Scourge.*[20] These newspapers were neither numerous nor long-lived.[21] More impressive was the backlash against them, including attempts at both the federal and state levels to prosecute printers for seditious libel.[22]

But structural considerations had begun to encourage partisanism. The monopoly local weekly and the daily "Advertiser" were the quintessential impartial papers, the first because it needed to serve a whole community and the second because it served a narrow constituency that turned its energies toward commerce rather than politics. Such papers thrived during the lulls in party controversy. But there was always a journeyman printer willing to set up a competing newspaper in the towns served by monopoly weeklies, and the larger cities came to support more and more dailies.

The Party Press of Jacksonian America

The 1820s created a national party press differing from the earlier period in a number of features: the articulation of national, state, and local political contests; the existence of competing newspapers in most localities; the institution of the office of editor; the solidification of national newspaper networks; the creation of a partisan ideology; and the estrangement of the ideology of rational liberty from mainstream newspapering. The trigger was Andrew Jackson's serial campaigns for the presidency, which took over the forms of advocacy honed during the Revolution and applied them to ordinary electoral politics.[23]

The new national party press was shocking. It shocked anti-Jacksonians because they were getting beat. It also shocked anyone thinking in classical terms about the public sphere: the new politics exploited irrational appeals to personal charisma or demonizations such as King Caucus or the Monster Bank. Anti-Jacksonians countered in kind and achieved partisan maturity in 1840 with the election of William Henry Harrison, an imitation of Old Hickory.

The Jacksonian system persisted through most of the nineteenth century and institutionalized certain features. The molecular unit was the local paper.[24] Partisan newspapering penetrated every locality. Local newspapers were autonomous nodes in national networks linking editors who were often surplus professionals or political aspirants—lawyers, usually, fond of prolixity and lawyerly habits of argument. Local autonomy was crucial. In theory, the system could have consisted of a few national papers—this had been the course of development in France and England, and it was the idea behind the national papers of the 1790s. This did not happen due to the absence of strong federal regulations, the absence of taxes on newspapers, the abundance of trained printers, the existence of local and state patronage, and especially the efficiencies of the system of newspaper exchange. Because the content of national papers could be clipped and copied by local printers as quickly as local readers could obtain a copy of that paper, there was little reason for local readers to prefer national publications over local ones. Further, local papers let the party claim to represent local public opinion, both locally and to the nation at large. (The decentralization of the party press stands in contrast to the increasing centralization of the commercial system; commercialization eventually introduced a tilt toward a more consolidated national system.)

This system of representing public opinion appalled many on both the left and the right. Hezekiah Niles of the influential *Weekly Register* characterized it as the "manufacture of public opinion." Niles castigated the Jacksonian newspaper regime (then directed by Francis Preston Blair) and described how, on the instigation of Blair, newspapers throughout the nation printed editorial comments on particular issues, which were then collected and republished as if they were the product of a genuine popular movement.[25]

The Revolution had proposed a national press system based on the metaphor of the town meeting. The party press proposed a different relationship to the public sphere. Party papers would address the electorate like a lawyer addressed a jury. Their pages would not be open to the opposition, which had its own newspaper. Citizens—again, like a jury—could choose between these two versions of reality. The role of citizen is reduced to the role of voter. In fact, partisan editors assumed that their readers did not read opposition newspapers and instead played a game of gotcha with opposing editors, taking a passage out of context and ridiculing it, heightening divisions between "us" and "them," and reinforcing the one-dimensionality of the voter's function. Party papers referred to voters in terms of a military metaphor, as the soldiers of the party, whose function was to organize, obey their leaders, and vote the ticket. Just as lawyerly training was almost mandatory for editors, so was military glory for candidates, especially presidential ones.

The military and courtroom metaphors institutionalized competition in much the same way as the marketplace. They are disingenuous in that they imply an arena in which arguments collide. In fact, readers of partisan newspapers did not comparison shop. But even had newspapers and readers behaved in an ideal fashion, the party press still represented a collapse of norms of public discourse, now composed primarily of insults and emotional appeals, designed to knit together discrete interest groups. Contemporaries recognized this as a deviation from one legacy of the Revolution.

Condemnation of partisanism in the press came from all sectors. Conservatives complained that it had unleashed the passions of the electorate and could lead only to ruin; they urged a return to the project of educating and enlightening the populace. Radicals such as the anarchist Josiah Warren and antislavery activists such as William Lloyd Garrison (himself a former partisan editor) criticized the prostitution of the press to the parties and, through them, to commercial interests in thrall to the slave power.[26] Anti-Masons established a series of newspapers with names like "The Free Press" because they were convinced that partisan editors, dependent on the financial support of Masons, would never print their arguments.[27] The claim that the mainstream press was enslaved to a party was, ironically, also shared by the most commercialized sector of the metropolitan press, the penny press.

Commercialization

The growth of printing reached two plateaus, first in the 1820s and then in the 1830s. First, the number of printers and newspapers multiplied so that most local markets supported competing papers. Meanwhile, especially in the cities, growing markets fueled the appearance of new genres of printed matter—literary, religious, and scientific periodicals; gossip papers; mechanics' papers; and penny papers. This tremendous growth preceded new technologies, such as the steam press. New technologies, however, allowed the most successful of these media to edge out their less technologically sophisticated rivals. The weeding out was slow in coming. Even in New York City, the most advanced newspaper market in the antebellum period,[28] the daily newspaper field remained highly competitive. Even after the emergence of a few dominant dailies there, printing remained relatively decentralized elsewhere, with the census of 1840 showing printing plants as generally quite small.[29] But the tendency of commercialization was to centralize print culture where politicization had distributed it.

The enduring symbol of commercialization is the penny daily, the rise of which is the most commonly mentioned media development in the histories of the period.[30] I have argued elsewhere that much of this attention has been miscast. Particularly, I dispute a fundamental contradiction between commercialization and partisanism, either within a particular newspaper or throughout the system of newspapering.[31]

Commercialization especially meant the rise of advertising. Newspapers undertook to manufacture an audience of consumers that was sold to advertisers just as papers were sold to readers. Just as politicization reformulated readers as voters (rather than as citizens), so did commercialization reconfigure readers as consumers.

On the surface, partisanism and commercialization sure look contradictory. Because of this apparent contradiction, and because of the twentieth-century allergy toward partisan newspapering, the history of the period has usually been understood as a battle between partisan and commercial newspapering, with commercial winning.[32] There is much to support this narrative, especially in New York City, where a stable corps of party papers was replaced by an equally stable elite of commercial papers. But, the new papers all became partisan. Their partisanism did not contradict their commercialization.

From the perspective of the public sphere, this period looks more like a battle of rational liberty against the combined forces of partisanism and commercialization. Both processes depended on a new abundance of printed material. Both also required a breakdown in traditional press norms. The reaction against both at either end of the political spectrum was the same. But, as outspoken as the initial penny papers were on the evils of party, party papers had little to say about penny papers. The penny press was not a disturbing *political* phenomenon; even Horace Greeley thought that these little papers were mostly amusements.[33] It was a disturbing *cultural* development. Opposition came less from the parties, who adopted its innovations and eventually co-opted the successful penny papers, than from old elements of the cultural elite—such as mainstream Protestant ministers, who condemned it in the same terms as novels and other profane literature. The evils of mass literature were not unlike the evils of mass politics. Each blurred the lines between private and public. Party papers personalized political contests, inverting the traditional motto, "Measures, not Men." Penny papers also blurred public and private, with a clear line of descent connecting them to gossip papers of the 1810s and 1820s, which had styled themselves the moral censors of their communities. Gossip papers usually failed quickly, succumbing to libel suits or physical assault.[34] Their publishers instead turned to crime reporting, which offered fewer dangers. This sort of content, coupled with producer-class moral judgment,[35] gave the first generation of penny papers its distinctive flavor.

Partisanism and commercialization both created newspaper elites. Partisanism created elite newspapers in Washington, D.C., monopolizing news from the federal government and taking advantage of federal printing contracts. Meanwhile, commercialization created elite newspapers in New York City, capturing the stream of European news, first by attracting steamship lines to the city, then by bankrolling telegraph lines to Halifax. The present-day Associated Press originated in schemes for New York's dailies to sell the latest European news to the rest of the nation.[36] Both the Washington and New York news regimes seemed to critics to bestow too much power on a few media barons. Niles's criticism of the manufacture of public opinion was matched by endless criticisms of the Associated Press. Both partisanism and commercialism relocated public discourse from the locality to a national center, turned citizen-voters into spectators, and marginalized an increasingly visible periphery, which would have to find expression and identity in its own newspapers. Commercialization carried the seeds of a further transformation of the newspaper, one that would eliminate the most striking feature of the newspaper culture of the mid-nineteenth century—its competitiveness.

Industrialization and Consolidation

It is with a mixture of awe and nostalgia that one browses the newspaper directories of the second half of the nineteenth century. There were so many papers, and so many kinds of papers, that one can't help but imagine a social and political world of unprecedented dynamism.[37] Local newspaper markets became natural monopolies because of economies of scale in the production of news, newspapers, audiences, and advertising. Resisting these economies of scale was the tradition of partisan newspapering. Parties looked for large readerships but never expected universal ones. Partisanism was premised on segmentation and justified by the continual competition of newspapers in a political marketplace, which, in turn, implied competition in an economic marketplace. The business strategies of partisanism and of advertising became incompatible when a universal readership became thinkable again—when the economies of scale began to work.

We can call this the industrialization of the newspaper: the integration of the newspaper into the emerging bureaucratic structures of industrial America. The newspaper became a carrier for the information, commerce, and culture of industrializing America. It became an ingredient of what has come to be called the culture industry and of the bureaucratic state, entering into a more and more symbiotic relationship with governmental institutions.

Ironically, it's at this point that it makes sense to understand American journalism in the way that a Pulitzer Prize committee does. Industrialization enabled the development of modern journalism: we begin to talk about the great journalists *because* of industrialization, even if industrialization is itself a depersonalizing process. The first generation of great reporters worked on metropolitan newspapers and national magazines that were highly dependent on economies of scale and advertising revenue; ironically, these same journalists—Lincoln Steffens, Ida Tarbell, and Jacob Riis—took as their subject matter the industrial enterprise, the industrial city, and the people that inhabited them. These reporters are the first generation of role models for today's student journalists, who glaze over when reading Benjamin Franklin, Hezekiah Niles, or Horace Greeley.

How did these journalists inscribe their readers as citizens? Thomas Leonard argues that the modern journalism of exposé configures readers as increasingly disillusioned spectators, endlessly bombarded with the story behind the story they'd like to believe—this is the journalism that arose with the industrialization of the newspaper at the end of the nineteenth century and remains the gold standard for reporters today. Leonard sees journalists as unindicted coconspirators in the twentieth-century decline of popular politics.[38]

The corollary is the elevation of the reporter to the status of super citizen. Professional reporters assumed the responsibility of speaking on behalf of citizens—in a world of big business and big government, people needed big media to supervise and opine on their behalf. The pressrooms in Washington and in the state capitals have been constituted as simulated public spheres, with reporters playing *Publius*. Objectivity and social responsibility replaced impersonality and impartiality.[39] But the modern reporter, required to be an observer, cannot possibly be a citizen. The reporter is not allowed to make morally compelling arguments in the presence of both citizens and the state—his or her credibility is sacrificed by doing so. Instead, the journalist takes his or her condemnation by everyone with a moral commitment as a point of pride—the excellence of a professional journalist is in the even-handedness with which one is despised. The modern regime of journalism allows neither journalists nor citizens to effectively simulate the public sphere. This is because journalism has colonized the space that citizens used to occupy and utilize.

The Modern Way of Representing the Public

The party period developed an ensemble of techniques for representing public opinion, including the open-air debate, the political convention, and the monster rally. The party press worked at the center of this array of techniques. The professional press has developed a new ensemble, including the interview, the press conference, and the devices of objective reporting—sourcing, balancing, and bylines. If the techniques of the party press seem to have manufactured the public opinion they represented, the techniques of the professional press are designed to repress any manipulation on the part of the press. The professional press is meant to let the public think for itself. This ambition is delusional.

Ironically, the excellence of journalism correlates negatively with the liveliness of the public sphere. I will not disagree with Michael Schudson's assertion that journalism is better now than it has ever been.[40] But that's exactly the point. Journalism is defined increasingly in professional terms, as a form of expertise; it is functionally a part of the system of expert control that has replaced politics as the basis of much of the government. Journalists produce reportage answering the needs of expert communities, just as Carey argued. Take the coverage of the 1996 Telecommunications Act. On the business pages, where the interests of investors are paramount, coverage was detailed and richly textured and centered around the contest of different sectors of the industry—the Baby Bells, broadcasters, long-distance providers, cable companies, wireless servers—for larger slices of the pie, preparatory to their deregulated and lusty mergings. In the general news sections, coverage was scant, and treated the act as aimed at increased competition to create savings for consumers, an aim invisible on the business pages.[41] The media conducted two (at least) almost entirely insulated public discussions. Newspapers remain a crossroads of different interests, but there is no danger that these interests will collide.

The people do not have much voice in the deliberations that direct their polity. In spite of the unprecedented flow of information to the public, the opportunity for a member of the public to make a public statement or do a public act has diminished. But most would not have been able to at any previous point in U.S. history. Gender would have been a prohibition: women entered the voting force just as voting became for Habermas a mere form of acclamation, and voting participation declined to alarming levels. The norms of the classical public sphere were erected on the foundation of social inequalities. Those norms implied liberation from social inequalities, but that aspiration has always been utopian. The actual forms of inequality always mutate, and our recognition of them has always lagged behind their mutations. History gives us no reason to think that inequalities can ever cease.

My point is not that the professional press has exiled the people from the public. Rather, it's to say that the people have always had only a represented voice in the public—indeed, that the public never exists unless it is represented. What we are considering, then, is not the decline from a participatory public sphere to a politics of spectacle, but a substitution of one system of representing the public sphere for another. This should save us from a simplistic populism and equally simplistic rebuttals and open up some room for nuanced judgments about how democratic public discourse really is and where in hell it's going.

Mobile Privatization and the Future of the Public Sphere

Carey's account of the trajectory of mobile privatization offers slim hope of a reversal in the decline of political culture. Since 1979, a series of new technologies have confirmed the previous trajectory. Cell phones allow domestic space to encroach on previously public spaces of sidewalks, cafes, bookstores, and commuter trains. The Internet ruptures the bounds of locality and draws people away from densely configured geographical communities to thin global interest communities. Wireless communication and new energy technologies promise to take you off the grid. All of which explains, in part, the idiocy of national politics.

Carey's account is tragic. Not only does it have an unhappy ending, the unhappy ending is a direct result of the flawed excellence of its protagonists.

People become freer, and information technologies allow them to get individually smarter, but, because they're freer, their individual knowledge choices make them collectively stupider. The people get smarter, but the People becomes an idiot. There is something reassuringly Irish about this irony. And, as Robert Putnam, Robert Entman, David Mindich, and many others have shown, if you're talking about the past forty years or so, there's no denying the curve of decline.[42]

But a happier story is available. In this story, the republic was constituted out of an enduring contradiction between two tendencies in its communications system. The first was a Jeffersonian vision, lately re-understood as Habermasian, of intelligent political community. Its antagonist is the social fact of mobile privatization. Although warring, these two tendencies are inherently linked, coming from the embrace of individual freedom implied in the notion of government by consent at the base of modern liberal democracy. Neither can exist without the other.

Torn between these two tendencies, public discourse in the United States has almost always been idiotic. In this, Schudson and Altschuler and Blumin are somewhat correct. It is a mistake to think (as Neil Postman did) that an earlier communication environment produced radically more intelligent citizens (although today's do seem to share far less political information than previous generations).[43] But surely this is the wrong question to ask. The strength of the system has never come from individual intelligence or the virtue of its citizens. It is rooted in the institutional, cultural, and ideological forces that keep its centrifugal forces in check and require its politics to be conducted by a certain etiquette. Politics seemed more rational at various times in the past because political leaders took seriously the injunction to act as if the public was a supervising agent of great intelligence and wisdom. At various points, advances in communication technologies encouraged political professionals to violate that etiquette. In the 1830s a new abundance of popular printed material encouraged frankly racist appeals about abolitionists in both major parties. In the 1880s and 1890s a similarly racist antiradicalism flourished, and again in the 1950s. Historians identify each of these periods as moments of tremendous growth and competition in the tools of communication. Each period was also a seedbed for a following generation of political reform and, frankly, enlightenment. Although derided as crazies in the 1830s and 1840s, abolitionists and feminists are the ones we cherish today; likewise Eugene V. Debs and Martin Luther King Jr.

Moreover, in these dark periods of public idiocy and media abundance, redemptive energy was being produced by nonmainstream groups operating at the margins of the public sphere. Here the argument over the party period has failed us. For the creative periphery of politics, the parties have always resisted movements until they became inevitable enough to be co-opted.

Party period romantics note that the era produced the most powerful third-party movements in the nation's history—as if this were a virtue and not evidence of the inherent conservatism of mass electoral politics. Their critics, in their haste to dismiss any evidence of citizen activism beyond today's expectations, simply ignore movements from the margins. Schudson's *The Good Citizen* has nothing to say about the labor press, the socialist movement, Populism, and the rest, though it does discuss abolitionism and the Civil Rights Movement. Altschuler and Blumin also avoid these topics. But the energy of public life, when it has been admirable, has come from an interaction between margin and mainstream or been the invention of the margins entirely.

Here one is tempted to lapse into Pollyannaish recitations of secret heliotropism and old moles burrowing well. Instead, let me invoke another fixture of the public sphere discourse, the 1920s debate between Walter Lippmann and John Dewey. Lippmann, steeped in his generation's disillusionment with the modern media following World War I, declared that ordinary citizens, captive in a "pseudoenvironment" composed of stereotyped characters and plots, lack the cognitive capacity to comprehend the modern world and function as democratic decision-makers. Instead he called for expert "intelligence bureaus" to explain the world and frame policy choices. Lippmann called for a version of the professional public sphere, in which an active class of decision-makers participates in meaningful debate, which a class of professional communicators then represents to a large passive public. Surely we live in Lippmann's world. Most of the functions of governance have been professionalized, and no ordinary citizen is expected to challenge the propriety of letting unelected officials such as the chairman of the Federal Reserve Board make the most important decisions according to an expertise claimed to be apolitical and scientific. Dewey's counterargument appeals to political education as the key to healthy democracy. Ordinary citizens are admittedly underinformed but, given the appropriate means of deliberation, are not only capable of intelligent debate but are in fact the indispensable legitimators of any policy decision.

Lippmann and Dewey represent the dialectic between mobile privatization and a Jeffersonian ideal of deliberative democracy. Neither will win, and we cannot expect to choose one over the other, though anyone with any heart prefers Dewey. The competition between the two tendencies is the very motor of communication history, and that history has not ended.

That also means that history in the second sense—not the past, but our account of the past—has not ended and continues to have work to do, and that this work is not simply neutral recording but actual intervention. The history of norms of public discourse is also a normative enterprise. No trope is more common in historical discourse than the claim to oppose ideology with reality, and it is exactly that trope that characterizes much debate over the party period. But no account is innocent of ideology, and every properly historical account is also a normative argument.

A new regime of deliberation seems imminent now, one in which new technologies and subjectivities will be harnessed to the representation of public opinion. In the development of the Internet, the World Wide Web, and the blogosphere, to name three slightly different manifestations of the interactive technologies that seem likely to drive this new regime, one sees the continual redeployment of the rhetoric of Jeffersonian democracy contesting the tendency of mobile privatization. For the most part, the discourse of the information revolution devolves into utopian and dystopian visions of either. The normative usefulness of history is to gray this all up. In the process, it makes it all a bit more actionable.

Notes

1. Carey, "A Plea for the University Tradition," *Journalism Quarterly* 55 (Winter 1978): 846–55.
2. Carey, "Technology and Ideology: The Case of the Telegraph," in *Communication as Culture: Essays on Media and Society* (Boston: Unwin Hyman, 1988).
3. Bill Kovach and Tom Rosenstiel, *The Elements of Journalism: What Newspeople Should Know and the Public Should Expect* (New York: Crown, 2001), p. 10.
4. Harry Watson, *Liberty and Power: The Politics of Jacksonian America* (New York: Noonday Press, 1990); Jean Baker, *Affairs of Party: The Political Culture of Northern Democrats in the Mid-Nineteenth Century* (Ithaca, NY: Cornell University Press, 1983); William E. Gienapp, "Politics Seems to Enter into Everything: Political Culture in the North, 1840–1860," in S. E. Maizlish and J. J. Kushma, eds., *Essays on American Antebellum Politics 1840–1860* (College Station: Texas A&M University Press, 1982), pp. 15–69; Ronald P. Formisano, *The Birth of Mass Political Parties: Michigan, 1827–1861* (Princeton, NJ: Princeton University Press, 1971); Ronald P. Formisano, The Party Period Revisited," *Journal of American History* 86, no. 1 (1990): 93–120.
5. John L. Brooke, "To Be Read by the Whole People: Press, Party, and Public Sphere in the United States, 1789–1840," *Proceedings of the American Antiquarian Society* 110, no. 1 (2000): 41–118; Jeff Pasley, *"The Tyranny of Printers": Newspaper Politics in the Early American Republic* (Charlottesville: University Press of Virginia, 2001); Gerald J. Baldasty, *The Commercialization of News in the Nineteenth Century* (Madison: University of Wisconsin Press, 1992).
6. Willard Grosvenor Bleyer, *Main Currents in the History of American Journalism* (Boston: Houghton Mifflin Company, 1927); Frank Luther Mott, *American Journalism: A History of Newspapers in the United States through 250 Years, 1690–1940* (New York : Macmillan, 1941); Edwin B. Emery and Henry Ladd Smith, *The Press and America* (New York: Prentice Hall, 1954); see the critique of this paradigm by Joseph P. McKerns, "The Limits of Progressive Journalism History," *Journalism History* 4, no. 3 (1977): 88–92.

7. Especially, Michael Schudson, *Discovering the News: A Social History of American Newspapers* (New York: Basic Books, 1978). See my critique in "The Mythology of the Penny Press," *Critical Studies in Mass Communication* 4, no. 4 (1987): 376–404, and replies to the same.

8. Baldasty, *The Commercialization of News in the Nineteenth Century*; Richard L. Kaplan, *Politics and the American Press: The Rise of Objectivity, 1865–1920* (New York: Cambridge University Press, 2001); Michael E. McGerr, *The Decline of Popular Politics: The American North, 1865–1928* (New York: Oxford University Press, 1986); Pasley, *"The Tyranny of Printers"*; Richard R. John, *Spreading the News: The American Postal System from Franklin to Morse* (Cambridge, MA: Harvard University Press, 1986).

9. Especially, Robert D. Putnam, *Bowling Alone: The Collapse and Revival of American Community* (New York: Simon and Schuster, 2000).

10. David M. Rabban, *Free Speech in Its Forgotten Years* (Cambridge, England: Cambridge University Press, 1997); David Kairys, ed., *The Politics of Law: A Progressive Critique* (New York: Pantheon, 1982); Eric Foner *The Story of American Freedom* (New York: Norton, 1998).

11. See, for instance, the papers reprinted in the *Communication Review* 4 (October 2000) from a conference hosted by Middle Tennessee State University.

12. Schudson's point in his essay, "Was There Ever a Public Sphere? If so, When? Reflections on the American Case," in Craig Calhoun, ed., *Habermas and the Public Sphere* (Cambridge, MA: MIT Press, 1992), pp. 143–63.

13. Stephen Botein, "Mere Mechanics and an Open Press: The Business and Political Strategies of Colonial American Printers," *Perspectives in American History* 9 (1975): 130–211; Charles Clark, *The Public Prints: The Newspaper in Anglo-American Culture, 1665–1740* (New York: Oxford University Press, 1994).

14. John Nerone, *Violence against the Press: Policing the Public Sphere in U.S. History* (New York: Oxford University Press, 1994), ch. 2.

15. The metaphor of the partisan editor as surrogate warrior comes from Robert Wiebe's *The Opening of American Society* (New York: Vintage, 1984), pp. 101–102.

16. "Etiquette among Publishers and Printers," *Weekly Register*, vol. 37 (20 February 1830), pp. 426–470

17. For example, a document dated 30 January 1807, sent by the Trustees of the Worcester MA *National Aegis,* itemized what they owed their printer, Samuel Nutting: 13 weeks of editing at $3 a week, or $39; and 21 weeks of printing at $17 per week, or $357. *National Aegis* Papers, AAS, box 1, folder 1. The same low value was placed on editorial work in the negotiations in 1830 to establish the anti-Masonic *We the People and Old Colony Press: We the People* Papers, AAS, box 1 folder 1.

18. "The Devil to Pay among Printers," *Plebeian,* 13 October 1805. In noting the indictment of the editors of the *Poughkeepsie Journal* for libel, the editor of the *Plebeian* (Jesse Buel, probably) quips that "Johnny Akin will have one consolation, . . . he will now have employ in his professional line."

19. John Bixler Hench notes an unprecedented seventy-one newspaper starts in 1800, easily surpassing the previous high of fifty-five in 1798, unmatched until 1808, when eighty were started: Hench, "The Newspaper in a Republic: Boston's Centinel and Chronicle, 1784–1801" (PhD. Dissertation, Clark University, 1979), appendix A, table 1, p. 280.

20. David Hackett Fischer, *The Revolution of American Conservatism: The Federalist Party in the Era of Jeffersonian Democracy* (New York: Knopf, 1965), pp. 141–142.

21. Brigham lists three *Bees,* one *Hornet,* four *Scourges,* and two *Wasps.* Of these, the *Hudson (New York) Bee,* the *New London (Connecticut) Bee,* and the *Frederickstown (Maryland) Hornet* lasted more than two years. Clarence S. Brigham, *History and Bibliography of American Newspapers, 1690–1820* (Worcester, MA: American Antiquarian Society, 1947).

22. The following are taken from the *Plebeian:* 18 February 1805, an item relating a controversy in the Massachusetts legislature over whether Young & Minns shall continue to enjoy state printing contracts after printing an "indecent and libellous publication against the public character of the President of the United States" in the New England *Palladium;* 8 January and 15 April 1805, the legislature of New York directed the attorney general to prosecute James Cheetham of the *American Citizen;* 13 October 1805, "Within a few days past we have seen mention made of seven new prosecutions against our brethren of the type, viz. five against the editor of the *American Citizen,* and two against Powers, Bowman, Akin & Co. editors of the Poughkeepsie journal."; 13 Oct 1805, copies a report from the *American Mercury* of the prosecution of Osborne, editor of the *Witness,* by a federal grand jury in Litchfield, Connecticut, for publishing the trial of General William Hart in the Superior Court; 10 Oct 1806, "Tit for Tat," notes indictment of Hudson & Godwin, editors of the *Courant,* for a libel upon the general government. Also notes the sentence of Mr. Wright, of the *Republican Spy* of Worcester, Massachusetts, to six months imprisonment, for a libel against Governor Strong. See also Leonard Levy, *Jefferson and Civil Liberties: The Darker Side* (Cambridge, MA: Harvard University Press, 1963), and Norman Rosenberg, *Protecting the Best Men: An Interpretive History of the Law of Libel* (Chapel Hill: University of North Carolina Press, 1985).

23. Robert Remini, *The Election of Andrew Jackson* (Philadelphia: Lippincott, 1963); Charles Sellers, *The Market Revolution: Jacksonian America, 1815–1846* (New York: Oxford University Press, 1991); John William Ward, *Andrew Jackson, Symbol for an Age* (New York: Oxford, 1955); Richard McCormick, *The Second American Party System: Party Formation in the Jacksonian Era* (Chapel Hill: University of North Carolina Press, 1966).

24. Ronald Formisano, "Deferential-Participant Politics: The Early Republic's Political Culture, 1789–1840," *American Political Science Review* 68, no. 2 (1974): 473–487, and "The 'Party Period' Revisited," *Journal of American History* 86, no. 1 (1999): 93–120. See also Richard Hofstadter, *The Idea of a Party System: The Rise of Legitimate Opposition in the United States, 1780–1840* (Berkeley: University of California Press, 1970).

25. "The Organized Press, and the Case of Gales & Seaton," *Weekly Register,* vol. 45 (4 Jan 1834), pp. 306–309.

26. On Josiah Warren, see Nerone, *The Culture of the Press in the Early Republic: Cincinnati, 1793–1848* (New York: Garland, 1988), ch. 8; on Garrison, see David Nord, "Tocqueville, Garrison, and the Perfection of Journalism," *Journalism History* 12 (1986): 56–63.

27. AAS, papers of *We the People* and *Old Colony Press.*

28. "Newspapers," Niles's *Weekly Register,* vol. 34 (21 June 1828), p. 268, reports that New York City had 12 daily newspapers, 8 am and 4 pm, with an aggregate circulation of 15,000. There are also 8 semiweekly and numerous weeklies, making for a

total annual aggregate circulation of 7,072,000. Nationally, 50 dailies plus semi-weeklies and weeklies produce 52,050,000 copies. New York City issued one seventh of all the newspapers and one-fourth of all the dailies in the United States.

29. The American Annual Almanac for 1843

	MA	NY	PA	VA	OH	TOTAL
printing offices	104	321	224	50	159	1,552
binderies	72	107	46	13	41	447
daily newspapers	10	34	12	4	9	138
weekly newspapers	67	198	165	35	107	1,141
periodicals	14	56	42	5	20	227

total capital investment = $5,873,815
total employees = 11,523
Divide by total # of printing offices, avg. value about $3,800, and average # of employees slightly less than 6. Compare with other contemporary industries, with subsequent newspaper industry.
potteries. . . . . . 659 establishments valued at $2,084,100
lumberyards. . . . 1,793 @ $9,848,307
cotton manufactories. . . . 1,240 @ $51,102,359

30. R. Laurence Moore, *Selling God: American Religion in the Marketplace of Culture* (New York: Oxford, 1994); David S. Reynolds, *Walt Whitman's America: A Cultural Biography* (New York: Knopf, 1995).

31. Nerone, "The Mythology of the Penny Press," *Critical Studies in Mass Communication* 4, no. 4 (1987):376–404

32. Typical treatment of the "penny press revolution" is found in Mott, *American Journalism,* Emery and Smith, *The Press and America,* and Schudson, *Discovering the News.*

33. Greeley notes in his autobiography that the penny *Tribune* was considered a Whig rival to other penny dailies with Democratic leanings but was in no way expected to be an alternative to serious political sheets.

34. The Boston *Castigator* ceased publication after losing a libel suit; the Cincinnati *True Blue and Castigator* stopped after its office was attacked by a small mob.

35. Dan Schiller, *Objectivity and the News: The Public and the Rise of Commercial Journalism* (Philadelphia: University of Pennsylvania Press, 1981); Alexander Saxton, *The Rise and Fall of the White Republic: Class Politics and Mass Culture in Nineteenth-Century America* (New York: Verso, 1990).

36. Menachem Blondheim, *News over the Wires: The Telegraph and the Flow of Public Information in America, 1844–1897* (Cambridge, MA: Harvard University Press, 1994).

37. Ben Bagdikian, *The Media Monopoly,* 2nd ed. (Boston: Beacon, 1987).

38. Michael Schudson, *The Power of the Press* (Cambridge. MA: Harvard University Press, 1995); see also McGerr, *Decline of Popular Politics,* who similarly accuses reformers.

39. Robert D. Leigh, ed., *A Free and Responsible Press* (The Hutchins Commission Report) (Chicago: University of Chicago Press, 1947).

40. Schudson, *The Power of News,* p. 187.

41. Robert W. McChesney, *Rich Media, Poor Democracy* (Urbana: University of Illinois Press, 1999), ch. 1.

42. Putnam, *Bowling Alone;* Robert Entman, *Democracy without Citizens: Media and the Decay of American Politics* (New York: Oxford, 1989); David Mindich, *Tuned Out* (New York: Oxford, 2004).

43. Neil Postman, *Amusing Ourselves to Death: Public Discourse in the Age of Show Business* (New York: Viking, 1985).

9. A Ritual of Verification? The Nation, the State, and the U.S. Passport

CRAIG ROBERTSON

In recent years James Carey has explicitly framed his work as a story of how the American nation came into being through communication technologies. Carey has taken to write of a nineteenth century "crisis of representation" in which the transmission model becomes "social representation" (the problem of scale) and the ritual model becomes "self-representation" (the problem of identity). Through this framework Carey offers another version of the argument that in the second half of the nineteenth century the local was eclipsed in structure by increasingly national organizational structures.[1] In this chapter, I present a parallel history of the relationship between communication, technology, and the nation. I offer this history to argue that Carey's symbolic model of communication as culture doesn't fully capture the importance of the social and cultural construction of communication technologies. Although Carey deftly makes gestures otherwise, I contend that for all intents and purposes he consistently defines communication as an object of analysis largely in terms of representation through a very specific understanding of the relationship between culture and society. He conceptualizes communication as culture to provide a "mode of understanding actions and motives as a manifestation of a basic cultural disposition to cast up experience in symbolic forms that are at once immediately pleasing and conceptually plausible, thus supplying the basis for felt identities and meaningfully apprehended realities."[2] While this admirably fulfills his agenda of foregrounding the agency of human subjects, it places limits on our understanding of communication and culture.

To illustrate the limits of Carey's approach I provide a history of the emergence of state authority to mediate identity through documents; that is the development of identification documents, specifically the passport. The issuance of the optional U.S. passport in the nineteenth century was less about securing geographic borders and more about securing the nation to the state. It became one way in which the federal government sought to challenge the claims of individual states to grant U.S. citizenship. My focus is the techniques and technologies through which the passport was constituted as proof of citizenship, as an authoritative answer to the question, "Who are you?" Through this example I conceptualize communication technologies in terms of technical practices, to complicate the relationship between communication technologies and representation. This provides a history in which administrative or instrumental practices (such as documentation) are productive of culture; they are cultural practices. This cultural approach to communication entails a different notion of culture from that which Carey uses to underpin his history of communication and the nation. While he does not directly dismiss these practices, his histories do not speak to them. Therefore, in contrast to Carey, I offer an understanding of culture that recognizes practices in a Foucauldian sense—something closer to a technical definition of culture rather than a focus on culture as the individual and collective apprehension and maintenance of reality.

I conceptualize the issuance, presentation, and reading of a passport, as practices, following Michel Foucault's definition of practices as "places where what is said and what is done, rules imposed and reasons given, the planned and the taken for granted, meet and interconnect."[3] It is from this definition that I argue we need a definition of culture that more comfortably incorporates these practices. In an attempt to make clear the stakes of this argument, I use "verification" to frame my analysis of the emergence of the passport. In contrast to representation, I employ verification to label (and privilege) a set of practices and procedures that authenticate and authorize or more generally to emphasize the technical work of gathering, storing, and authorizing information. In this sense I present the passport as a "technology of verification."[4] To think of the passport as a technology of verification is to argue that representation is not only mediated through procedures and institutional forms, but the technical possibilities that limit and constitute the passport produce the very context in which representations make sense. Approaching the passport as a technology of verification allows me to "objectify" the emergence of practices that enabled a reconceptualization of authority as impersonal within the changing scalar dynamics of the nineteenth-century articulation of the modern state. I take this as the initial site of analysis, rather than documents or passports as symbolic forms, to emphasize the need to recognize the always possible importance of institutional and structural practices in how communication is produced and enacted.

To explain why I understand this approach to be an awkward fit within a ritual model I want to look at a distinction that has underpinned much of Carey's writing and that he makes explicit in one of his more recent articles:

as members of a nation, citizens and subjects live in both the "geographic space" and the "symbolic space" of the nation.[5] Carey makes clear that he prioritizes symbolic space over geographic space to argue that nations are in part the products of communication media. Symbolic space (primarily media space) is "the systems of meanings, values and identities that legitimate membership" that are "continuously contested and reshaped in the very media that implant and express them."[6] This contestation constitutes the *internal* border of the nation that determines who belongs to the nation and who doesn't. This formative relationship of communication to the (symbolic space of the) nation is analyzed through a ritual model. The nation is fundamental to Carey's understanding of communication as culture because it provides analytical access to shared representations—the memory through which people make sense of their world.

In contrast to the "inherently vague" internal borders of symbolic space, the external border of the geographic space of the nation is clearly marked through customs and immigration points—a "space where one is 'known' and protected or unknown and unprotected."[7] For Carey, one is required to present an identity document to pass through these points because of the "simple fact that in the modern world everyone belongs to a nation; that is the one nonpsychological fact of human identity in our time."[8] At such points "identities are confirmed and implanted." Therefore, the immigration office is a site where the geographic and symbolic spaces of the nation converge. By briefly invoking the immigration *office* Carey seemingly intends to convey the institutional origin of this need for a nonpsychological (or legal?) identity. To me this implicitly foregrounds that the geographic space of the nation, the administrative space of the nation, the space of transmission, is "the state." Although Carey argues the border is the basic political institution of the nation (the articulation of uncontested sovereignty with secure spatial borders that makes the modern nation a distinct form of social organization), the fixed nature of geographic space seems be of little interest to him.[9] Thus, after this mention of the passport, Carey does not dwell on this right of passage. Rather he moves quickly to the rites of passage within the symbolic space of the nation where he defines communication as culture. The institutional (the border) and the structural (the state)—the geographic space of the nation—are not prioritized as spaces determined by, and productive of, cultural practices. Critically they are fixed and, therefore, Carey is more interested in the contested symbolic space where geography matters, in some sense, in terms of social structure.

I want to use the passport as a communication technology to dwell a little longer in, what Carey terms, the "geographic space" of the nation. From there I intend to argue, more forcefully than Carey does, that geography matters; I believe that his definition of culture can limit attempts to under-

stand how geography matters. Put simply, despite offering a robust definition of culture, Carey has struggled to use it to articulate his understanding
of power. He moves from geographic space to symbolic space because for
him the former is fixed, and the latter is a space of contestation. In contrast I
understand geographic space as an important space of contestation. As
Carey's example of the geographic space of the nation illustrates, it can only
exist with any useful consequences if state agencies are able to police who can
enter and leave. This is achieved through state monopoly over the authority
and means for identification. In this sense geographic space can only exist,
and is in effect created, through the mechanisms that police it. In Carey's
terms I want to consider the institutional and structural production of the
nonpsychological identity that enables a right of passage across the external
borders of the nation. I agree with Carey that the presentation of a passport
produces a space where "identities are confirmed and implanted." But I want
to foreground how the passport comes to confirm and implant an identity, as
a way to understand what made the passport possible, and what the passport
makes possible. This history of the passport is part of the problem of scale
that Carey isolates—the simple fact that by the middle of the nineteenth century the United States was too big to be a republic. Specifically, the authority of the passport, enacted through the confirmation of identity, involves
trust in the absent authority of strangers. This trust had to be established
through the introduction of specific techniques, as new technologies such as
the passport enabled government at a distance. The passport thus provides an
example of the need to recognize, within a cultural definition of communication technologies, the "complex of mundane programs, calculations, techniques, apparatuses, documents and procedures through which authorities
seek to embody and give effect to governmental ambitions."[10] As I have
already indicated, this involves a focus less on the symbolic utility of the passport and more on the practices that constitute the claim to truth represented
in the passport. It demands a focus on the production of this truth rather
than the apprehension of it through the symbolic form of the passport.

This chapter produces a historical context for the emergence of the passport to ask, what makes the passport a practicable and thinkable solution to
policing the border? The passport did not simply emerge. It was contested;
there was a challenge to the authority of the passport to transmit information. The emergence of authority to mediate identity through state-produced
documents is outlined through a section on documents and bureaucracy and
a subsequent section on the development of the U.S. passport. I then conclude the paper with an attempt to engage this Foucauldian history with
Carey's project of foregrounding the problem of democracy.

Documents and the Articulation of the Nation and the State

The historical context that Carey provides for his understanding of American communications is the connection of previously autonomous local practices into a national space. This loss of the local community associated with the advent of nineteenth-century modernity produced a crisis of representation. Carey analyzes the creation of nationally produced communication as a response from a "society lacking the terms or vocabulary necessary to ingest these changes into consciousness."[11] In the following analysis, this crisis of representation is approached through the procedures and practices by which the geographic space of the nation became a thinkable and practicable space to govern.

As an example of a gradual but general paperization of everyday life, the contested emergence of paper money in the United States speaks to Carey's contention (via Harold Innis) of the importance of print technologies to binding the space of the nation. However, I use paper money, official documents, and the passport as explicit examples of technologies grounded in a new bureaucratic objectivity that increasingly produced the structure of government in the United States. Through this, a "memory of the state"[12] developed in which a simultaneous reconceptualization of trust grounded in the impersonal enabled documents to form a new model of communication separate from personal authority. Although technologies were used to transmit authority and information prior to the middle of the nineteenth century, the examples of paper money and the passport show that through the nineteenth century there was a conscious pedagogical attempt to educate people to recognize this authority in terms of their relationship to a still emerging nation and state. Authority had to be created, techniques taught, and trust established. A focus on practices of documentation through the gradual emergence of paper money as a new form of communication provides an example of how the (symbolic space of the) nation-state became meaningful to its residents. However, I use it to ground an analysis of how the use of official documents and the practice of documentation were critical to making the geographical space of the nation a viable space of government. To change the notion of who can grant legitimacy, the techniques that granted legitimacy also had to be altered. This involved a reconstitution of trust away from personal authority to what Anthony Giddens calls "abstract capacities." For Giddens the emergence of the modern state as a successful and efficient site of governing was founded on this change from trust grounded in presence to trust in absence.[13]

Literary critic Marc Shell contends that paper money, particularly the permanent introduction of legal tender in 1862, provided the "main public forum for discussing the relationship between symbols and things" in the

United States during the middle of the nineteenth century.[14] As one opponent of the greenback argued, "the law of legal tender . . . [is] an attempt by artificial legislation to make something true which is false."[15] The debate between "gold bugs" and supporters of "greenbacks" turned on this apparent dilemma; unlike coins, which were understood both as symbols and commodities, paper money appeared "to be a symbol entirely dissociated from the commodity it symbolizes."[16]

The historian David Henkin argues paper money is a critical example of the spread and acceptance of a specific form of authority that is exercised impersonally and, therefore, depends on trust in the medium through which it is expressed. Henkin is interested in paper money as one form of text, which in New York City in the second quarter of the nineteenth century produced an "impersonal public discourse through which new forms of written authority became part of urban life."[17] He links banknotes to signs, cards, posters, and newspapers to explain how this public discourse developed separately from personal authority to "circulate promiscuously in a world of strangers," as he labels this a new model for communication.[18] These urban texts went beyond the control of their authors to, in effect, bracket personal authority. However, Henkin argues that the authority of paper money in large part still depended on the personal signature of the bank president or bank cashier that appeared on notes. These signatures represented the notes as a personal agreement but one that in circulation registered personal absence—a critical example for Henkin of the particular interplay of replication and singularity that formed part of the paradox of the still-developing print culture.[19]

In a similar vein, the legal historian Jennifer Mnookin argues that "increasing urbanization led to business transactions among a wide circle and resulted in less secure reputational knowledge among members of a community."[20] She argues this was part of the context for a challenge to the common law rule against "comparison of hands" in handwriting identification. Until the middle of the nineteenth century, most U.S. states utilized English legal precedent that sought proof of authentic handwriting from a witness familiar with the person and his or her character and reputation; similarities, or lack of, between two examples of handwriting did not constitute legal evidence in disputes based on handwriting.[21] From 1850 to 1900, at least twenty states passed statutes that abolished restrictions on the comparison of handwriting examples in courtrooms. Mnookin's insightful history shows that handwriting became separated from the knowledge of the individual as a whole and reconceptualized as an act that could only be reliably articulated to an individual through the expert knowledge of a specific act—personal knowledge was no longer necessary for identification. Reliability became grounded in the judgment of a "stranger" whose claimed knowledge of handwriting techniques and lack of familiarity with the person produced a detachment or expertise that could "objectively" determine the authenticity of handwriting.

The changing evidence required to prove the authenticity of a signature in this period emphasizes the changing status of personal authority and a new trust in expertise (particularly to read and use documents). I contend this is critical to the constitution of the geographical space of the nation. The increasing use of official documents, specifically the trust in the authority of documents in absence of known or unknown individuals, produced distance as something that could be more effectively governed or administered.

In the United States the increased use of documents to administer distance began in large corporations before gradually being adopted in the federal government. In discussing the importance of the railroad and the telegraph, Carey cites Alfred Chandler's landmark book, *The Visible Hand.*[22] However, Chandler uses the development of the railroad and the telegraph to foreground a different story from Carey—the emergence of modern management techniques to supplant the informal, ad hoc, and largely oral exchanges that dominant small-scale businesses had employed. Chandler argues that geographical dispersion of corporate activities required a form of administration through which distance could be ordered and contained.

The "systematic management" developed in specialized journals, and increasingly implemented in manufacturing and mass-market oriented firms, stressed two key principles: (1) the need to transcend individuals (owners, managers, and workers) by documenting duties and procedures; and, (2) a systematic approach to gathering and analyzing information as the basis for coordination.[23] Advocates of "efficiency" and "system" valued the information produced and administered within the office for the archive it created, hence the importance placed on recording and retrieval mechanisms: preprinted forms, press copy, carbon paper, adding machines, and vertical filing cabinets.[24] As one proponent argued in the late 1880s, "except in the rudest of industries, carried on as if from hand to mouth, all recognize that the present must prepare for the demands of the future, and hence records, more or less elaborate, are kept."[25] These bureaucratic and corporate measures only haphazardly appeared in the federal government prior to the twentieth century. Cindy Aron argues the nineteenth-century operation of the federal government generally remained "irrational and idiosyncratic" operating "in ways that were more reminiscent of small, informal, and even family-run businesses."[26]

I want to extract from these histories the importance of the document as a governing technology. In this context, the document is an example of "the ways in which the problem of modern governing has been the development of ways to manage the distribution of people and resources over increasingly greater territory (as an 'arrangement') increasingly at a distance through new systems of mobility and transfer."[27] Documents solved this problem in the scale of modern government through the construction of a "memory of the state."[28] Allan Sekula conceptualizes this development through "archival rationalization," which Antoinette Burton has usefully defined as "a process whereby archives became part of the quest for a 'truth apparatus,' which undergirded a variety of social practices."[29] Sekula isolates a "bureaucratic-clerical-statistical system of intelligence," the central artifact of which is the filing cabinet.[30] Within the federal government the filing cabinet provided a "memory" that did not depend on any specific individual. This impersonal memory became the site of bureaucratic objectivity; determined by the organization of files, it accommodated the authorship of reports within the nonsubjective space of the cabinet. The collection and classification of information premised on an archival logic of anticipation that allowed for information to be retrieved, therefore, made the administration of territory dependent on the temporal construction of knowledge.

In recent years, in a variety of contexts, a series of arguments have been offered that articulate "the document" and the collection of knowledge to practices of governing and modern statecraft. These arguments make explicit how the techniques and technologies used to collect information have a constitutive effect on the production of knowledge; they produce objects to be governed. The constitutive power of the administrative structure of modern states has been most thoroughly analyzed in terms of the British government of India, regarding which Bernard Cohn has isolated a "documentation project" that "involved the coding of India in ways that rendered it increasingly available to colonization."[31] The production of usable knowledge is made possible through what Cohn labels "investigative modalities": "the definition of a body of information that is needed, the procedures by which appropriate knowledge is gathered, its ordering and classification, and then how it is transformed into usable forms such as published reports, statistical returns, histories, gazetteers, legal codes and encyclopedias."[32] Perhaps more provocatively, James Scott describes modern statecraft as a never completely realized project of "legibility." He argues that officials used "state simplifications" (practices of rationalization and standardization) that "did not successfully represent the actual activity of the society they depicted, nor were they intended to; they represented only the slice of it that interested the official observer."[33] Scott isolates the "administrative simplification of nature (for example, the forest) and space (for example, land tenure) and the invention of permanent, inherited patronyms" as critical to establishing the foundation of modern statecraft.[34]

From these varied sources, a history emerges in which documents as a technology, and documentation as a practice, are critical to governing. They "simplified" objects and practices and thus make them governable; the technological limitations of documents also assisted in "reducing" the scale of resources and people to a level that made them thinkable. Therefore, the use of documents in governing and management provides a history to the geographic space of the nation—how centralized practices, usually in the form of documentation, introduced a standardized and mobile form of knowledge production. In this context, I follow Peter Miller and Nikolas Rose and define knowledge not "simply [to] mean ideas, but [to refer] to the vast assemblage of persons, theories, projects, experiments, and techniques that has become such a central component of governing."[35] A more specific example of the use of documents to constitute the geographic space of the nation comes from the practice that Carey argues symbolizes it—the presentation of the passport at a national border. This practice also foregrounds the specific techniques and procedures that were used to articulate local practices to the centralized, bureaucratic tendencies of state practices from the second half of the nineteenth century.

The U.S. Passport, 1845–1930

The U.S. government (along with most foreign governments) kept passports optional for most of the nineteenth century. However, the State Department still issued almost 500,000 throughout the century, more than 200,000 in the last quarter of the century.[36] Throughout this period applications indicate that many citizens tended to think of the passport as a letter of introduction. In contrast federal officials increasingly considered it a certificate of citizenship and, eventually, by the early twentieth century, an identification document. In line with this changed role, at the end of the century State Department officials sought to more rigorously enforce the application process—a point made explicit in the replacement of the "General Instructions" with "Rules Governing Applications for Passports" in 1897.[37]

The State Department published its first "General Instructions to Passport Bearers" in 1845. This occurred more than fifty years after the federal government issued its first passport and a decade before Congress made the federal government the only authority able to issue passports in 1856. These initial instructions included the demand that applicants use the department's preprinted form and that they provide proof through official documents of both their personal identity and their claim to citizenship. Therefore, instead of applying for a passport through a personal letter to the secretary of state (as had been the practice), U.S. citizens, albeit somewhat inconsistently, began to "formally" apply for the optional passport through official forms and documents. All applicants had to prove their personal identity through affidavits sworn by themselves and a citizen-friend in front of a notary public. In the absence of universal birth registration, those born in the United States also had to prove their citizenship by affidavit; naturalized citizens had to provide their naturalization certificates. Precision, standardization, unity, and impersonal written rules were the practices that redefined reliability as the eradication of the possibility of individual bias and thus constituted bureaucratic objectivity. The gradual introduction and the hesitant deployment of these requirements are an example of the piecemeal emergence of bureaucratic objectivity in practices of the federal government.

The demand for documents effectively centralized personal identification. This challenged the dominant local practice of verification—self-vouching. The increased territorial scope of government had exposed the limited geographical reach of this form of personal trust. This local practice, what Mnookin labels "reputational knowledge,"[38] constituted a form of trust that, in the nineteenth century many citizens and residents considered trumped the need for documents. The replacement of this practice tended to be perceived as unjustified mistrust on the part of government officials, not warranted by any behavior on the part of the applicant. Identification documents, and official forms, were seen as justified only in the case of marginal and suspect populations. Into the last decades of the nineteenth century many applicants continued to believe that personal statements and relationships should be, and were, the primary mode to establish identity. These concerns, expressed in letters to the State Department, contested the new standardization that was redefining reliability, such that state officials increasingly deemed varied local customs "illegible." The clash between the novelty of a centralized need for stabilization and local practices is apparent even in one of the oldest forms of identification—the personal name.

In 1873 the State Department's "General Instructions" clarified that an applicant's name had to be spelled consistently across all the documents in the application—a clarification directed at naturalized citizens. Discrepancies in names regularly appeared in applications for a number of reasons: the result of a clerical error at the time of naturalization, the subsequent formal or informal Americanization of a name, sloppiness on the part of the notary or attorney overseeing the application, or limited literacy.[39] Regardless of the exact circumstance, the explicit request for a consistent name recognizes the problems that occurred in the move from a local and oral culture of identification to one that privileged documents as a more reliable form of interaction. In an 1885 letter to the State Department, an attorney read the requirement for consistent spelling across documents against a claim for an understandable variance in the spelling of names. Irrespective of his motivation, the attorney's argument for discounting the misspelling of his client's name on a naturalization certificate is only plausible in an environment where an individual is not remembered consistently in and through documents and, therefore, in which a person's name is infrequently written. He argued, that "there are so many ways of spelling names that this mistake can easily occur, each one thinks his way is the proper one."[40] In this argument the written or printed version of a personal name is presented as an interpretation, not necessarily a standardized technique for the exact description of an individual.

A similar controversy occurred in the 1920s, this time centered on the standardization of evidence of birth in the United States. Native-born U.S. passport applicants contested the post–World War I requirement that they prove their citizenship through the presentation of a birth certificate. This protest had a significant impetus, as passports were now required for international travel. Despite attempts at standardization, the limited administrative reach of the federal government often made the passport application a process of negotiation—universal birth registration was not achieved in the United States until 1933. If a birth certificate or baptismal certificate could not be offered, the State Department required affidavits from individuals whom it considered had to have witnessed the birth (mother, doctor, or midwife). In the event these were unavailable the State Department resorted to its pre-war requirement—affidavits from citizens known to the applicant whom the department deemed "respectable." The complaints generated by this, and the application process in general, congealed into the "passport nuisance"; newspaper and magazine editors used this label to describe the public response to the annoyance caused through passport requirements. Travelers and businessmen directed their complaints at official attempts to rigorously adhere to practices of standardization and centralization. They articulated their concerns through discourses of respectability, trust, and privacy. The bureaucratic application practices were perceived to dehumanize; documents replaced an individual's word as proof of his or her identity. Such concerns were expressed in the, presumably humorous, suggestion that soon passports would be worn "in some sort of frame tied around our neck, in order that they may be more continuously and conspicuously in evidence, like—pardon me—the tax tags on the collar of a dog."[41]

In this same period certain government officials also contested the authority of documents in the establishment of a secure national border. Through the first decades of the twentieth century, border officials had resisted the challenge that, in their view, the passport made to their personal authority. Prior to the war, and the 1920s immigration acts, officials believed they could use an individual's appearance to accurately determine if an individual belonged to a group that represented a threat to the United States. However, security concerns during World War I, and the introduction of nationality-based immigration quotas, produced a new individual identity that, it was argued, could only be verified through documents. A person's individual identity became important, not just the articulation of their identity through their belonging to a particular group. The passport became a thinkable and practicable identification technology as a response to the problem of verifying this specific identity.

Immigration restrictions originated in the problematization of whiteness as a guarantee of civic competence. Nationality provided a "finer set of gradated exclusions"[42] that was increasingly difficult for officials to read from the body of immigrants. Nationality could not be as easily read off a body as whiteness. The need to enforce annual quotas also required a record of who had entered the United States. The system of identification documents thus provided a memory for the state, necessary to ensure that only a designated number of certain nationals entered each year. Thus, identification documents were required to police the spatial (national) and temporal (annual quotas) limits imposed in the 1921 and 1924 immigration acts.

To be clear, the passport did not completely replace the personal judgment and knowledge of state officials. Rather, it became acceptable at the border only when official identification necessitated an archival dimension—an individual identity that could be rendered through bureaucratic practices of classification and retrieval. Border policing still required moments of personal judgment, when "intuition and identity are collapsed."[43] The moments when immigration officials did exercise their personal judgment over the authority of documents tended to occur at ports of entry along the Canadian and Mexican borders. There, not all faces centrally classified as "alien" were locally viewed as strangers. Officials could recognize many as members of a local community that happened to exist on both sides of an international boundary; the face of the bearer could still trump the face of the document.

A Technology of Verification

The unsettling of privilege, the diminishing authority granted to reputational knowledge, acknowledged that in official terms identification had become less about who you knew and more about how you were known. The introduction of standardized applications and specific criteria for evidence was intended to make citizens more "legible." The U.S. passport developed as part of a solution to a specifically modern problematic of identification. Within the increased scale of government the given of identification had developed into a problem. This was an archival problem dependent on an institutional memory constituted through the collection and retrieval of information; it required an identity that was manageable and thinkable as an object of government practices. In terms of identification at the margins of the modern nation-state, the passport provided a technical solution to the need to constantly and consistently know the individuals who entered and left the United States on an individual basis. This problem replaced previous official concern with the infrequent need to identify certain groups (for example, Chinese, insane, prostitutes) at the border.

The passport, as a technology of verification, produced an official identity. As the organizing unit for bureaucratic procedures, Pamela Sankar argues the existence of an official identity should remind "us of the state's right to know who we are, and what we have done."[44] In the form of the passport nuisance, the emergence of the modern passport until the 1930s is one way in which the development of this right was negotiated. By the 1930s, it appears the heightened degree of anxiety that produced the passport nuisance disappeared, as people become accustomed to the documentation of individual identity and the general paperization of everyday life; precisely when, in fact, the ubiquity of practices began to more closely approximate the concern about general surveillance that had, in part, triggered the passport nuisance.

An official identity was produced through standardized practices. These fixed a citizen's identity according to specific criteria and, therefore, stabilized it as a consistent object. In this way the application process produced a reality, an identity fixed in the document, to which the individual had to adequately compare himself or herself to the satisfaction of the official. I define this as a practice of verification. Verification is a practice of comparison, usually a comparison of a fact or theory to "reality." As I characterized it at the beginning of this chapter, verification suggests a set of practices that "authenticate" the technical work of gathering information. These practices involve standards of objectivity applied to not only evidence but also a clearly defined or stable object to which to compare evidence. The passport conceptualized as a technology of verification is offered as a critique of claims to accurately and truthfully verify personal identity. It does this by forcing us to consider both identification and verification in terms of the production of "truth." The passport does not simply represent an existing identity by presenting it in a document—through the passport, citizenship and personal identity are redefined to assist in the constitution of a memory of the state.

The passport in the act of verification establishes a correspondence between a bureaucratic expression (what, following Sankar, I have called official identity) and a person; it establishes the terms such that the bearer then has to convince an official he or she is in effect the document. That is, what becomes accepted as objective practices of verification in "fact" produce the very criteria they utilize—verification produces the verifiable object it requires.[45] The contested and negotiated emergence of this practice provides the passport with the history I have briefly summarized—the passport nuisance as a resistance to the novelty of the production of official identity, a challenge to the practices of verification producing a verifiable object.

Carey, Culture, and Power

The tension between centralized practices of documentation and local, subjective claims to identity fit into the general narrative of the articulation of the local into a national network that frames Carey's analysis of nineteenth-century communication. Within the normative terms of the ritual model this is a narrative of loss because the spatial bias of modern communication (control over distance) is prioritized over the "primitive equality" inherent in traditional oral practices of community formation. In contrast, Carey privileges oral practices for the ongoing possibility they offer for the establishment of publics.[46] However, I have sought to locate the emergence of official identity simultaneously in the geographic space of the nation as well as this symbolic space. The production of citizenship through documents as an administrative fact is part of a general strategy of the modern state to manage difference. I have used Scott's idea of "simplification" to explain the importance of practices of rationalization and standardization to the production of knowledge. In terms of Carey's work this is the geographic space of the nation—the administrative space constituted through legal practices and state agencies. The development of bureaucratic practices through the use of documents, and specifically the passport, suggests an important aspect of how the geographic space of the nation is created as a manageable and governable space. These bureaucratic practices and documents establish the geographic space of the nation by giving the state a memory.

This returns me to the question I formulated at the beginning of the paper—how effectively does Carey's cultural approach to communication accommodate a cultural analysis of forms of communication within an institutional and administrative context? In a very different context Carey urged cultural studies scholars to think more broadly about cultural practices when he argued that they needed to include an analysis of state and legal institutions in work on consumption and media.[47] But what about when the focus of communication research is not media, consumption and representation, but the state and legal institutions—when research is focused on communications and governing and the transmission of information? Carey asks us to analyze these practices within a ritual model, for he argues a ritual model enables us to "understand these processes [of information transmission] aright."[48] However, I contend that the theory of culture Carey uses to underwrite the ritual model does not enable an effective or specific cultural analysis when the focus is on institutions and structures. Rather, such a cultural analysis of distinctive institutions or technical relations and processes is enhanced by a Foucauldian idea of practices rather than the grounding of culture in subjective interpretations. In terms of this chapter, the documentation of individual identity needs to be understood through practices of verification not simply as a symbolic representation of identity and thus the nation. To clarify what is actually being argued here, I want to first more explicitly locate Carey's definition of culture in terms of his argument for a cultural approach to communication and, second, use his critique of Michel Foucault to make explicit why I consider the history of communication and the state that I have outlined fits awkwardly within Carey's ritual model.

In his challenge to the foundation of communication in positivism, Carey argued that "to reconceive transmission as ritual is to reveal communications not as a means of sending messages but as the constitution of a form of life."[49] For Carey this means the processes and technologies through which "messages are transmitted and distributed in space for the control of distance and people" can only be effectively understood within a ritual view of communication which *privileges symbolic forms* as the basis for "felt identities and meaningfully apprehended realities."[50] Thus, to avoid an analysis of transmission that merely evaluates communication in terms of the ability to send messages over distance, in a ritual model Carey identifies communication as culture, and culture in the first instance with ritual and conversation. The spatial bias inherent in a transmission model is avoided as Carey prioritizes the cultural function of technologies in the maintenance of society in time through the *representation* of shared beliefs over the act of imparting information over distance (the latter I have sought to understand through *verification*). Communication technologies, therefore, are analyzed within a model of communication that defines culture as a way of life in terms of tradition and community. It is a model that perceives mediated communication as precisely that—a mediated form of the primary act of communication embodied within individuals.[51]

Carey's formulation of culture and ritual constitutes a model that privileges an oral formation of culture for descriptive and normative reasons.[52] In contrast to what he perceived as the politically redundant transmission model it offered a foundation for what Carey articulated as the aim of his cultural approach to communication—to renew a public sphere and democratic dialogue. It is the disjuncture between this project and his reading of Foucault that initiates his critique of the latter. Put simply, for Carey, Foucault's "framework . . . was a bad prescription for democratic politics."[53] However, I want to dwell on the specifics of Carey's subsequent demolition job on Foucault to tease out the limitations of Carey's understanding of power and "the state." It is in these terms that I suggest that culture as knowledge and expertise, as technical practice, struggles to make sense within Carey's ritual view of culture as the individual and collective apprehension of representations.

Carey's rejection of Foucault is based on a caricature of Foucault not dissimilar to other critiques—power is everywhere, power is domination. In his eloquent dismissal Carey contends that "In writing an allegory of endless domination, Foucault . . . constituted not only an analysis of power, but a lust and idolatry towards it, for he spurned any middle ground between total power and total anarchy. In short, in Foucault's rendition power is simply another name for culture, for the webs of significance and meaning, in which the self is suspended, but that web is one of intrinsic cruelty."[54] However, these comments read into Foucault's work an understanding of power that for much of his career he sought to contest. In presenting his analytics of power Foucault argued that it was necessary to recognize our understanding of power was derived from a repressive model (state power), which dominated and limited our ability to analyze power, as Carey's reading of Foucault illustrates. While domination exists, for Foucault, it is domination and explicitly not power. Power is understood in terms of relations, and relations of power are only such if they are changeable, reversible and unstable. Critically Foucault understood power as productive not repressive; his analytics of power are offered to illustrate the production of truth and the production of subjects. He used the idea of power/knowledge to refuse to separate forms of knowledge and relations of power. Through power/knowledge he argued that discourses of social and human sciences constituted practices through which individuals were objectivized (classified, examined, trained, and divided from others) and encouraged (usually by "experts") to understand themselves through these categories, that is, formed as subjects.

Foucault contended that power was, therefore, more effectively understood in terms of techniques and technologies, that "this question of 'who exercises power?' cannot be resolved unless that other question, 'how does it happen?' is resolved at the same time."[55] The sociologist Philip Corrigan has argued approaching power in terms of "how questions" "transcends the 'boundary maintenance' practices that detach subjectivity from culture, culture from power, power from knowledge, 'the state' from subjectivities."[56] In this analysis "the state" is approached in terms of practices, not as an anthropomorphized object. Thus, unlike Carey who views power as something that should be primarily analyzed as an attribute of those who dominate, in terms of who possesses it, for Foucault it is a question of what power produces, a question that can be answered through a descriptive analysis of practices and technologies.

In the preceding history of documents and the passport I focused on institutions and structures in terms of practices: "places where what is said and what is done, rules imposed and reasons given, the planned and the taken for granted meet and interconnect."[57] This presents a definition of cultural practices that includes a distinctive set of knowledges, expertise and techniques, not solely the symbolic construction of meaning. The conceptualization of documents and the passport as technologies of verification, derived from this more Foucauldian definition of culture, does not exist separately from Carey's exclusively symbolic definition of culture. However, nor is it encompassed by this definition, rather it suggests the limitation of this definition.

An analysis of the passport as communications history is possible within Carey's cultural approach to communication—for him it represents the point where the symbolic and geographic spaces of the nation meet. The ritual model enables a cultural analysis of the passport in the symbolic space of the nation in terms of the representation of shared beliefs and the maintenance of society in time. However, less accessible in Carey's model is a broader history of the passport in terms of the institutional and the structural, in which culture includes not only symbolic representation but prioritizes a critique of the "technical" production of meaning. That is, it becomes difficult to carry out an effective descriptive analysis of the passport as a communication technology within a ritual model. I argue this is because the culture that defines the symbolic space of the nation produces a specific cultural history. Carey's symbolic culture does not allow for a history of how the passport produced an official identity, or specifically the establishment of the authority through which the passport could secure national borders and, therefore, produce the border as a governable space. I argue that such a cultural and political history of the geographic space of the nation requires an understanding of power not in terms of "the state" but in terms of a decentering of power through a focus on technologies, on practices as practices. Significantly, for Carey, this would require a strategic decentering of his humanist actor. In Carey's terms this would be a history of how the passport produces the nonpsychological fact of identity. This chapter offers such a history, written as a description of practices of verification as an attempt to analyze how information, in this example identity, is transmitted. The need to govern over distance made identification a problem. The production of the passport as a technology of verification is an example of the "archival" solution to this modern problem of identification. The practices that enabled this solution (documentation) produced official identity. Verification, instead of representation, foregrounds how a technology, the passport, produces the object it requires. Therefore, I have offered verification as a way to understand transmission that is neither instrumental nor ritual but positions transmission as a site of contestation that provides a way to analyze changing conceptions of "effectiveness." In this sense verification offers a critique of scientific accuracy in sympathy with the frustration that motivated Carey's attack on a behaviorist model of communication; it offers another front to Carey's project to "make scientific practices one of many."[58]

A focus on knowledge and expertise facilitates a conceptualization of the geographic space of the nation, of the state, that does not collapse it into the symbolic space, what becomes the "nation" for Carey. It is necessary to maintain this distinction I have read into Carey's own distinction to emphasize two specific definitions of culture: the "symbolic" and what I have awkwardly labeled the "technical." The technical definition of culture privileges verification over representation and the production of culture over the apprehension of it. As such it indicates the limitations of Carey's specific deployment of culture in terms of the maintenance of society as community and tradition through symbolic meanings. As my history of the passport indicates, in a descriptive analysis of communication as culture, it is not easy to keep them distinct. For the purposes of this chapter I have tried to tease them apart to highlight an important aspect of culture that is too easily discounted in cultural conceptions of communication.

The limitations that I am reading into Carey's conception of communication as culture are perhaps understandable in a model of communication offered to challenge a focus on communication as transmission. However, taking for granted the victory of Carey's cultural approach, I have offered verification as another perspective to enable "transmission" to be understood culturally. That is, I have read the strategic privileging of ritual over transmission in practice to be equated with a downplaying of the forms of communication, of communication as techniques and practices. Thus, verification offers another dimension to a definition of culture. To be clear, I am not arguing that it is always necessary to frame projects through a technical definition of culture nor always to attend to practices of verification. Rather I am arguing that we should not unquestioningly limit culture to an analysis of representation and symbols. We need to recognize the possibility of going beyond the margins of a ritual model if we are to comprehend all the implications of the transmission of information in and over territory, if we are to understand it culturally and "productively."

Notes

1. See discussion of this in the introduction to this volume.
2. James Carey, "Reflections on the Project of (American) Cultural Studies," in *Cultural Studies in Question*, eds. Marjorie Ferguson and Peter Golding (London: Sage, 1997), p. 11.
3. Michel Foucault, "Questions of Method," in *The Foucault Effect: Studies in Governmentality*, ed. Graham Burchell et al. (Chicago: University of Chicago Press, 1991), p. 75.
4. Thanks to Lacey Torge and Vivek Kanwar for helping me begin to think about the passport as a technology of verification.
5. James Carey, "The Sense of an Ending: On Nations, Communications and Culture," in Catherine A. Warren and Mary Douglas Vavrus, eds. *American Cultural Studies*, (Urbana, IL: University of Illinois, 2002), pp. 196–238.
6. Ibid., pp. 204, 205.
7. Ibid., p. 204.

8. Ibid., p. 204.
9. Ibid., p. 199.
10. Nikolas Rose and Peter Miller, "Political Power beyond the State: Problematics of Government," *British Journal of Sociology* 43 (1992): 175.
11. Carey, "Sense of an Ending," p. 210. See also James Carey, "Afterword: The Culture in Question," in Eve Stryker Munson and Catherine A. Warren, eds., *James Carey: A Critical Reader* (Minneapolis: University of Minnesota Press, 1997), pp. 322–323.
12. Matt Matsuda, *The Memory of the Modern* (New York: Oxford, 1996), pp. 212–213.
13. This is the basis for Giddens's oft-cited explanation of modernity and the state through the concept of "disembedding: the lifting out of social relations from local contexts of interaction and their restructuring across indefinite spans of time-space." Giddens also uses money as an example of this. Anthony Giddens, *Consequences of Modernity* (Stanford, CA: Stanford University Press, 1990), p. 25.
14. Marc Shell, *Money, Language, and Thought: Literary and Philosophic Economies from the Medieval to the Modern Era* (Berkeley: University of California Press, 1982), p. 14.
15. Michael O'Malley, "Specie and Species: Race and the Money Question in Nineteenth-Century America," *American Historical Review* 99 (1994): 378.
16. Shell, *Money, Language, and Thought,* p. 105.
17. David Henkin, *City Reading: Written Word and Public Spaces in Antebellum New York* (New York: Columbia University Press, 1998), p. 14.
18. Ibid., p. 7.
19. Ibid, pp. 157–159.
20. Jennifer Mnookin, "Scripting Expertise: The History of Handwriting Identification Evidence and the Judicial Construction of Reliability," *Virginia Law Review* 87 (2001): 1773.
21. Randell McGowen, "Knowing the Hand: Forgery and Proof of Writing in Eighteenth-Century England," *Historical Reflections* 24 (1998): 385–414.
22. Alfred Chandler, *The Visible Hand: The Managerial Revolution in American Business* (Cambridge, MA: Belknap Press, 1977).
23. JoAnne Yates, "Business Use of Information and Technology during the Industrial Age," in *A Nation Transformed by Information,* ed. A. Chandler Jr. and J. Corteda (New York: Oxford University Press, 2000), p. 110.
24. JoAnne Yates, *Control through Communication* (Baltimore: Johns Hopkins University Press, 1989).
25. Ibid., p. 111.
26. Cindy Aron, *Ladies and Gentleman of the Civil Service: Middle-Class Workers in Victorian America* (New York: Oxford University Press, 1987), p. 134. For example, into the 1880s, the State Department continued to rely on long-term officials such as William Hunter who was described as the "personification of the department's work . . . its memory, its guiding hand." On one occasion Hunter alerted the secretary of state that a treaty the Dutch government had recently made a claim under had in fact been abrogated, although it took considerable time to confirm this as his initial remembrance of the date proved inaccurate. Graham Stuart, *The Department of State: A History of Its Organization, Procedure, and Personnel* (New York: Macmillan, 1949), pp. 130–131, 142–143.
27. James Hay, "Unaided Virtues: The (Neo)Liberalization of the Domestic Sphere and the New Architecture of Community" in *Foucault, Cultural Studies, and Govern-*

mentality, ed. Jack Bratich et al. (Albany: State University of New York Press, 2003), p. 171.

28. Matsuda, *The Memory of the Modern.* These are relatively recent developments. In Canadian colonial administration only in the 1840s did an increased scale of documents result in the inclusion of methods of standardization—filing classifications (number, date, subject, and list of enclosures)—in the heading of any report sent to London. Using changes in the existing institutions, such as census and civil registration, and implicitly recognizing the importance of the project of colonialism to these developments Edward Higgs argues that the foundation of the modern information state in England did not fully develop until 1870–1920. Bruce Curtis, "Official Documentary Systems and Colonial Government," *Journal of Historical Sociology* 10 (1997): 394; Edward Higgs, "The Rise of the Information State," *Journal of Historical Sociology* 14 (2001): 183.

29. Antoinette Burton, *Dwelling in the Archive: Women Writing House, Home, and History in Late Colonial India* (New York: Oxford University Press, 2003), p. 18; Allan Sekula, "The Body and the Archive," *October,* 39:3 (1986): 3–64.

30. Sekula, "The Body and the Archive," p. 45.

31. Bernard Cohn, *Colonialism and Its Forms of Knowledge* (Princeton, NJ: Princeton University Press, 1996), pp. xii, xv.

32. Ibid., p. 5.

33. Scott outlines five characteristics of state simplifications: (1) interested, utilitarian facts (2) written (verbal or numerical) documentary facts (3) static facts (4) aggregate facts (5) standardized facts. James Scott, *Seeing Like a State: How Certain Schemes To Improve the Human Condition Have Failed* (New Haven, CT: Yale University Press, 1998), pp. 3, 80.

34. Ibid., p. 65

35. Miller and Rose, "Political Power beyond the State," p. 177.

36. Passport Office, *The United States Passport: Past, Present, Future* (Washington, DC: Government Printing Office, 1976), p. 220.

37. Galliard Hunt, *The American Passport: Its History and a Digest of Laws, Rulings, and Regulations Governing Its Issuance by the Department of State* (Washington, DC: Government Printing Office, 1898), pp. 46–47, 59.

38. Mnookin, "Scripting Expertise," p. 165.

39. Kantowitz to secretary of state, 18 October 1884, RG 59, Entry 509 Box 79, NARA; George Russell (Superior Court of the City of New York) to Passport Bureau, Department of State, 14 March 1885, RG 59 Entry 509, Box 79, NARA.

40. T. Zimmerman to Benedict (Passport Clerk), 23 September 1885, RG 59 Entry 509, Box 80, NARA.

41. A. Fraccaroli, "Crossing Frontiers," *Living Age* (9 October 1920), p. 89.

42. Ann Stoler, *Race and the Education of Desire: Foucault's History of Sexuality and the Colonial Order of Things* (Durham, NC: Duke University Press, 1995), p. 93. For a insightful analysis of nationality as an alibi for race based on a history of pre–WWI passport policy in the British Empire, see Radhika Mongia, "Race, Nationality, and Migration," *Public Culture* 11 (1999): 527–556.

43. Amy Robinson, "It Takes One to Know One: Passing and Communities of Common Interest," *Critical Inquiry* 20 (1994): 719.

44. Pamela Sankar, "State Power and Record-Keeping: The History of Individualized Surveillance in the United States, 1790–1935" (Ph.D. dissertation, University of Pennsylvania, 1992), 26.

45. Michael Power makes a similar argument in his critique of auditing. He argues, through "social consensus" audits construct the context in which auditing occurs. For Power, "audibility is not a function of things themselves (of an absolute property of the transactions themselves) but of agreements within a specialist community which learns to observe and verify in a certain way." He does not specifically define audit because he argues it is a practice that is constantly negotiated. Michael Power, *The Audit Society: Rituals of Verification* (Oxford, England: Oxford University Press, 1999), p. 80.

46. Carey, "Afterword," p. 322.

47. Carey, "Reflections on the Project of (American) Cultural Studies," p. 18.

48. Carey, *Communication as Culture*, 21–22.

49. Carey, "Reflections on the Project of (American) Cultural Studies," p. 11.

50. Ibid., p. 11.

51. Carey, "Afterword," pp. 316–323.

52. Ibid., p. 322.

53. Carey, "Reflections on the Project of (American) Cultural Studies," p. 18.

54. Ibid., pp. 18–19.

55. Michel Foucault, "On Power," in *Michel Foucault: Politics, Philosophy, Culture*, ed. Lawrence Kritzman (New York: Routledge, 1988), p. 103.

56. Philip Corrigan, *Social Forms/Human Capacities: Essays in Authority and Difference* (London: Routledge, 1990), p. 265.

57. Foucault, "Questions of Method," p. 75.

58. This is Chris Russill's description of Carey's project—see his chapter in this volume.

10. Configurations of Culture, History and Politics

JAMES CAREY IN CONVERSATION WITH LAWRENCE GROSSBERG, PART 2

Grossberg

I want to come back to the idea of the essay as something that you can revisit. The essay of yours most widely quoted, and most widely known, is "A Cultural Approach to Communication."[1] You've revisited it occasionally, but not in a major way, and you haven't revisited it for a long time. What do you think of it now? Do you still believe it? Do you still think it's right? If you were to do it again, would you do it differently? Are there major changes you would make in your argument? Do you still think positivism is the bad guy?

Carey

Well, the first thing that I would say is that, as a few of the contributors point out, whether I think positivism is the bad guy or not, it was necessary to write such things at that time to try to clear some space in the academy so other things could be done. That was the same kind of thing that was happening at Birmingham as you can detect when you read the early working papers. They were trying to ask how can we create a space in a literary tradition to take it beyond the paradigmatic, and you had to fight for that space. I wouldn't have to do that anymore; that's been done. But there has been an enormous resurgence of positivist modes of thought as part of the conservative reaction. I'm always astonished by those who write essays about universities as hotbeds of liberal radicalism and revolution. You've got whole faculties in business, agriculture, and engineering who are to the right of George Bush, and yet there is this image based upon a few departments, or a few people in the humanities. But anyway, I wouldn't have to do that now. And I wouldn't have to argue for a more symbolist or culturalist point of view. It's all much better known now and one could get on with other things. And I might even rename notions like ritual and transmission and illustrate them in quite different ways than I did at that time. Culturalist and positivist might do. I remain happy with the conclusion of the paper, which is indirectly a tribute to Raymond Williams; it was time to reiterate publicly the things Williams was saying at the time so as to express a certain kind of alignment in that way. But there are a lot of changes and improvements that could be made in adapting it to much different circumstances. And, I've learned a lot in the meantime as well. I remember when I showed it to you, you said something to me like, "You write too well."

Grossberg

Part of what it seems to me has happened to that paper is that the binarism between the ritual and transmission has been almost fetishized, absolutely in ways that a careful reading of the essay, of its complexity and nuances, mitigates somewhat. You do talk, for example about the religious and moral origins of the transmission view, but then this sort of gets lost. And, then science intervenes into that history, and it takes on a different trajectory, but it has a common root with the cultural, with the ritual view in some ways.

Carey

We'll get back to that again with the communication/transportation distinction discussed in this book. My own forms of binary thinking get in the way. I certainly did not intend that reading. What I was trying to say is, first, that the dominant ways in which communication has been thought about and understood, which I call the transmission model, contain a political project to which I object. Second, that reading ignores something, whether religiously inspired or not, which for me is much more fundamental: all these forms of interaction are necessarily the anticipation and creation of forms of social relations and, therefore, of forms of institutionalized modes of conduct and ways of dealing with one another. In the essay I was trying to find a way of saying what was neglected and left out. But I realize that it often becomes interpreted as one is altogether different than the other one, that you have to make a choice in all of this. Whereas, I don't believe that. I think there are a lot of interesting studies to be done, aspects of which are talked about in this book, particularly about the way in which, as a cultural proclivity, there are certain extraordinary consequences of transmission models that can get examined within the normal course of doing research. I don't know how to get away from that. I don't know how to get away from certain native forms of thinking, and phrasing, even when I recognize the difficulties that they inspire.

Grossberg

Could you, perhaps in a quick way, distinguish for us how you use the terms? What's the difference in your usage between "culture" and "communication"? In the "Cultural Approach" essay and others, you say things like "culture constitutes communication as practices." What in your mind is the relation? Because then, of course, I'm going to put in the third term of "ideology" and ask you to distinguish culture, communication, and ideology.

Carey

I don't particularly make a distinction between culture and communication. Culture is not something you find in some hidden recess of the society, locked away in some vault. You find it active as meanings and practices in the daily life of the society. In the case of ideology, what I want to say is that ideology is one particular form of a cultural practice, one particular mode of deploying language for political purposes; I want to reserve it for that. In other words, I don't want to get into a position where everything is ideological. Everything may have a political consequence or ramification to it of some kind. But I think that it is helpful to say that ideology is a particular form of discourse aimed at changing the political order and using certain tropes and stylistic devices in order to accomplish it. And thus to contain ideology in some sense such that it doesn't become the whole of culture, meaning, practice. This would go back to what I was saying about religion [in part 1]. If all we can say is that religion is just another face of an ideological project, which in some sense is true, but, if that is all, then I think you lose something very valuable in terms of examining religion.

Grossberg

Is the relation between culture and communication something like the relation in Williams between a whole way of life and the forms of expression?

Carey

Yes or between the project and the formation, maybe. I have to think about that.

Grossberg

Part of the complexity and I think the nuance, but also in a sense the ambiguity, of that piece is you want both to talk about the symbolic in relation to culture and to communication but to refuse what you describe as the textualist kind of move, that is, the reduction of culture to a system of texts. You want to hold on to that system of social relationships, presumably, within which the symbolic texts function to give order to . . .

Carey

For example, Williams says we don't find the culture of the Welsh working class in texts particularly. We find it in the institutions they built and created. Now, you can call the institutions textual in some sense. You can use it metaphorically, but I don't know that it helps you to do that, to treat what is distinctive about a group of people whose life is more firmly realized through forms of association, institutions, patterns of daily living that seem to have little symbolic content on the surface of them as texts. I wanted to resist converting the whole of the real into a text. But, you're right insofar as Williams talks about the relations within a whole way of life, which includes much more than ideology and particular forms of expression of the ideological way of life.

Grossberg

But, it seems to me, your pragmatism puts you in a different position, perhaps a different set of problems than Williams, because Williams, while he wants to hold that position, constantly slides back into a privileging of the aesthetic, of the textual, even while he tries to hold on to the experience, the living. Whereas, your pragmatism puts you in the position of privileging the system of social relations . . . within which then communication is the process that fits into the forms of culture.

Carey

Yes, well, communication is the process that creates the social relations, which it then fits within. Those kind of phrases I use, it creates what it pretends only to display, I use to get at that particular kind of complication. And no, I don't privilege the aesthetic in this case partly because what I thought of . . . if I go back to the biographical part. To come from an uneducated family but one that practiced quite radical politics, as really tough street corner orators and terrific organizers of people in factories and this sort of thing, and to textualize this, you know, seems to lose something very important. That this *was* their culture, their way of life, their systems of meaning, and their pattern of social relations, all brought together. And by privileging the aesthetic, we lose to some degree the greatness of the accomplishment. It's like aestheticizing the civil rights movement and ignoring the black women in the basements of churches organizing a bus boycott. If I want to privilege anything, that's what I want to hold on to and privilege.

Grossberg

I want to come back to something, because a few moments ago you talked about ritual and transmission embedded in these ways of organizing and controlling the conduct of people's lives. I want to come back to that through Foucault. But there's one other question I want to ask about the way in which that article is read and your own sense of it. It is often read in relation to your Innis and McLuhan work, so that the ritual view is time biased and the transmission view is space biased. And, correlatively, it is read as if you located politics on the side of the transmission view and religion on the ritual side. And so the dichotomy gets established in a system of connotativeness. How do you respond to that reading, which puts the ritual view, time bias and religion on one side and the transmission view, space bias and politics on the another?

Carey

I would like to take politics away from both of them and say that it's an autonomous category, that is not grafted prematurely onto either of these types. If I say to you, for example, that I think the best studies that we've been able to do answer the question why, with very high rates of literacy in the colonies, did the colonialists read the British papers and not the American ones? Why did they want news of Britain? Why were they relatively uninterested in what was happening in Virginia? The answer is that they got up in the morning and said, "I'm a subject of the British Crown," and by reading, by entering the newspaper, I enter the world of being that subject, that person. Now, I learned things that have happened in England as a result of that, but I make that entrance into that world in order to confirm a particular set of social relations in which I'm embedded, of who I am. Now, that in some sense is time biased. It is a reaffirmation and an underscoring of tradition, of the past, of who I am, of who I will continue to be. That is the point that I really want to hold on to—to enter any medium of communication is to enter a world of often predefined, but negotiable, identities, and, at the same time, in which a positive affirmation takes place. When Hegel writes, "The modern world begins with reading the newspapers," in some sense, that says it all. To get up and to make the choice to say that I'm going to enter the secular world, the political world in this case, the world of being a citizen or a subject, and I'm this, before I'm that now in my life. Now, these are political acts.

But, to say on the other hand, if we (New York merchants) can get to Chicago faster than the Boston merchants because we go up the Hudson, and build the Erie Canal, which empties into the Great Lakes, we will control Chicago, and we'll cut off Boston. And we'll do it by reducing signaling time between these two points and isolate Boston so it can't compete with us. That's a transmission view of it. It doesn't talk about this being a world of consumers or nations or nationalism or frontiers or expansion. It simply talks about a limited, instrumental goal of profit maximization, of the control of space, the control of time in the interest of controlling space. And, it's a one-day world in this sense. It's a view of the world to be understood in one day. Both of these are political acts done under the control of different images of what a social relation is and how it's solidified and made permanent. Does that speak to your question?

Grossberg

Let me take a different route into the same thing. I have taught this essay many times, and one of the things the students always ask, undergraduates in particular, is whether you are describing two theories of communication or two practices of communication? And I think this is where, or rather an answer is always, "they're the same," because culture produces the world it describes. But I do think people read this in a way that transportation is the embodiment of the transmission view and some other forms of communication embody a ritual view. So communication and transportation become binary representations of ritual and transmission, and then communication itself gets split off into two. As opposed to saying, no, one could treat transportation with a ritual view. One could understand that although the New York merchants viewed the railroad system and viewed the Erie Canal with a transmission view, they were also re-creating the map of how people understood their reality and understood their world: I mean reconfiguring the spatial relations was also a reconfiguration of the maps.

Carey

Well, when I read the essays in this book on this point, I had the acute feeling that I unconsciously, by using transportation and transmission to refer to two different kinds of problems I was wrestling with, tended to obscure what those problems are. A few people, for example, cited Wolfgang Schivelbusch's work on the railway journey. Surely, transportation remains primarily a form of communication. I mean, people still walk, bicycle, go by train. These established social relations . . .

Grossberg

. . . Baudelaire's *flaneur* . . .

Carey

Exactly. And just how they do it. So that a railroad system that emphasizes end point connections and not midpoint connections means you establish a long-distance relationship between New York and Chicago, and you don't care about anything in between except as something to get through, as something that does not inhibit the flow. And, so, in some sense, as Schivelbusch argues, the space between disappears for us, and we think of our social relations now being conducted in terms of a particular kind of geography. At the same time, Schivelbusch in his work on the railroad adds all sorts of complications. He also argues it created new ways of perception, new forms of entertaining one's self, new types of social relations within the railroad car itself that were a function of speed. But I was after a more limited point and that's where I failed. It may have helped if I said this: In Wiener's introduction to *Cybernetics* he says something like "the age of power engineering is over." And he meant by that, after the age of the railroad and the jetliner, we've solved all the problems, or they're marginal, and I suppose you can say that now that we can get to the moon, we can get anywhere. But the real problem became communications engineering, the economy of a signal—it's a difference between strong signal and weak signal engineering. That's the point I was trying to get at. What the telegraph then shifted was the kinds of problems people started to think about as central. It did this accidentally, in this case, seeing that you could utilize the signaling system as a means of controlling the transportation system and a means of controlling the elements within it, whether they're human beings or boxcars or any other thing. It is an abrupt shift here, that in the long run, frees communication from many of the constraints of geography.

But, it's a bit of an illusion. I'm driving on Interstate 90 going from New York City to Chicago. I look out the window. There's the Erie Canal. There's the Erie Railroad. There are the telegraph wires. There are the telephone wires. If we went down and did a little archaeological digging, we would find an old Indian trail and probably even a deer lick. Now, these are all slight modifications on what came before. They're simply overlays, one on the other. But what I was trying to say is, while it was not realized until we really came to an age of packet switching, you no longer have to get to Chicago by following that route. You may get to Chicago faster by going through Charlotte. And all of a sudden Charlotte starts to grow, even though it's off the route. It grows because of relative factors of speed and course, and so now we have cities growing that are off the old trunk lines that ran east to west, cities like Atlanta and Houston. Other places now become able to compete effectively because the transaction costs of the geography of transportation are relatively low. That's what I was trying to get at.

Grossberg

Would you accept the statement that while the dominant way in which the telegraph was rationalized, and then in retrospect theorized, was through a kind of transmission view of communication, it was also possible, and perhaps done by you among others, to offer a kind of ritual view of the telegraph?

Carey

Yes, that's right.

Grossberg

And that, in fact, your reading of the emergence of the transmission view of the telegraph is itself a kind of ritual, cultural interpretation, a ritual view of the conjunction of the telegraph and the transmission view . . .

Carey

Sure. For many people, a map of the United States that is a map of the railroad system and the telegraph system is a better representation of the United States than any other kind of map because it's a map of its linkages, its connections, its most powerful circuits. It's all of those things at once. I was only trying to talk about communication versus transportation in the limited sense that an electrical engineer might say that the problems associated with figuring out how to economize a symbol, if you will, or a message, are different than the engineering problem of how to get more power into the system to move it faster between point A and point B. And, that this difference becomes decisive over a long period of time. Now, there is something that John Peters gets at in his essay that's both right and wrong. I also was trying to say that in fact, modern communications engineering has been to some degree a struggle to understand the telegraph and what it is, and to take some of these principles and apply them to as many different places as possible and to incorporate human operators into it as kind of seamless participants, so that no longer does the telegraph operator have any independence; he is seamlessly integrated into the system in terms of what he can and cannot do. I don't want to call this integration a revolution. I think the kind of language I was trying to use was that of a "decisive change" that had taken place.

Grossberg

But, I guess my question would be is it really a decisive change outside of the fact that it's a kind of reconstitution of the language with which people are rationalizing. The thing is, the engineer and the cyber-manager and the telegraph operator are all operating, as it were, in scientific terms, as measuring efficiency, efficiency of power versus the efficiency of speed. So, in that sense, they're all operating within a common universe. But now, within that scientific worldview, it's like biology breaking off from physics. You know, they've sort of broken off and said, well, we have two relatively autonomous sciences here: the science of communication and the science of transportation.

Carey

Yes, and when they start to bring them back together, the question they're asking is how can the signaling system control the human operator and the physical system that goes with it. That becomes the central problem of cybernetic engineering. Now, the thing that makes it, in my view, less of a more fully realized ritual understanding, is that for the people doing this, at least, doing these things and saying these things and talking in that almost utopian language, they do not see how they are also changing the structures and contours of politics and social life. That the signal engineering is central to a much bigger project, the project of building large nations and keeping them under control. And, that is where forms of political support come into play. It's not just a pure love of science. It is a matter of what kinds of markets we create, whether they're commercial or they're political or whatever. And that seems to me to be the accomplishment, to be able to control places where there is no transportation system to undergird it. We may not have a train track or even a highway that gets in to this space, but a signal will get into it, and maybe that can be a sufficient mode of control.

Grossberg

Let me turn to a different question, which is about your political correctness piece.[2] And there are two sides of the question. One is in the essay you wrote on resistance to cultural studies, you talk about the phenomenological resistance to cultural studies, which is precisely defined by its opposition to a kind of structuralist/poststructuralist turn.[3] And you say in that essay that you have some sympathies for that, but you resist the phenomenological resistance. But, then, some years later, you seem to have given into it. And, so, I guess one question is what changed so that you thought now that it was right. But on the other hand, if you remember, when that essay came out, I called you somewhat upset. I think the way I phrased it was, "But, what about Stuart [Hall]?" And you said, "Oh no, I didn't mean Stuart. Stuart isn't included." But, I think everyone who reads that essay assumes Stuart is because you attacked the turn to French theory, to structuralism, Althusser, ideology critique, etc. So the two sides of the question are: what changed that you felt you had to make a fairly strong attack on these developments (and I realize it was strengthened by the context of that book), and, second, how would you explain why you might think that Stuart isn't included? What is the object of your critique such that you wouldn't necessarily include Stuart in the description of what you're critiquing?

Carey

Well, I think that the paragraph that you're repeating to me was probably mentally composed one night that I heard Cary Nelson [an English professor at the University of Illinois]. He was just going on about economics but he didn't know anything about the subject. He took it as a subject he didn't have to study, and I said to myself, God, this is what happens when cultural studies becomes literary studies. That's really what the critique is. You understand that I encountered French poststructuralist theory in a certain institution and a certain moment, as a literary formation.

If we think of cultural studies as a kind of open intellectual formation in which, in principle, you could say, "I'm not only going to examine literature and the growth of the global economy, but I'm going to look at other things, policing and surveillance, human welfare, population, immigration, these sorts of things." For me, that's what I wanted cultural studies to be. It would be a place in which people were interested, and willing, to transverse certain disciplinary lines. But at the same time, I recognized that there were forces turning it into an adjunct of the literary disciplines. That's what the frustration was. I certainly don't blame Stuart for doing that. In fact, he did much the opposite of that. He kept it open to all sorts of things; you can see that just by looking at the title of his works. Now, it wasn't that I always agreed with him about it, but it seemed to me that he represented a kind of authentic spirit. He was moving from literature to other things. But, he was always very careful to recognize the integrity of what he was moving to and his own intellectual responsibility. For example, on the question of ideology he says that Weber's *Protestant Ethic and the Spirit of Capitalism* is a tour de force that has to be dealt with. Anyone who wants to deal with this problem has to deal with Weber, has to deal with the tradition of sociology, with the question of how the state monopolizes violence, with what the modern state wants to be.

But, unfortunately, I think that cultural studies created a kind of license that led to many of the charges of political correctness, and it became too much of an adoption of certain kinds of attitudes about things without trying to back those attitudes with understanding. I felt this very intensely because I thought in addition the Left was losing the war, at least in politics. I thought it was losing the war because it would not address certain problems that were on everyone's mind, right or wrong, like crime, welfare, population, immigration, and the loss of state control under globalization. These seemed to me to be things that everyone was facing one way or another—a great sense of personal loss: I'm losing my job, losing this, losing that. And I thought that in order to have a political movement, to have an ideology, you had to address these kinds of issues and not, what should I say, textualize them by saying that learning how to read a text adequately provides it.

The only time I remember being disappointed with Stuart in these terms was in a lecture he gave in the Home Economics building one year on the campus at Illinois. It was a wonderful lecture on, as I remember, among other things, the circulation of what we call primitive objects throughout the world and the creation of a market for the primitive. And toward the end of it he said, and I hope I get this right, he turned to Jamaica and Rastafarianism, and he pointed out the power of this religious formation within Jamaican society as the creation of a space within which black Jamaicans could live their own life and make their own achievements and serve as some kind of self-protection. And I thought it was very smart, but then he said something that seemed to me not a cultural studies statement. He said, "Of course, I don't believe this stuff," and I said to myself, now that's a functionalist argument. It's doesn't make any difference whether you believe it or not, Stuart. It couldn't have done the things it did if they didn't believe it. They were not just building a shell of protection, they were building a system of belief to confer upon themselves, a form of dignity and purpose. And, even if we can't understand it, we have to honor it as a cultural formation. That's the *only* time I can remember . . .

Grossberg

I have to admit that I only vaguely recall the event. I think that his distancing himself was in response to a question, when someone pressed him to declare where he stood, in more personal terms, on the question of Rastafarianism and religion. Stuart has of course published an essay on Rastafarianism and religion in Jamaica, perhaps a version of at least part of that talk. I do agree with you, however, that the issue of our own beliefs is, as cultural studies scholars, not directly relevant; the issue is not whether we agree with people's assumptions or find them rational.

Carey

I think that so much of the centrality of cultural studies, no matter where we deploy it, has to start from saying, "these people who worry about their jobs being shipped overseas may be crazy, they may be selfish, they may be all these things, but let us try to find out what the hell they're thinking, and what is bothering them so we can engage them." To engage them, not necessarily to agree with them, but to argue with them. But not to caricature them and to assume that there's not a certain density to their thought, and a system of beliefs that's very important to them. And, I know I said this to you at the time . . . too much of what I started to see as cultural studies, at least in some of the literary circles, and too much of what I see on the Left, does not take this task seriously. I've always had trouble with literary disciplines.

Grossberg

Is that where I inherited that from?

Carey

I said, the old high culture/mass culture debate is creeping back in, in a disguised form. You know, these forms of popular life are being visited, but with a kind of spiritual traveler's check that we understand this is all crap. That was the moment. . . . And it was also the moment when I think you had to deal with some of the criticisms, only some of them, of the political correctness thing. I think you had to take them seriously, but also you had to redefine some of what we meant by cultural studies and go on the attack and say, that's *not* what we believe. That's *not* what we are trying to do. . . . That's the sense of exasperation in overcoming . . .

Grossberg

It might be said that the French theorist who comes closest to cultural studies in his own work and project is Foucault. In particular, in recent days, a number of cultural studies types have taken up his notion of governmentality, the notion that culture or discourse is deployed to produce subjects and control the conduct of populations. Do you read Foucault as someone sympathetic to your own work? Do you see the relationships? They are certainly there in this collection of essays.

Carey

I don't know how we develop these complicated relations to people . . . where it all comes from. There's too much of a body of work there to say that I've read it all. I've certainly read the major books. There are many aspects of *The Order of Things* that I liked. I must confess, and it may be a very bad book for all I know; the portrait of him in James Miller's biography scared me.

Grossberg

I do think it is a bad book. I don't know James Miller, and I don't think this was his intention, but it is the moment at which there was kind of an attack on Foucault. And Miller's book, which constructed Foucault as this sado-masochistic figure, living life on the edge, certainly played into that.

Carey

I understand . . . I'm admitting to influences here that are imperfectly understood. I think that the force that these essays together are going to have, is to get me to rethink and reread Foucault. Because so many of the essays raise this question with me, I have to deal with it in some way . . . I didn't find a democratic spirit in his work. Now, this is a difficult thing to do, to both admit to the excessiveness, the lasciviousness of these forms of control and identity formation and all and yet to try to maintain some kind of hope and optimism for some better way of life. But, beyond the beauty of some of the empirical investigations, I didn't find any of that spirit that I was looking for, that I wanted to keep company with, and perhaps I even became afraid of him, afraid of what he might do to me if I took him too seriously.

One of the things I liked in Soderlund's chapter on trafficking women is that there is in the essay a kind of forgiving spirit in some sense. What I mean by this is she seems to want to say at some point, . . . If a Muslim woman as one I was listening to last night says, "Allah, be praised my son is dead as a martyr. My life is fulfilled." Now I don't find this a very cheery idea, but I have no doubt that's what she believes. I have no doubt that you just can't treat her as being an object of patriarchy, or whatever, and that there is a serious commitment to a way of life however repugnant we may find it.

And there's something in me that I suppose tenses up at the notion of governmentality. All culture is a form of control because it narrows the distribution of, at least, legitimate behaviors. The difficult problem is deciding when it is that those controls seem to legitimately arise out of the life ways of people, and which we may aggressively criticize and try to talk them out of, even as we recognize the dangers of simply imposing upon them our own way of life as if it is one that is unproblematically superior. This goes to contemporary politics. If you look at the distribution of wealth in the United States, the great beneficiaries of George Bush's tax cut all live in the blue states: Connecticut, New Jersey, New York, California. New York used to send, let us say, two dollars to Washington, for every dollar that came back. Under Bush, New Yorkers only have to send about $1.40 now. These numbers are plucked from the air but nonetheless illustrate the paradox. So much is coming back in these damn tax cuts. And, yet, it's the people out in Oklahoma, where there aren't many millionaires, who support this kind of economic policy. I mean, I'm perplexed by it . . .

It strikes me as a purely irrational belief, and if someone would just point this out to them, they would do something about it. But because it's part of a larger conception of how society is put together. . . . Every human organization that is not completely demoralized and anomic sets boundaries or borders. It has some things it values. It says, if you want to be one of us, you must honor this, too. It's a very arbitrary process. Universities say, we honor truth, so if you've been caught cheating, we throw you out. (But, we throw out very few cheaters.) There's a moral boundary to the university. You can transgress it. There are things that you can't do without the university saying, we're not going to let you be part of this community anymore. I'm interested in these symbolic boundaries, which are in part supported by paper and documents and governmentality. And, in part, more ethereally embodied somehow in the ether of social organization. These are the interlocking relationships, the symbolic spaces of and between the national boundaries, or the boundaries of a nation, or the boundaries of a family. I haven't found Foucault helpful with that. Even though he denies that he's using the notion of power in a repressive way, rather, he's using it in a productive way, looking at how knowledge is made productive in social life. I just feel uneasy with the whole thing. I always think it is important to remember that as we experience these changes, some of them seem to be driven by technology, it's almost always true that as old borders and social relations come down new ones go up at the same time. And, it's much harder to see the erection of new borders than the fall of the old ones. We're trying to find out the way the world gets repartitioned on the basis of new technologies; this is the real challenge.

Grossberg

One of the things people who use Foucault forget is that Foucault argues that we can only analyze structures of power when they're already disappearing. And so, for example, we can talk about the human subject now in a particular Enlightenment form because that's already disappearing. We can't yet talk about that individuality that is emerging, which is that organization of power that we live in. That's always the most difficult challenge. In any case, in one of your early essays, when you are laying out the problem with positivism in its various forms (utilitarianism, behaviorism, functionalism), you say that the basic assumption is that the ends of human action are random and exogenous and therefore, it concludes, and I quote now, "Hence, politics should not try to form the character or cultivate the virtue of its citizens. But, to do so would be to legislate morality." And so positivism throws morality out. In a sense, Foucault says, that's exactly what culture's always been like. And, that's what governmentality is, right? It is that culture is always cultivating the virtue of its citizens, however virtue is defined. So, what's your answer to positivism's rejection of this position? Foucault says, well, you can't reject it because this is the very nature of culture. Would you agree with that? Would you say, well, this isn't the nature of culture, but its one possible thing culture can do, and we ought to encourage it? What is the place of morality and politics in your alternative intellectual formation?

Carey

Well, you are very close to some contemporary questions. I believe that when positivism ruled out issues of morality to substitute the issue of choice, by which I mean simply that whatever is moral is what you choose, positivism sets out to help maximize the utility of *human* choice without entering into judgments about those choices. I want to say, in the long run, that won't work. I mean, it's always I suppose about the formation of character and virtue, even though it tries to rule it out. But what often then comes in are characters and virtues that are less admirable than those that have been ushered out the front door. And, that for me is in part from an inadequate theory of democracy as involving the making of these choices in collective ways.

Grossberg

I'll come back to that because I want to get into democracy and politics. Before that, there's one question I want to ask. It has to do with the inexact fit between your work on technology and the cultural approach. How do you fit the two sides of your work together? At one point you describe them as "two halves of a sometimes discordant conversation I carry on with myself." You talk about them as point counterpoint, "I'm unable to seamlessly integrate the terms." At another point you say, "I'm aiming to develop the cultural theory in Innis' work." At some points you refer to technology as culture, as symbols of and for reality, as forms of life. At other points, you say that "technology is a privileged insight into the social totality," and you compare it with the status of the commodity in Marx. You say our national storytelling is, to an unusual extent, embedded in the history of technology. All of these are different ways of trying to fit those two pieces together. Can you fit them? Do you have a way? Do you think they fit together?

Carey

Well, the thing is that they all fit together in my mind, yet I can't express this fitting together in a way that can convince anyone else to think that they fit together or that I'm not just being schizophrenic about it. There's a real tension there because the different essays serve different purposes and call forth different events and different arguments that I was having at different times and that I would like to see fit together better while resisting what Jonathan [Sterne] in this collection almost calls essentially another base superstructure kind of argument, which I'm well aware of, and that I don't want to get into, not only for all the reasons we learned from Marxism but because it just makes me uncomfortable to think about it that way. I want to say that to enter given technological worlds is to enter actual social relations and that a way of conceiving of these social relations is in terms of their temporal and spatial character and as representation of . . .

Grossberg

Therefore, technologies are cultures . . .

Carey

Technologies are cultures. I think that technology as an artifact operates differently, functions differently, in different cultures. One of the nicest sentences in this collection was when John Peters said that I tried to read a whole way of life out of technologies as a series of suggestions. That's what I want to do. And, therefore, not to separate medium and message or, in other ways, ritual and transmission . . . and to reconcile it in some way by bringing them together so that they mutually inform one another.

Grossberg

Yes, that seems to me half of the work that needs to be done. And, I propose a possible other half. Because what you've done is to say, so, technology can be a culture. And, my question is, is communication or culture a technology? And as I was doing this, I actually went back to my notes from Communication 474 [a class on the history and theory of technology that Carey taught at the University of Illinois], and I came upon your lecture on Mumford. And, Mumford argues that language is a technology. Would you agree with that? So, if technology is a culture, is communication, in its form as symbolic expression, language, etc., is it a technology?

Carey

I hesitate, because I know I'm committing myself to more than I want to commit myself to. I'll use the example from a recent paper that I haven't quite finished. Prior to the advent of Western musical notations, the musical tradition was carried in memory, and deliberately so carried. And that's why we had boy's choirs that memorized Gregorian chant, which derived from Hebrew chant. The longest continuous body of music we had until the fifteenth century was essentially this chant that was, in some sense, universally known and understood throughout the West, including the Jewish West in diaspora. And, then, written notation was invented. This is a technology of making music, too. It is quite a different technology because it means now the music can go where the choirboys don't go. You can send the score and play the music. . . . So, yes I want to say it is a technology. But I fear at times someone will take my saying that *too* seriously, and rather than seeing relationships along the way will simply say, well, it's just another machine. It's not what I mean, and it can't be that simply because it was the first machine that evolved within the human species for accomplishing certain forms of work. So, I can live with the notion that communication is a technology, if we recognize the limits of that statement.

Grossberg

But, it's a privileged technology in a Deweyan sense, in a pragmatist sense?

Carey

Yes, because ontogeny recapitulates phylogeny. It's the first command we learn to make of our environment. The first grasping on to it other than through some instinctual way, so it is in each of our lives, you know, it has a kind of privilege that nothing else has, and it has a certain privilege in the evolution of the species as well. I think it did evolutionary work. It is in Marx's notion of work as an attempt to externalize thought and understanding, and to share . . . so, I find it in a variety of ways, including political ways, obviously . . . as a kind of baseline of comparison to all sorts of things. But, I do want to see the interesting relationships between memorized music and written music and different devices of recording this sort of thing as having derivative characteristics.

Grossberg

To use a bad analogy, are you saying language is to other forms of technology much as the human body is to other forms of transportation, and, as we walk, we understand what motion through space is through our body, and, then, develop forms of technology? Similarly, we learn to symbolically represent . . .

Carey

. . . Yes, I would say this, and I would also say it also happens to be, in both cases, the thing that is generally most under the control of the person and is the most flexible. You can get almost anywhere by foot, even places you can't even get to on a bicycle . . . let's forget about the SUV. What I want to say is that, each addition involves a kind of process of capital formation to make it work, which becomes a series of constraints on it even as it becomes a system of liberation. And, I really think that the gains that have been made for me in some ways in the kind of technological studies over the course I've been doing them is that now people can see relationships. There were real political consequences that flowed from the West's invention of written music: Western music conquered the world before the West conquered the world. Such music was everywhere, and the Western system of notation is used to translate every musical idiom of the world. I mean, if you want an example of cultural imperialism, look at the classical tradition of music in the West. Such inventions have led to real gains in what we can see in the relationships between cultural and political forms.

Grossberg

I want to turn to the politics of the day. It seems to me that you are recently going through a kind of rethinking of your politics and your political analysis of what's going on. "A Sense of an Ending" is a wonderfully Careyite essay but also different than anything you've published before.[4] You seem to have gone from earlier rejecting claims of postmodernity to now embracing them or at least being willing to talk about living in a certain kind of postmodern, disorienting time. You seemed to have gone from an emphasis on consensus in your work to more wanting to put up front the notions of dissensus and antagonism as part of the process of culture. And, you seem at the same time to be fighting between a kind of optimism and a kind of pessimism about this. I found two quotes, for example, in "The Culture in Question" that talk about the United States in seemingly contradictory ways: "The membrane of civilization is especially thin." I take that to be a rather pessimistic judgment. Yet, you also talk about "the persistence of underlying forces in American culture": "However new this all seems, Americans are learning how to live together by experimenting with new ways of living apart." That seems rather optimistic.[5] So, I guess I want to ask an open question first. What are you struggling with? What is your sense of what you want to grapple with about the contemporary world as a cultural studies scholar?

Carey

Well, I'll utter a series of contradictions. Many of the views of politics that you can quote from me started to come crashing down around 1972. The election of Nixon to a second term and the nomination of McGovern, the purging of the Democratic Party, and the adoption of the primary system were I thought enormous errors. And, therefore, the cheery optimism of early years started to turn, not only because I think, and Todd Gitlin now agrees, that allowing Nixon to beat Humphrey in '68 was a terrible mistake. It started to establish a kind of conservative hegemony, which has simply grown over the course of time, and I don't think that that hegemony is a particularly democratic one. Now, if I go from there to where we are now, there are days in which I wake up and say, 'Oh my God, was I wrong about everything?' Or, was I right at the time but it turned out wrong for reasons no one could anticipate? So, there is no doubt that I am much more pessimistic for the same reasons I suspect everyone on the Upper West Side of Manhattan is pessimistic. And, you know, I am now wondering what's going to be left to us at the end of Bush's second four-year term. Whether or not this is going to be the securing of not just a conservatism but a particular kind of conservatism that comes out of the marriage of the South and the Southwest with cosmopolitan economic elites, and whether the Bush policies are going to end up permanently damaging the culture.

Now, and this is more difficult to talk about, I think that certain beliefs associated with the Left, or at least parts of the Left, have caused some of the problems as well, and we are as guilty, if you will, on this as anyone else. I think essentially the Democratic Party by abandoning the working class—working-class economics—gave away an important part of their base. I think the purging of the city machines was a mistake. I'm more of an admirer of the first Mayor Daley than I should be. The city machines were built upon a minor kind of graft. They paid off the tow truck operator and took care of their brothers-in-law. But the real graft in America flows between the federal government and major corporations, e.g., Enron, WorldCom, Tyco, etc. I would rather live with certain forms of urban corruption, if I have to make that kind of a choice. I think because of the tensions over the Vietnam War, there was too much of a writing off of the working class and making them available, eventually, to Ronald Reagan and then to some degree George W. Bush. At the same time, I thought the political strategies of the Left were the wrong ones. For example, I do believe that if we had not "won" *Roe* v. *Wade,* abortion would be universal in the United States; the issue would be settled by now, unavailable as a moral issue used to discredit both the Left and the Democratic Party. It's not going to be settled now because you can't settle those kinds of questions through the courts. We can fight about gay marriage all we want, but unless you work things out democratically one is destined to fail.

I think that the Democratic strategy of essentially trying to work through the courts and to a lesser extent through the media rather than through the legislative process, which involves winning majorities at the legislative level, turned out to be, in the long run, a bad choice. Now, when you try to make these arguments, people too easily read into what you're saying certain kinds of moral commitments, and my only position on these things has been, essentially, that these are not the kinds of issues that courts handle very easily or can resolve, and I think cumulatively they've come back to haunt the Left. At the same time, the Left has been unimaginative. We allow George Bush to get away with moral values, a culture of life platform despite his enthusiastic use of the death penalty in Texas. You know, he talks about the culture of life but with cynicism. If you want to talk about the culture of life, you ought to have some reasonably unified position on it. I can live with the French position on abortion, which goes about as follows: we don't particularly like abortion around here, but we're not going to deny it. The state takes a stand against it, does not think this is the best practice you can engage in but does not get into the business of legislating it. Now, there is a lack of imaginative formulations that might present alternatives to the Right. Instead, the Democratic Party gets so caught up in the Right's culture, the choice culture, if you will, rather than what I call the democratic culture. It's not only that we've abandoned the working class, we've pretty much abandoned trying to reform work, to make the workplace someplace we can learn about democracy because it functions in some way with some reasonable set of democratic procedures, and there is a similar problem with universities. We've become increasingly more hierarchical and dictatorial. So, there's plenty of blame to go around and plenty of things that are not understood. But I've increasingly found myself becoming more stridently Leftist, simply because I'm so troubled by the dominance of the Right at the moment and what it means. I think it's very dangerous.

It's a complicated series of dislocations and we have to create a more democratic Leftist politics, but I'm not sure how we can do it now. It has to be one that has a little more patience. A swing to the Left is not going to happen overnight. It's going to happen, if it happens at all, over the course of twenty years or so.

Grossberg

To what extent do you think that this complex situation is the result of changes that have happened in and around culture? To what extent is culture implicated in these changes? In "Culture and Economy" in 1994, you wrote, "The entire history of modern communication has been turning the resources not only of information but of meaning itself into a phenomenon of the market." And, then, you go on to talk about how a major project has to be "to revitalize our understanding of communication independent of economics."[6] To what extent is the situation you described above the result of the inability of the Left to imagine alternative ways? Do you think that, in the end, the political economists have been proved correct, that we are now living in a world in which culture has become entirely commodified?

Carey

I don't believe this. I think the Left has placed too much weight on what is commodified. I'm not going to give you any plea for the Jimmy Swaggarts of the world or for these southern families who are voting overwhelmingly for conservative congressmen, but I don't think they're doing this on a commodity basis. I think they're acting against their economic interest . . . which should be pointed out to them, for one thing. But, I don't think they're living in this commodified world, except in so far as they've seized control of that world. That is to say they've seized control of the channels of culture so that certain southern understandings of religion, and certain southern understandings of who is and who is not an American, what patriotism is, what loyalty is, certain militaristic habits, which have always been part of the old South, a certain worship of oil in the oil patch, have simply now gone from South and West into the North, and they've undercut the basis of the more reasonable, that's not to say perfect, northern liberalism. And, this southernization has not been engaged. It hasn't been answered and the organization necessary to do it is absent.

When I lived in Iowa in the 1970s, five of the six congressional seats were Democrats, the sixth was Jim Leach, a very liberal republican. Both senators were Democrats, the governor was a liberal Republican. It was among the first states in the union to pass the Equal Rights Amendment. It was pro-choice. Now, all of a sudden, it's in George Bush's camp. How did these old Scandinavian states with their tradition of social democracy like Iowa and Minnesota get taken away from the Democratic Party or those old loyalties undermined? What are the possibilities of reclaiming the border states like Missouri and Kansas, which were always on the margins?

Grossberg

But how would you respond to Thomas Franks's *What's the Matter with Kansas?* Basically, they're suffering from false consciousness, voting against their own economic interests, being distracted by cultural issues, etc.

Carey

What I want to say is whether consciousness is true or false, it's the only consciousness we have, and you have to deal with it. And you're not going to deal with it by calling it false, because it is not false to those people . . . they don't think of it that way. Now, as I say, you can thank them for all the money they're sending to New York. You can do certain things but you have to do it tactically, you have to do it organizationally, and you have to deal with the underlying beliefs that are there. Meanwhile, there is a very wide range of things we can do. I think we should be mounting legal challenges under the First Amendment to the concentration in the communication/telecommunication sector by requiring that if an entertainment company owns a news operation, they either have to sell it or they have to organize it into a wholly owned subsidiary with an independent board of trustees such that journalism is not forced to conform to profit expectations laid on, say, the Disney company as a whole.

Grossberg

Why is this an issue that could be decided by the courts if the Left has already gone overboard in having the courts make all these other decisions? Don't we have to win that battle in popular opinion?

Carey

Yes, we have to win it, but we have to win it in popular opinion in order to win it in the courts. The court counts votes in elections as well. But, there are legislative ways of doing this, too. You pass the legislation; the court can strike it down, then you can fight in the court. This is a lot different than the old, forgive me, ACLU pattern, which goes back to the Scopes Monkey Trial. You run ads in southern papers that ask, "Do any of you dislike the new rules on science textbooks? If so, the ACLU will become your champion?" This case didn't emerge from this Tennessee town; it emerged from New York, as a deliberative attack upon the law. Now, it would have been one thing to try to go in there and to try to get the Tennessee legislature to recognize your argument, to lose, and then to take the case into court under the Tennessee constitution, which I'm sure is far more liberal than in fact Tennessee politics are. But that is a reorientation, and it's a reorientation towards the legislature. This requires you to face some of these beliefs that people hold, some of them right, some wrong, some false, some true, and take them seriously. I think people have condescended to them too much. We need to learn to respond to differences, to the fact that different groups of people may seem very strange to us, and often their beliefs will be different from and even conflict with our own. We have to find a way to say, look, we don't have to agree with one another, we need to figure out a way of living with one another. But, we have to find ways that don't involve ceding the dominance in the political to the Right. These people are not going away. They are not going to disappear. Whether they will foster a revolution is another matter.

Grossberg

I often argue that the Right is doing much better cultural studies than the Left.

Carey

Yes, I believe they are.

Grossberg

One of the ways in which you buck current intellectual fashion is that you argue that one of the great strengths of cultural studies is its ethnocentrism. And many people have pointed out that you are a decidedly American author. And, you celebrate that; in the face of people arguing against the national for the global, you have consistently maintained that kind of national focus. How would you defend that? Or, would you? Or, do you think it's so obvious in the contemporary world that we need to fight this battle at the scale of the nation?

Carey

Well, there are three or four different responses. One, I think, at one point, I call it a useful ethnocentrism. Second, I like Ken Cmiel's phrase of "exceptionalism without hubris."[7] I don't mean by exceptional the kind of positive evaluation that would exempt us from the laws of history and the problems that beset all people. Third, exceptional is a political judgment. Now, and for the foreseeable future, sovereignty will be located in nation-states, even if it's gradually absorbed upward. We don't even know the fate of supranational formations like the European Union, which still has a long way to go. Our political battles inevitably are at the level of the nation or the subnation. I mean, that's where we can have some influence. The more global institutions will have to be taken on through the nation-state. If we want to get to the World Bank, the International Monetary Fund, we get at them through the power of the nation. To go further, I don't want to be a citizen of the world. The speeches I gave before Bush's election kind of said, look, up until now it's George Bush's war, after Tuesday it's our war, if we reelect him. I mean, you know, there's a taking of responsibility that's inevitable here.

And, finally, is that my own thinking, and I believe most people's thinking, begins not merely with the encounter with theories and texts and thinkers, it begins within the pressures of our own lives and our own experience of family, community, of work, of troubles. These things all mark our thought in some sense. And these things are almost always particularistic, and they force us to define our problems that way. And, so if I sometimes react against, let us say, the French thinkers, it's more because I want to say to people, take these ideas and get them translated into modes of language that resonate with experience elsewhere. If a term "governmentality" doesn't seem to work here, try to find some other way of putting it that will do it. Raymond Williams was very ethnocentric. He pretty much lived his life within Great Britain, and he was pushed to take on Althusser, but it seems he always preferred to debate it within the English traditions, because that's what he felt *in* himself. And so, I think that there are many more people who are more ethnocentric than they'll say they are. I'm just doing a bit of confession.

But, also, for all the criticism, there are certain aspects of American life, of Western civilization at large, that are real gains that we should be careful not to inadvertently abandon. The notion of human rights, natural rights, democracy, etc., are very valuable even though they emerged in a particular context.

I'm sad always when someone thinks that I'm giving the American exceptionalist argument, because most of the time I've been saying, it can happen here, too. You know, there are worse things that you can imagine. It doesn't give us any protection. It just means that this is the way we are, and our thought begins within this context. And, we have to be prepared to address our fellow citizens as well as one another.

Grossberg

What do you make of the resurgence of interest in Dewey. For example, as Chris Russill shows, one of the things coming to light now is how much this generation of French intellectuals actually read Dewey.

Carey

I was very surprised, even astonished by that.

Grossberg

Dewey has been and continues to be influential, but you won't see it in their politics. . . . It is not *The Public and Its Problems* that they are reading.

Carey

Yes, I know . . .

Grossberg

And how do you respond to the charge that you have an individualistic point of view?

Carey

I have to say that I don't understand it. I think of myself as an interactionist.

Matters of individual will and imagining are always social matters for me.

Grossberg

You started out your intellectual trajectory in economics, as it were. Do you ever miss it? Do you ever regret having gone so far from it?

Carey

I wish at times that I didn't put it on hold for such a long period of time, as I went off and struggled with other things. I don't so much like economics as a discipline anymore, but I like certain ideas within economics that I find very useful and I feel very comfortable thinking about in economic terms. So, I wish that I had more self-consciously continued it. It was hard to do within the circles in which I was traveling, in part because of political economy, and in part because economics departments became so conservative, and it was the stray person I could find to talk with who could think a little bit outside of the box. But, I do like economic forms of analysis and reasoning, and I find them very helpful at times.

Grossberg

Do you think it will ever be possible to bring cultural studies and economics together? It seems to me hard to know how one can talk about the culture of the world today without bringing economics in.

Carey

Yes, it will be hard. But if you think of cultural studies, as a project, as a formation, the problems that it takes up are somewhat unpredictable because they're responses to particular conjunctures and certain things that emerge out of history. More people are going to study it, and there's going to be less literary theory because they're going to find that there are other games that need to be played.

Grossberg

Thank you, Jim.

Carey

It was very nice of you to do this and to work so hard, Larry. And as I say, I appreciated the essays more than I can say.

Notes

1. James Carey, "A Cultural Approach to Communication," *Communication* 2 (December, 1975), 1–22; James Carey, *Communication as Culture: Essays on Media and Society* (New York: Routledge, 1989), pp. 13–36.
2. James Carey, "Political Correctness and Cultural Studies," *Journal of Communication* 42:2 (1992), 56–72. Reprinted in Eve Stryker Munson and Catherine A. Warren, eds., *James Carey: A Critical Reader* (Minneapolis: University of Minnesota Press, 1997), pp. 270–291.
3. James Carey, "Reflections on the Project of (American) Cultural Studies," in Marjorie Ferguson and Peter Golding, eds., *Cultural Studies in Question* (London: Sage, 1997)
4. James Carey, "The Sense of an Ending: On Nations, Communications and Culture," in Catherine A. Warren and Mary Douglas Vavrus, eds. *American Cultural Studies* (Urbana, IL: University of Illinois, 2002), pp. 196–238.
5. James Carey, "Afterword: The Culture in Question," in Eve Stryker Munson and Catherine A. Warren, eds., *James Carey: A Critical Reader* (Minneapolis: University of Minnesota Press, 1997), pp. 308–340.
6. James Carey, "Communications and Economics," in Robert Babe, ed., *Information and Communication in Economics* (Boston: Kluwer, 1994), pp. 321–36. Reprinted in Eve Stryker Munson and Catherine A. Warren, eds., *James Carey: A Critical Reader* (Minneapolis: University of Minnesota Press, 1997), pp. 60–78.
7. Kenneth Cmiel, "Review: *Culture as Communication: Essays on Media and Society,*" *Theory and Society* 21:2 (1992), 289.

Contributors

James W. Carey is currently CBS Professor of International Journalism at Columbia University. He has been president, Association for Education in Journalism; president, American Association of Schools and Departments of Journalism; National Endowment for the Humanities fellow; Gannett Center for Media Studies fellow; member of advisory board, Poynter Institute for Media Studies; member, board of directors, Public Broadcasting System; board member, Peabody Awards for Broadcasting. He has authored *Media, Myths, and Narrative : Television and the Press* (Sage, 1988), *Communication as Culture* (Routledge, 1989) and *James Carey: A Critical Reader* (University of Minnesota Press, 1997), as well as dozens of influential essays across a wide range of topics over the past 40 years.

Lawrence Grossberg is the Morris Davis Distinguished Professor of Communication Studies and Cultural Studies, and the director of the University Program in Cultural Studies at the University of North Carolina at Chapel Hill. His most recent books are *Caught in the Crossfire: Kids, Politics and America's Future* (Paradigm, 2005) and *New Keywords* (co-edited with Tony Bennett and Meaghan Morris).

James Hay is Associate Professor in the Department of Speech Communication, the Graduate Program in Cultural Studies, the Unit for Criticism and Interpretive Theory and the Unit for Cinema Studies at the University of Illinois at Champaign–Urbana. He is author of *Popular Film Culture in Fascist Italy* (Indiana University Press, 1987) and co-editor (with Lawrence Grossberg and Ellen Wartella) of *The Audience and Its Landscape* (Westview Press, 1996) as well as the author of numerous essays about media and social space.

John Nerone is Professor in the Institute of Communications Research at the University of Illinois at Urbana–Champaign. He is the author of *Vio-*

lence against the Press: Policing the Public Sphere in US History (1994) and the coauthor (with Kevin Barnhurst) of *The Form of News: A History* (2001).

Jeremy Packer is Assistant Professor of Film/Video & Media Studies in the College of Communications at The Pennsylvania State University–University Park. He is the author of the forthcoming book *Mobility Without Mayhem: Mass Mediating Safety and Automobility* (Duke University Press) and a co-editor (with Jack Bratich and Cameron McCarthy) of *Foucault, Cultural Studies and Governmentality* (SUNY Press, 2003).

John Durham Peters is Wendell Miller Distinguished Professor in the Department of Communication Studies at the University of Iowa. He is the author of *Courting the Abyss: Free Speech and the Liberal Tradition* (University of Chicago Press, 2005) and *Speaking into the Air: A History of the Idea of Communication* (Chicago University Press, 1999) as well as co-editor (with Elihu Katz, Tamar Liebes, and Avril Orloff) of *Canonic Texts in Media Research: Are There Any? Should There Be? How About These?* (Polity Press, 2003) and (with Peter Simonson) *Mass Communication and American Social Thought: Key Texts, 1919–1968* (Rowman and Littlefield, 2004).

Craig Robertson is an assistant professor in the Communications Studies Department at Northeastern University. He is the author of articles on media and globalization and the writing of history in cultural studies. Currently he is working on a history of the passport in the United States.

Chris Russill is a lecturer in communication studies at the University of Otago in New Zealand. Recent articles have explored the importance of William James's radical empiricism for communication theory and cultural studies. He is currently studying forms of environmental activism as they respond to extensions of regulatory power.

Gretchen Soderlund is Assistant Director of the Center for the Study of Communication and Society at the University of Chicago. She is currently working on a book about journalism and moral panics in the early 20th century.

Jonathan Sterne teaches in the Department of Art History and Communication Studies and the History and Philosophy of Science Program at McGill University. He is author of *The Audible Past: Cultural Origins of Sound Reproduction* (Duke, 2003), and numerous articles on media, technologies and the politics of culture. His next book considers mp3s and digital audio culture. He is also an editor of *Bad Subjects: Political Education for Everyday Life* (http://badsubjects.org), one of the longest continuously running publications on the Internet.

Index

A

Albig, Bill 20
Althuser, Louis 42, 60, 208, 222
Altschuter, Glenn 159
anti-masons 165
Arendt, Hannah 50, 131
Aron, Cindy 183
Auxier, Randell 64–70

B

Babbage, Charles 148–149
Barber, Benjamin 62
Barry, Andrew 82
Baudrillard, Jean 46, 125
Becker, Howard 59
Benjamin, Walter 62, 130, 138–141, 149
Berger, Bennet 20
Bernstein, Richard 62
Blair, Francisi Preston 164
blogosphere 172
Blondheim, Menochem 120, 125–126, 148
Blumin, Stuart 159, 170–171
bodies 47, 49, 108, 111, 112–120, 122, 131, 139, 142–147
Brain, Robert 145
Braudel, Ferdinand 127–129
Buchanan, James 159
Burke, Kenneth 20, 21
Burton, Antoinette 184

C

Carey, Bette 15
Carey, James
On
   current communication scholarship 5
   cultural studies 20–25, 208–211
   Columbia Journalism Review 27–28
   communication/transportation thesis 6, 7, 200–206
   "A Cultural Approach to Communication" 199–203
   Dewey 2
   his education 12–10
   his family and childhood 12
   face to face communication 7–8
   Foucault 211–214
   French Post-structuralism 208
   George W. Bush 199, 212, 218–222
   historical research 2–3
   Innis 2, 17, 26, 39
   journalism 16, 19, 27, 220
   McLuhan 17, 20
   Marx 23–26, 214, 216
   modes of travel and speed 204–206
   politics of the day 217–223
   political economy vs cultural studies 224
   ritual 11, 25, 200, 203, 206, 207, 210, 215
   technologies as culture 214–217

Williams 200–202
Wittgenstein and Baseball 19
Essays
  "Abolishing the Old Spirit World"
    60, 62, 141
  "Afterword: The Culture in
    Question" 59, 122, 129, 181,
    190, 191, 217
  "The Ambiguity of Policy Research"
    2, 94
  "A Plea for the University Tradition"
    157
  "The Chicago School and the History
    of Mass Communication
    Research" 4
  "Canadian Communication Theory:
    Extensions and Interpretations of
    Harold Innis" 37
  "Commentary: Communications and
    the Progressives" 7, 60, 62
  "Communication and Culture: A
    Review Essay of Clifford Geertz"
    36, 38
  "Communication and Economics" 33,
    219
  "The Communication Revolution and
    the Professional Communicator"
    58, 140
  "A Cultural Approach to
    Communication" 33, 35, 58, 61,
    80, 199
  "Culture, Geography, and
    Communications: The Work of
    Harold Innis in an American
    Context" 34, 37, 39
  "Graduate Education in Mass
    Communication" 95
  "Harold Adam Innis and Marshal
    McLuhan" 17, 152
  "The History of the Future" 92
  "The Language of Technology: Talk,
    Text, and Template as Metaphors
    for Communication" 2
  "Mass Communication and Cultural
    Studies" 32
  "The Mythos of the Electronic
    Revolution" (with John Quirk) 22

  "Overcoming Resistance to Cultural
    Studies" 61
  "The Politics of the Electronic
    Revolution: Further Notes on
    Marshal McLuhan" 81
  "Political Correctness and Cultural
    Studies" 60, 208
  "The Problem with Journalism
    History" 2, 57, 61
  "Reconcieving Mass" and "Media"
    58, 61, 139
  "Reflections on the Project of
    (American) Cultural Studies"
    20, 31, 57–61, 177, 190, 191,
    192, 208
  "The Sense of an Ending: On
    Nations, Communications and
    Culture" 7, 179, 181, 217
  "Space, Time, and Communication:
    A Tribute to Harold Innis" 1,
    3, 81–82, 85, 94
  "Technology and Ideology: The Case
    of the Telegraph" 5, 6, 48,
    80–82, 84, 158
Books
  *Communications as Culture: Essays on
    Media and Society* 16, 29, 34,
    35, 46, 81–82, 117–120, 125,
    140, 190
Cartesionism 131
Castells, Manuel 125
Center for Contemporary Cultural
  Studies, Birminghan 22, 23, 199
Chandler, Alfred 141, 183
Chappe's Semaphoric Telegraph 127,
  139
Chicago School 4, 21, 22, 35–37, 40,
  51, 54, 58–59, 62, 119
circuit model of communication 146
Citizens Band Radio 6, 90–91
Civil Rights Movement 171, 203
Cohn, Bernard 184
colonial press 161
conversational model 122–123, 135
Cook and Wheatsone's Electrical
  Telegraph 127
Cooley, Charles 128
'combat zones that see' 92

Committee of Concerned Journalists 158
communication and communications
 126–128
communication and the individual 121
communication and transportation 1, 2,
 5–7, 29–34, 40, 43, 47,49, 55, 58,
 79, 81–85, 88, 91–95, 110–12,
 117–132, 147–148
communication and geography 7, 29–31,
 35–37, 40, 44, 48–49, 147–148,
 179–180, 205–206
Corrigan, Philip 192
Cowan, Ruth Schwartz 131
Croly, Herbert 74
Cronen, Vernon 75
cultural materialism 29–55
cultural studies 4, 8, 11–27, 29–32, 37,
 39–45, 49–51, 53, 57–62, 70, 73,
 79, 96, 141, 152, 190, 208–211,
 217, 221, 224

D

Debs, V. Eugene 170
de Certeau, Michel 43
Deledalle, Gerard 64–65
Deleuze, Gilles 60,128
Derrida, Jacques 60, 121–122
de Saussure, Ferdinand 146
Dewey, John 61–76, 95, 106, 122, 138,
 152, 157, 171, 215, 223
the "Dewey Group" 60–62, 75
'digital model of language' 145, 147
Douglas, Susan 85
Durkheim, Emile 5, 22, 33, 101–104,
 108, 113
Dworkin, Andrea 111

E

Edelman, Murray 20
Edison, Thomas 144–145, 150
Einstein, Albert 138, 150–152
Entman, Robert 170

F

face to face communication 7, 123, 141,
 161
'fantasy of functionless transmission' 148
FCC 80
Federalist Papers 161
Fiedler, Leslie 21
Flanders, Dwight 19
Foucault, Michel 3, 4, 57, 60–75, 79,
 81, 96, 97, 178, 191–194, 203,
 211–212
Frankfurt School 36, 50
the 'French Group' 60–61

G

Galison, Robert 151
Geertz, Clifford 37–38, 51, 76, 101, 102
'general theory of communication' 58
Gerbner, George 16,18,20–23
Gilroy, Paul 128
global positioning systems 91
Goffman, Erving 19–22, 58
governmentality 61, 63, 70, 71, 74, 79,
 81, 211–213, 222
'govern at a distance' 6, 82, 90, 95,
Gramsci, Antonio 39, 42, 53
Greeley, Horace 166–167
Guattari, Felix 76, 128
Gusfield, Joe 20–21

H

Habermas, Jurgen 121, 158–159, 162,
 169–170
Hall, Stuart 37, 22, 25, 208
hand signaling 89
Harvey, David 125
Hegel, 14, 39, 131,139, 161, 203
Heidegger, Martin 119
Heisenberg uncertainty principal, 148
Henkin, David 182
historical materialism 38–42, 45, 51, 54
Hobbes, Thomas 67–68, 130
Hoggart, Richard 22, 32, 37, 39, 51, 53
Hook, Sidney 24

Huntington, Samuel 59

I

Innis, Harold Adam 1–2, 4, 9, 17,
    20–22, 26, 37–43, 50–53, 57–58,
    81–82, 95, 128, 135, 137, 141,
    152, 157–158, 181, 203, 214
Institute of Communication Research
    (ICR), Illinois 16
interpersonal communication 94, 121,
    128
invisible media 5, 105

J

Jackson, Andrew 163
Jacksonian era 163–172
James, William 57, 60, 152
Jeffersonian ideal of public 171, 64
Jensen, Jay 57, 60, 152
Jensen, Joli 62
journalism 2, 6, 16, 42, 57, 61, 65,
    73–74, 137, 157–172

K

Kafka, Franz 151
Kant, Immanuel 73, 143
Kern, Stephen 125
King Jr., Martin-Luther 170
Kittler, Fredreich 128, 131, 138
Kracauer, Siegfried 36
Kuhn, Thomas 21, 60

L

La Capra. Dominick 123
Laclau, Ernesto 42
Latour, Bruno 118
Le Bon, Gustave 129
Lenoir, Timothy 143
Leonard, Jean Francis 126
Leonard, Thomas 167
Lefebvre, Henri 5, 44–46, 54

Levi-Strauss, Claude 5, 103, 105, 106,
    108
Lippman, Walter 61,74,171
Lipset, Seymour Martin 19
Locke, John 130

M

Mackinnon, Catherine 111
Mann Act 109
maps 21, 46–49, 60, 73, 140, 204–206
Marey, Etinne Jules 144,146,149
Marx, Karl 131
Marx, Leo 21–22
marxism 24–25, 37, 42, 44, 214
mass media 4, 36, 45, 94, 101–114, 122
mass society debate 59, 62, 129–130
Massey, Doreen 48
Mattelart, Armand 55, 81, 82, 119, 127
Mattelart, Michelle 119
McLuhan, Marshall 1, 4, 17, 21–22, 38,
    58, 122, 143, 152, 203
'memory of the state' 181
'metaphysics of presence' 121
'metaphysic of democracy' 57
Miller, Peter 185
Mindich, David 170
MIT MediaLab 92
Mnookin, Jennifer 184, 186
mobility, 6, 48, 49, 52, 83, 87, 90–94,
    109, 128, 159, 184
Mumford, Lewis 4, 122, 128, 139, 215
Munsterberg, Hugo 152

N

the nation 7, 129, 158, 161, 164,
    177–185, 190, 193, 212, 222
newspapers 110–111, 126, 129,
    148–149, 160–172
news 86, 112, 125, 129, 148, 158–162,
    165–169, 220
Niles, Hezekiah 162,164,166–167
non-symbolic communication 117–118,
    123, 132
Northwestern University 19

O

Oersted, Hans Christian 143
Ong, Walter 122
orality 9, 51, 58, 95, 122, 157, 183,
    186, 190–191
Osgood, Charlie 20–21

P

Park, Robert 36,38,58
party press (1820–1890) 158–172
passport (as technology) 177–194
Poe, Edgar Allan 142
police radio 6, 90, 91
positivism 21, 30, 33, 38–41, 43, 54,
    103, 140, 191,199, 213
Postal Act (1972) 161–162
postal roads 86,128–129
Postman, Neil 170
power, Carey's concept of, 42–49
pragmatism 57, 60, 62, 66, 139, 202
problematization 4, 61–67, 70–75, 82,
    188
the public sphere 8, 62, 93, 108,
    158–164, 166, 168–171,191
publics 57–59, 61–74,161–162, 190
public space 157, 160, 169
Putnam, Robert 170

Q

Quirk, John 21

R

Rabinow, Paul 66
radio 6, 80, 84–92, 121, 128–129, 131,
    148
railroad 11, 80, 82, 84, 85, 87, 120,
    121, 125–127, 140, 142, 148, 151,
    158, 183, 204, 205, 206
religion 24–25, 33–34, 50, 102, 104,
    201–203, 210
Riis, Jacob 167

ritual model 4–8, 11, 25, 29–44, 46–49,
    58, 61, 80, 82, 92, 95, 101–107,
    109, 111, 113–114, 117–118, 122,
    148, 157–158, 177–179, 181, 183,
    185, 187, 180–191, 193–195, 200,
    203–204, 206–207, 210, 215
Rorty, Richard 60
Rose, Nikolas 185
Rubin, Gayle 105–106

S

Sankar, Pamela 189
Schiller, Dan 131
Schiller, Herbert 23,24
Schivelbusch, Wolfgang 124–126, 133,
    138, 158, 205
Schudson, Michael 159, 168, 170, 171
Sconce, Jeff 121,131
Scott, James 184
Sekula, Allan 184
semiotics 37, 44, 46
Shell, Marc 181, 209
Siegert, Bernhardt 144,147
Simmel, Georg 36, 129–130
Skornia, Harry 17
Smee, Alfred 142, 150
Smelser, Neil 19
Smith, Adam 131
Smythe, Dallas 16–17, 20, 23
Snow, C.P. 33
social purity campaigns 108–110
space/spatial-bias 5, 29–47, 50–53, 82,
    190–191
spatial materialism 29, 31–50
standard time 120, 148
Stanford University 19, 143
Steffens, Lincoln 167
structuralism 2, 37, 42, 46, 63, 103,
    120, 146, 148, 208
surveillance 71, 90–94, 111, 148, 189
systems of representation 160, 169
symbolic communication 113, 118

T

Tarbell, Ida 167

technological determinism 126, 140
telecommunication 146, 220
Telecommunications Act (1996) 168
telegraphic split 147
'tele' and 'graph' 143
Telegraph 5–8, 33, 42–43, 48–49, 58,
    79–85, 118–121, 123, 125–132,
    137–153, 158, 160, 166, 183,
    205–207
television 17, 52, 102, 121, 128, 157
Thompson, E.P. 39, 141
time 40, 42, 44, 48, 57, 82, 95, 101,
    104, 120–121, 125–127, 137–141,
    144, 147–152
time-bias 38–39, 52, 203
time-space compression 82, 125–126,
    151
Tonnies, Ferdinand 33–34, 36, 41
Toronto School 1
trafficking of woman 101–115
transmission 4, 5, 7–8, 29–35, 38, 40,
    41, 43, 46–49, 53, 58, 61, 80, 86,
    90, 95, 103, 104, 108, 114, 118,
    122, 124, 127, 142, 144, 148, 150,
    152, 157–158, 177, 179, 190–194,
    200, 203–206, 215
transportation model of communication
    29, 83, 104, 124, 125,160, 200

Williams, Raymond 21–22, 32, 37–41,
    52–53, 72, 107, 115, 128–129,
    133, 200–202, 222

V

Virilio, Paul 125

W

Warren, Josiah 165
Weber, Max 21–22, 33, 36, 41, 101,
    141, 209
Wells, Paul 18
West, Cornel 62
Westbrook, Robert 62
Whannel, Paddy 23
White, Hayden 123
white slavery scare (1907–1911) 5–6,
    108–112, 115
Wilde, Oscar 1
Will, Fred 19

Intersections
in Communications
and Culture

Global Approaches and Transdisciplinary Perspectives

General Editors: Cameron McCarthy & Angharad N. Valdivia

An Institute of Communications Research, University of Illinois Commemorative Series

This series aims to publish a range of new critical scholarship that seeks to engage and transcend the disciplinary isolationism and genre confinement that now characterizes so much of contemporary research in communication studies and related fields. The editors are particularly interested in manuscripts that address the broad intersections, movement, and hybrid trajectories that currently define the encounters between human groups in modern institutions and societies and the way these dynamic intersections are coded and represented in contemporary popular cultural forms and in the organization of knowledge. Works that emphasize methodological nuance, texture and dialogue across traditions and disciplines (communications, feminist studies, area and ethnic studies, arts, humanities, sciences, education, philosophy, etc.) and that engage the dynamics of variation, diversity and discontinuity in the local and international settings are strongly encouraged.

LIST OF TOPICS

- Multidisciplinary Media Studies
- Cultural Studies
- Gender, Race, & Class
- Postcolonialism
- Globalization
- Diaspora Studies
- Border Studies
- Popular Culture
- Art & Representation
- Body Politics
- Governing Practices

- Histories of the Present
- Health (Policy) Studies
- Space and Identity
- (Im)migration
- Global Ethnographies
- Public Intellectuals
- World Music
- Virtual Identity Studies
- Queer Theory
- Critical Multiculturalism

Manuscripts should be sent to:
Cameron McCarthy OR Angharad N. Valdivia
Institute of Communications Research
University of Illinois at Urbana-Champaign
222B Armory Bldg., 555 E. Armory Avenue
Champaign, IL 61820

To order other books in this series, please contact our Customer Service Department:
(800) 770-LANG (within the U.S.)
(212) 647-7706 (outside the U.S.)
(212) 647-7707 FAX

Or browse online by series:
www.peterlangusa.com